T0146581

A PUSH
FROM BELOW

How the Black Power Movement Changed
Higher Education

DR. KINAYA C. SOKOYA

authorHOUSE

AuthorHouse™
1663 Liberty Drive
Bloomington, IN 47403
www.authorhouse.com
Phone: 1 (800) 839-8640

Published by AuthorHouse 10/24/2018

ISBN: 978-1-5462-6188-9 (sc)
ISBN: 978-1-5462-6187-2 (e)

Dedication

I would like to thank the creator and my ancestors for the successful completion of this book. The journey, which has been long and arduous, has played a key role in my effort to continue to grow as a person and contribute to society. Through this endeavor, I have been able to give voice to the many African American activists who devoted their lives to ensure a better life for all people. I thank them for contributing to this effort. I would also like to give tribute to my deceased parents and my siblings, who laid the foundation for me to become the first child in our family to become a college graduate. Special recognition is given to my brother, James, who was one of my primary educational mentors during my formative years. Their unconditional support has taught me that nothing is unachievable if you believe in yourself and work hard to realize your dreams. I would like to also acknowledge Mr. Gugliano, my high school guidance counselor, who encouraged me to pursue a college education. I thank my husband, Babatu Olubayo, who devoted many hours proofreading my drafts; and, my children, Sitawi, Ayinde, and Omotunwase; and, my grandchildren, Kaliq, Sharif, Quinn, Jamar, and Caden; who provided unwavering moral support for completion of this effort. For them, my message is you too can achieve unlimited heights if you follow your dreams.

Acknowledgements

I want to thank the faculty of George Washington University, specifically members of my book committee. Dr. Kim has provided tremendous ongoing support and guidance for me from completion of coursework to writing this book. She has mentored me and provided support while demanding excellence. Without her help, this book would not have been possible. Dr. Zimmerman and Dr. Villarreal are special individuals. Thank you, Dr. Zimmerman, for your insight and guidance for completion of this qualitative educational study of a historical topic. Thank you, Dr. Villarreal, for your support and guidance in methodology. I also would like to thank my two outside readers, Dr. Komozi Woodard and Dr. Wells-Wilbon for their willingness to serve as evaluators.

Dr. Woodard's feedback was invaluable. He was a true mentor. Dr. Wells-Wilbon's support was also invaluable. I am and will be eternally grateful to them. Finally, I would like to thank Dr. Kochhar-Bryant for agreeing to serve as presider for my oral defense and the GSEHD faculty for their support and patience. I thank all for believing in me and encouraging me to complete this process.

Abstract

A Push from Below: *How the Black Power Movement Changed Higher Education*

The purpose of this research was to study the link between the Black Power Movement and changes that occurred in higher education between 1960 and 1980. The main research question study was, —What effect did the Black Power Movement have on changes in higher education from 1960 – 1980? The intent of this historical research is to reconstruct knowledge on the complexity of the African American freedom struggle through the voices of thirteen Black Power activists, who were leaders of Black Power organizations, faculty in Black Studies programs, and students.

The study used an interview process to conduct the study. Data was collected through semi-structured interviews and a document analysis. The document analysis included primary documents, books, scholarly journals, and organizational websites. The sampling strategy was purposive because of the special knowledge of the participants.

The findings were presented within organizations and across organizations. Lewin's model of change was used to analyze the catalysts for change and the response of higher educational institutions.

There was a consensus among the participants interviewed and the literature reviewed that the Black Power Movement was a student-driven movement that was responsible for the formation of Black student organizations on campuses, particularly Black student unions, establishment of Black studies departments, an increase in African American faculty, and changes in curricula. The researcher discerned five major themes that describe the era, 1) the challenges of first-generation African American students on predominately White campuses, 2) the role of Black student unions in the success of African American students, 3) the lack of representation of Africans and African Americans in college courses, 4) the role of Black studies departments in providing information on Africans and African Americans, and 5) confusion between the accomplishments of the Civil Right Movement and the Black Power Movement.

The major findings of the study have implications for higher education institutions in 1) student affairs, 2) adragogy, 3) curricula, and 4) diversity education. Based on the findings, it is recommended that higher education institutions maintain and build on changes made in the past based on the lessons learned from the Black Power Movement.

Contents

CHAPTER I

CHAPTER II

CHAPTER III

CHAPTER IV

CHAPTER V

List of Figures

List of Tables

INTRODUCTION

The period between 1960 and 1980 is remembered as a period of discontent, unrest, and, at the same time, a belief in the ability to change the status quo. The problem is multi-faceted with problems in practice and problems in research. This section will address each area. Following are (a) a statement of the problem in practice, (b) a statement of the problem in research, (c) the purpose of the study, (d) research questions, (e) the significance of the study, (e) the paradigm of inquiry, (f) the methodology and context, (g) definitions oterminology, (h) delimitations and limitations of the study, and (i) an overview of chapters I–V. The chapter will conclude with a summary.

Context of the Problem

The context for this book is the period from 1960 to 1980, which is remembered by many people as a turbulent period (Grant, 1968; Heath, 1976; Hill, 2004). During this period, President Kennedy, Martin Luther King, Jr., and Malcolm X (El Hajj Malik El Shabazz) were assassinated and President Nixon resigned. Civil Rights groups protested unequal treatment of African Americans by marching, helping African Americans to register to vote, conducting boycotts of businesses, staging sit-ins, and sponsoring teach- ins. For the first time, on televisions in their living rooms, Americans and the world were seeing protesters being beaten, attacked by police dogs, and hosed with water (Grant, 1968; Robinson, Battle, & Robinson, Jr., 1987). It was also a period of Black uprisings in communities across the United States in response to a lack of opportunity, resulting frustrations, reaction to the assassinations of Martin Luther King, Jr. and President John F. Kennedy, and police brutality. Young people began to question the traditional values of their parents and authorities. Several activist groups emerged to challenge the status quo. In addition to Black activism, other activist groups protested issues such as American involvement in the Vietnam and Cambodian wars, nuclear proliferation, and capitalism among other issues (Sparks Notes, 2007; Williams, 1998). The 1960s and 1970s were years of unrest in America.

Higher education institutions were not insulated from this unrest (Biondi, 2012; Grant, 1968; Ture & Hamilton, 1992). Campuses across the country were the sites of student protests where students expressed concern and outrage about the same issues that were being protested by community activists. Two infamous incidents were student occupations of administrative buildings at Columbia University in 1965 (Columbia University, 2007) and at Cornell University in 1969 (Joseph, 2006). After passage of civil rights legislation (Grant, 1968) and the Higher Education Act of 1965 (U. S. Department of Education, 2008), there was a sharp increase in the number of minority students that enrolled in predominantly White colleges and universities (PWCU). Failure to prepare for the needs of this sudden influx of minority students was, in part, the catalyst for student unrest.

After enrollment in PWCUs, many African American students experienced racial hostility, alienation, and isolation on these campuses (Williamson, 1999). They felt a need for an organization of their own on campus to ensure their academic survival. The purpose of the organization was to serve as a safe zone and provide a power base for the students. The first Black student union was founded in 1966 at San Francisco State College (Joseph, 2006; Williamson, 1999). Similar organizations rapidly emerged at PWCUs across the country. Organizations, such as the Student Nonviolent Coordinating Committee (SNCC), the Student Organization of Black Unity (SOBU), and the Congress of African People (CAP) played major roles in organizing Black student unions on college campuses. The demands student activists submitted to university administrations often mirrored the tenets of Black Power organizations.

The first Black studies department was established at San Francisco State College in 1969 as a result of a strike held by student activists at the college. Students in the newly formed Black student union led this strike. The outcome was the establishment of the Division of Ethnic Studies and departments of Black, Asian, Chicano, and Native American studies. These departments were considered the first of their kind. A position paper written by members of the Black student union entitled *"The Justification for African American Studies"* provided the rationale for the institutional change. The paper was subsequently used as a prototype to promote the establishment of Black studies departments at more than 60 universities (Okafor, 1999).

Problem in practice.

Scholars have included some of the activities of Black activists in American higher education history classes; however, the information taught includes several inaccuracies and gaps (Carson, 1981; Joseph, 2006). This is largely due to the absence of information in major higher education texts. Professors are forced to find other references to teach the subject. The content of the material taught is highly dependent on the resourcefulness of professors. In addition, some information on Black activism during the 1960s and 1970s has not been documented. This paucity of information has limited professors' ability to provide rich, thick data on the complexity of Black activism during this period.

Problem in research.

Little research has been conducted on the rich diversity of African American activism during the 1960s and 1970s. During a review of the literature, only two documents were found that presented the voices of Black Power activists on their efforts to effect changes in higher education. In the text, *A History of American Higher Education* (2004), Thelin devoted minimal attention to the topic, focusing on affirmative action, historically Black colleges and universities, and need-based scholarships.

However, he acknowledged the impact the presence of diverse populations on college campuses in the 1980s had on university life relative to policy discussions. He also noted the growth of Black sororities and fraternities. When he discussed activism, he focused on violence, opposition to the Vietnam War, and the threat to higher education curriculum. The information lacked depth and an understanding of the complexity of activism during the period.

Clayborne Carson served as director of the Martin Luther King, Jr. Papers Project at Stanford University's Center for Nonviolent Social Change. In his book, *Martin Luther King, Jr.: Charismatic Leadership in a Mass Struggle* (1987), Carson lamented the portrayal of Dr. Martin Luther King, Jr. as a leader who singularly spearheaded the Civil Rights Movement. He stated that the Black struggle was a locally based mass movement, rather than a reform effort led by national civil rights leaders, and there were many protest movements in which King had little or no direct involvement. Although there were hints at the complexity of the African American movement in the higher education history texts, few details were provided.

In *Race in Higher Education*, Chang, Altbach, and Lomotey (2005) stated that the most visible issues race presented to higher education were enrollment gaps, the viability of the historically Black colleges and universities, curricular challenges, campus balkanization, and affirmative action. They noted the significant increase in the enrollment of African Americans in four-year institutions during the 1970s following passage of civil rights legislation. With the increase in enrollment of African American students, there were calls for the addition of African American studies to college course offerings. Although these events were briefly mentioned, the authors provided no contextual information on the impetus for the demands.

College and university press have published several books and journals on selected areas of African American activism or on African American personalities. These include works such as *Radio Free Dixie: Robert F. Williams & the Roots of Black Power* (Tyson, 1999) and *The Deacons for Defense: Armed Resistance and the Civil Rights Movement* (Hill, 2004). However, this information has not been integrated into major texts. This omission has contributed to a lack of understanding of the activism of African Americans who devoted their lives to the advancement of equal opportunity for African American people. Cultural competency related to any people requires an accurate depiction of their history. This research is an effort to begin to document their legacy.

Purpose of the Study

The purpose of this research is to analyze the role of the Black Power Movement in changes in higher education during the period from 1960 – 1980. Currently, there is unevenness in the portrayal of these contributions. The two seminal texts used for teaching the history of higher education, *the ASHE Reader on the History of Higher Education* (Astin, Astin, Bayer, & Bisconti; 1997) and *A History of American Higher Education* (Thelin, 2004), attribute the contributions of African American activism to higher education from 1960 to 1980 to the Civil Rights Movement. Although, this movement did facilitate significant changes in higher education, there were other Black movements operating simultaneously in the same and different arenas (Austin, 2006;

Carson, 1981; Columbia University, 2007; Grant, 1968; Gilliam, 2005; Hill, 2004; Joseph, 2006; Lang, 2001; Marable, 1997; Robinson, Battle, & Robinson, Jr., 1987; Sparks Notes, 2002; Ture & Hamilton, 1992; Tyson, 1999; University of Michigan, 2007; Warren, 1990; Williams, 1998; Williamson, 1999; X, 1990). Because the activities of Black activists have been attributed to the Civil Rights Movement, there is a lack of understanding of the existence of other groups, their leaders, their varied philosophies, their activities, and the contributions that resulted. This study focuses on the structure of the Black Power Movement, activities of Black Power organizations that affected student populations on and off college campuses; and, the contributions to higher education of African American individuals and organizations that were part of the Black Power Movement. The intent of this research is to construct new information.

Conceptual Frameworks

This study was analyzed through the perspective of one of the advocacy or political paradigms of the social constructivist paradigm, critical race theory (Crotty, 2003; Creswell, 2007). According to critical race theory, racism is normal. Because of racism, people of color endure macro and micro aggressions. Macroaggressions are structural problems, such as segregation and poor education that impact African Americans and other people of color. These aggressions were addressed and continue to be addressed through the activism of civil rights organizations. The activism, however, has not addressed microaggressions, which are small injuries, which may be unintended, that African Americans endure multiple times daily. White culture is employed as the standard, making people of color feel like outsiders or —the other. Because the critical race theory paradigm (CRT) assumes multiple realities, the perspective is appropriate for this study.

The reality of many African Americans differs from those in mainstream society.

This difference helped trigger African American activism. In this paradigm, the researcher participates in reconstructing reality. Based on the findings of the research, it is my intent to construct information to influence changes in higher education texts and andragogy, including recognition of the complexity of African American activism during this period and the contributions of those in the Black Power Movement to changes at higher education institutions.

Research Questions

The general research question was, —What effect did the Black Power Movement have on changes in higher education from 1960 – 1980? Four research sub-questions were:

1. What role did the Black Power Movement play in the development of Black student organizations, particularly Black student unions?
2. What role did the Black Power Movement play in the development of Black studies departments?
3. What does the San Francisco State University experience in the development of a Black student union and Black studies department suggest about the Black Power Movement and higher education?

4. What other important cases provide information on the effect of the Black Power Movement on changes in higher education?

To answer the general research question on the relationship of the Black Power Movement to changes in higher education in curriculum and student development, the four sub-questions were analyzed.

Significance of the Study

This study can contribute to knowledge on the role the Black Power Movement played in changes made in higher education from 1960-1980. It informs higher education curriculum and advances the aims of an accurate representation and inclusion of African Americans as contributors to higher education. Efforts have been made to include the activities of Blacks in the history of American higher education; however, the information is primarily limited to the activities of the Civil Rights Movement (Joseph, 2006). The voices of African Americans who were leaders or activists in the Black Power Movement have not been included in literature relative to their efforts to foster change at higher education institutions. Without this type of research, the practice of excluding and/or misinterpreting the contributions of the Black Power Movement to higher education will continue.

Everyday new information on the history of humankind is discovered. It is an ever-changing process that requires ongoing research, analysis, and revision. Because inclusion of racial minorities in technical and social advancements in the United States is an area that is still evolving, accuracy and completeness of this information are critical for the knowledge of students and scholars. It is also an educational ideal, building the furniture of the mind (Yale University, 1828).

Summary of the Methodology

Through a literature review; review of primary documents; interviews with representatives from activist groups, students, faculty, and personal testimony; the researcher provides a historical analysis of the activities of African American activists related to higher education during the period of 1960-1980. The study differentiates between the philosophies and activities of those in the Civil Rights Movement and those in the Black Power Movement. Primary documents and repositories of archival information were examined and semi-structured interviews were held with selected African American leaders in the Black Power Movement, students, and faculty at San Francisco State University.

Delimitations

Relative to African American activism, there is little data on the Black Power Movement as opposed to the Civil Rights Movement; therefore, the study focused on the Black Power Movement. During the period from 1960–1980, there were several social and political movements that aimed to effect changes in a variety of areas, such as employment, the wars in Viet Nam and Cambodia, the rights of women, etc.(Heath, 1976). The Black Power Movement was part of this activism. Numerous organizations participated in the Black Power Movement. Following is a partial list of organizations and associations that were active in the Black Power Movement, including organizations that were led by higher education students.

- Afro-American Association,

- African Federation of Black Educational Institutions,

- African Heritage Studies Association,

- African Liberation Day Committee,

- African Study Tour Movement,

- All African People's Revolutionary Party,

- Black Panther Party,

- Black Political Prisoners Association,

- Black Youth Organization,

- Coalition of Black Trade Unions,

- Committee for Unified Newark,

- Communiversity,

- Congress of African People,

- Council of Independent Black Institutions (CIBI),

- Harambee House,

- Institute of the Black World (IBW),

- Kemetic Institute,

- League of Black Revolutionary Workers,

- Marcus Garvey Institute,

- National Association of Black Social Workers (NABSW),

- National Black Independent Party,

- National Black Political Agenda, National Black Teachers Association,

- National Black United Fund,

- National Council on Black Studies,

- Nation House,

- Nation of Islam,

- Payton House of the Lord Church - Brooklyn, NY,

- Republic of New Africa,

- Revolutionary Action Movement (RAM),

- Student Nonviolent Coordinating Committee (SNCC),

- Student Organization for Black Unity (SOBU),

- Task Force for Political Empowerment,

- The East,

- The New Ark School,

- Third World Press,

- TransAfrica,

- Trinity United Church of Christ,

- United Negro Improvement Association (UNIA), and The US

- Organization (Worhill, 2008).

Some Black Power organizations or associations contributed to higher education - others did not. This study does not include the universe of Black Power organizations that were active at the time but documents the activities of selected Black Power organizations relative to their contributions to changes in higher education during the period.

Even though the Black Power Movement may have contributed to higher education in several areas, such as changes in curricula and an increase in the number of African American professors (Furniss, 1969; Jennings, 2007; Okafor, 1999), this research is limited to the development of Black student organizations and Black studies departments. It should be noted that the period that is covered, 1960–1980, does not cover the full breath or longevity of Black activism. Efforts predate the 1960s and continue to present times (Joseph, 2006; Robinson, Battle, & Robinson, Jr., 1987).

Limitations of the Study

Because of the sensitivity of some areas of the topic and activists' experiences with the FBI's Counter Intelligence Program (COINTELPRO), some of the individuals interviewed were hesitant to fully disclose details of events or were inclined to report events through ideological lenses. The information provided in their responses was cross- referenced with information found in primary documents, public records, books, and peer-reviewed journals to augment and verify information obtained through interviews.

Opinion was separated from facts by cross-referencing the information provided from interviews with data from other interviews and print data. The scarcity and/or inaccessibility of primary documents affected the researcher's ability to address some knowledge gaps. Some documents reviewed had incomplete information or omitted critical information.

The period that was studied occurred more than 30 years ago. Some details were forgotten and/ or records lost. Published information on this period is scarce and disjointed. Many of the Black leaders and activists of the period have died. Many of those who remain are senior citizens. In some cases, their memories were faulty and their accounts were affected by their biases.

Definition of Key Terms

Definitions of terms used in this book follow.

Black Nationalism is a term that is used interchangeably with Cultural Nationalism (Joseph, 2006; Karenga, 2008).

The Black Power Movement in this study focuses on two segments: the Revolutionary Nationalist Movement and the Cultural Nationalist Movement (Joseph, 2006; Lang, 2001; Woodard, 1999). The foci of the Revolutionary Nationalists were the self- determination and self-defense of African American people (Joseph, 2006; Williams, 1998; Woodard, 1999). The foci of the Cultural Nationalists were re-connecting African Americans to continental Africa, searching for and revealing the truth about the history of Africans in Africa and in the Diasporas, and instilling pride in African American people (Joseph, 2006; University of Michigan, 2007; Woodard, 1999).

The Civil Rights Movement is comprised of the individuals and organizations that worked to eliminate systemic discriminatory practices (i.e. voting rights, housing, education, etc.) and advance the integration of African Americans into all areas of American life (Joseph, 2006; Lang, 2001).

COINTELPRO is an acronym for the Counter Intelligence Program of the Federal Bureau of Investigation (FBI), which existed since the 1920's during the activism of Marcus Garvey. The surveillance program continued to be used to monitor and sabotage the activities of African American activists during the period studied (Joseph, 2006; Woodard, 1999).

Kawaida Doctrine is a document created by Dr. Maulana Karenga that prescribes how cultural nationalists should conduct their lives. *Kwanzaa* is an African American holiday that falls on December 26 – January 1(Karenga, 2008).

The Nguzo Saba means the seven Principles of Blackness. These principles; which include unity, self-determination, collective work and responsibility, cooperative economics, purpose, creativity, and faith; are the values that are celebrated during Kwanzaa (Karenga, 2008).

Pan-Africanism is the belief that all people of African descent, whether living on the continent of Africa or in the diaspora, are connected (Ture & Hamilton, 1992).

Platform is a list of the demands of organizations such as the Black Panther Party and students advocating for changes at universities (Austin, 2006; Williamson, 1999).

Overview of the Study

In this chapter, the researcher provided a statement of the problem in practice, the problem in research, the purpose of the research, research questions, the significance of the study, the theoretical framework and paradigm of inquiry, the methodology and rationale for the research, definitions of key terms, and delimitations and limitations of the study.

In Chapter II, the researcher reviews the literature on African American activism and changes in higher education from 1960 to 1980. Information includes a brief history of African American activism, the scholarship that already exists on the subject, primary sources that were used for the project, and tentative conclusions based on the review.

In Chapter III, the methods followed to gather and report the data are presented. Methodology includes the examination of primary documents and repositories of archival information; and, conducting semi-structured interviews with selected leaders, professors, and students in the Black Power Movement. The chapter provides the research design, description of the population, research questions, instrumentation, data collection, data preparation and handling, data analysis, design issues, ethical issues, and the timeline for the research.

Chapter IV provides an analysis of the findings of this study based on the responses of participants to the general research questions and the four research sub- questions, the characteristics of the population sampled, and contributions by organization. A summary of the history and status of the African American Black Power organizations researched and the history of the development of the Black Student Union (BSU) and Black Studies Program at San Francisco State College (SFSC) are presented. Through triangulation, correlations between the responses given during the interviews and literature are provided.

Chapter V presents the interpretations, conclusions, and recommendations of the study. Findings are presented for each research question. Recommendations are offered for improvements in practice and future research.

CHAPTER II

REVIEW OF LITERATURE

This chapter provides (a) primary sources that were used for the project (b) a brief history of African American activism from 1960 to 1980, (c) information on the scholarship that currently exists on the Black Power Movement, and (d) tentative conclusions based on a review of the literature.

Purposes and Methods of the Literature Review

Summaries of Black activism, its causes and outcomes, are included in numerous articles on the history of higher education in the United States. However, most of the articles, including those in the ASHE Reader Series: *The History of Higher Education* (1997), attribute Black activism to the Civil Rights Movement. Treatment of the Black Power Movement during this period in American history is absent, incomplete, or factually flawed on the relationship of the Black Power Movement to the history of higher education in the United States (Carson, 1987; Joseph, 2006). To address this problem, the researcher reviewed primary data found in collections and organizational websites, interviewed key participants, and conducted member checks through feedback from participants and a review by outside readers. The researcher triangulated the data to increase knowledge and gain more clarity on the dynamics of this period.

The History of African American Activism

Africans have struggled for freedom since the beginning of their enslavement.

According to Robinson et al. (1987), African Americans have revolted since the beginning of their enslavement, throughout their enslavement, post slavery, and the Jim Crow period; and, efforts continue to present times. Resistance to enslavement can be traced back to events such as revolts of Africans en route to the Americas in slave ships (e.g., the Amistad), slave revolts throughout the southern states, and the Haitian Revolution (Robinson, Battle, & Robinson, Jr., 1987). Several different strategies to realize Black liberation have been pursued by many individuals and organizations.

These efforts have been overt and covert, violent and non-violent. During the years of enslavement, African Americans communicated in code through song, revolted, and escaped plantations employing strategies such as the Underground Railroad. During the Civil War under President Lincoln, African Americans joined the Union Army to fight for their freedom. Since then, African Americans have fought in every American war. During the Reconstruction Period that immediately followed the end of the Civil War and the end of slavery, African Americans ran for elected office and were leaders in developing and passing legislation to rescind discriminatory Black Codes or Jim Crow laws in the South. Race riots occurred in 1909, 1920, 1921, 1964, 1965, 1966, 1967, and 1968. These activities are examples of the myriad of efforts employed by African Americans to achieve equal opportunity.

African Americans in the Civil Rights Movement led the effort to end segregation in schools and services. African Americans and Whites in this Movement protested inequities and injustices through marches, sit-ins, boycotts, and picket lines; adapting the non-violent principles of Mahatma Gandhi to guide their efforts (Grant, 1968). The National Association for the Advancement of Colored People (NAACP) is a premiere civil rights organization that was founded in 1909. Its advocacy efforts in 1955 are recognized as the launch of the Civil Rights Movement. Several significant events occurred in 1955. Several African Americans were killed in Springfield, Illinois;

Rosa Parks was arrested in Montgomery, Alabama for refusing to give her seat to a White person and sit in the back of a bus; and, Emmet Till, a 14-year old boy, was mutilated and lynched for allegedly whistling at a White woman. The results were the beginning of the Montgomery Bus Boycott, led by Rev. Dr. Martin Luther King, Jr. of the Montgomery Improvement Association, and the emergence of a number of organizations whose goal was to fight for civil rights.

African American churches were major players in the Civil Rights Movement, lending their human and material resources. Many of the heads of civil rights organizations were ministers. The first organization that used the pacifist tactics of Mahatma Gandhi was the Fellowship for Reconciliation. In 1941 in Chicago, Illinois, this organization formed the Congress of Racial Equality (CORE). In 1957, the Southern Christian Leadership Conference (SCLC), with Dr. King as president, was founded. The objectives of these organizations were to strike down discriminatory laws that prohibited service to African Americans in public facilities, to obtain the right to vote, and, through integration, to open access to employment, education, housing, and neighborhoods. The end of segregation in public schools (Brown v. the Board of Education, 1954) was the first major accomplishment followed by passage of the Civil Rights Act of 1964 (Grant, 1968; Robinson, Battle, & Robinson, Jr., 1987), the National Voting Rights Act in 1965 (Grant, 1968; Robinson, Battle, & Robinson, Jr., 1987), and the Higher Education Act of 1965 (Grant, 1968; Robinson, Battle, & Robinson, Jr., 1987). Although the Civil Rights Movement's advocacy resulted insignificant achievements, during the same period there were African Americans who rejected the philosophy of non-violent resistance and integration. Many of these individuals would become leaders and activists in the Black Power Movement.

The Black Power Movement

The Black Power Movement emerged in 1966following the shooting of James Meredith as he attempted to integrate the University of Mississippi. The term, "Black Power" was coined by Mukasa (aka Willie Ricks) and popularized by Stokely Carmichael during a march in honor of

James Meredith (Joseph, 2006; Tyson, 1999). The term was condemned by Martin Luther King, Jr. and other civil rights leaders but was embraced by other organizations. The Black Power Movement grew significantly after the assassinations of Rev. Dr. King, Jr., Malcolm X, and President John F. Kennedy (Joseph, 2006; Robinson, Battle, & Robinson, Jr., 1987).

In *Black Power, The Politics of Liberation in America*, Ture (aka Stokely Carmichael) and Hamilton (1992) defined Black Power as "...a call for black people in this country to unite, to recognize their heritage, to build a sense of community...to define their own goals, to lead their own organizations and to support those organizations" (p. 44). The premise of Black Power was articulated in the words, "Before a group can enter the open society, it must first close ranks... group solidarity is necessary before a group can operate effectively from a bargaining position of strength in a pluralistic society" (p. 44). To this end, Black Power activists purported that Black people must lead and run their own organizations. Black Power activists called for Black self-determination, Black self-identity, Black self-defense, and the creation of power bases for proper representation and sharing control. The goals of these constructs were "...full participation in the decision-making processes affecting the lives of Black people, and recognition of the virtues in themselves as Black people" (p. 47).

The Black Power Movement rejected non-violence and integration as accepted strategies (Ture & Hamilton, 1992) for Black freedom. The Black Power philosophy was influenced by the writings of Harold Cruse and Malcolm X, who promulgated the need for African Americans to have self-determination, self-defense, and self-respect (Joseph, 2006; Woodward, 1999). Ture and Hamilton (1992) stated there could be no social order without social justice. Black people must fight back and meet aggression with defense.

They saw integration as devaluing the Black community, requiring Black people to give up their identity and deny their heritage for acceptance in White society. The importance of the Black community winning its freedom while preserving its racial and cultural integrity was stressed. The authors saw integration as working against this preservation.

Black Power did not reject the participation of Whites in the movement but defined their role as educative, organizational, and supportive (Carmichael, 1971; Ture & Hamilton, 1992). Whites were encouraged to educate White groups that Black activists could not reach on the need for Black power. They were urged to go into White communities and work to end racism. Organizationally, Whites were urged to form a White power block that would join with Black groups to end racism. The leaders of Black Power organizations stated that Whites should play a supportive role, offering specific skills and techniques, but the organizations should be led and staffed by Blacks.

In *Black Liberation in Conservative America*, Marable (1997) called for a new Black Power Movement stating, "Whenever there is a crisis in confidence in middle-class Black leadership, and whenever this occurs at a time when White political and corporate power turns aggressively against Black folk; the conditions are ripe for an upsurge of Black nationalism and Black awareness. This social eruption is cultural, educational, political, economic, and ideological" (p. 229). Marable noted the gap created by what he considered the demise of the Black Power Movement. He asserted that the Black Panther Party was largely destroyed by the Federal Bureau of Investigation's (FBI) Counter- Intelligence Program (COINTELPRO). Black activists that favored political and social change were isolated, harassed, and/or imprisoned. Marable defined "power" as "...the ability or capacity to realize your specific, objective interests. Power is not a thing, but a process…" (p. 247). Because of the gap, he believed that a new movement was needed.

Although there was general agreement on the tenets of Black Power among Black Power activists, there were divergent views on emphases and strategies. One segment – the Revolutionary Nationalists - embraced the idea of self-defense and focused on defending the Black community. Another segment – the Cultural Nationalists - promoted fostering a reconnection with Africa, African history, African American history, African culture, and the development of parallel Black institutions to fill the void in the Black community (Marable, 1997; Woodard, 1999). Other organizations, such as the Nation of Islam, embraced both self-defense and cultural renewal through religion. The passion and difference of opinions of Black Power activists on these issues led to dissension and conflict. To address the conflict, Karenga called for "unity without uniformity" (Woodard, 1999, p. 104) at the 1967 Black Power Conference in Newark, New Jersey. The groups agreed to work together on certain issues and, at the same time, continue to employ their own strategies to accomplish Black liberation.

In 1968, Black activists held a Black convention in Philadelphia, Pennsylvania.

Participants included activists from the Black Arts Convention held in Detroit, Michigan and the Black Power Planning Summit held in Washington, DC. Organizations/coalitions that spun off from the meeting included the Congress of African People, the African Liberation Support Committee, the National Black Assembly, the Congressional Black Caucus, the Black Women's United Front, and the Federation of Pan-African Educational Institutions (Woodard, 1999).Many of the organizations that were part of the coalitions continue to exist today.

The Black Power Movement and Revolutionary Nationalism.

Revolutionary nationalists embraced the notion of self-defense. A number of organizations emerged with an emphasis on self-defense. Among these were the Deacons for Defense and Justice (Hill, 2004; Tyson, 1999), the Black Panther Party (Austin, 2006), and the Student Nonviolent Coordinating Committee (Carmichael, 1971; Carson, 1995; Ture & Hamilton, 1997). The Deacons for Defense and Justice was founded in 1964 in Jonesboro, Louisiana in response to attacks on Blacks by the Ku Klux Klan and police brutality. Several chapters were organized throughout the southern states. The Black Panther Party was one of the most infamous Black self-defense organizations in America. It was founded in 1966 in Oakland, California to defend the Black community from police brutality. Because of African Americans' intense concern about police brutality, chapters quickly spread throughout the United States. The Student Nonviolent Coordinating Committee (SNCC) emerged from the Civil Rights Movement. Members were college students who took time off from college to help Blacks in the South obtain voting rights. They also worked to end segregation of public facilities. During these activities, students were victims of shootings and beatings. Because of the violence they experienced, members of the organization became disillusioned with the principle of nonviolence. After James Meredith was killed, they rejected the tenets of nonviolence and adopted "Black Power" (Ture & Hamilton, 1997, p. 1) under the leadership of Stokely Carmichael. There were many other Revolutionary Nationalist groups, too numerous to list in this writing (Joseph, 2006), however, the three organizations highlighted are representative of this approach to Black liberation.

The Black Power Movement and Cultural Nationalism (Black Nationalism).

According to Joseph (2006) and Warren (1990), Dr. Maulana Karenga and Amiri Baraka were major forces in the Cultural Nationalist Movement, which is also known as the Black Nationalist Movement. Karenga formed the US Organization in September 1965 in Los Angeles, California. From 1965 to 1980, the US Organization played a central role in virtually every African-centered movement in the United States (Karenga, 2008).

Karenga wrote and promulgated the tenets of the Kawaida Doctrine, which provided guiding principles for the conduct of cultural nationalist activists throughout the United States. He also created the Nguzo Saba (Seven Principles of Blackness) and Kwanzaa, an African American holiday that celebrates the survival of African Americans (Karenga, 2008). In 1967, Amiri Baraka, under the mentorship of Karenga, formed the Committee for Unified New Ark (CFUN) in Newark, New Jersey, and later in 1970, Baraka helped to form the Congress of African People (CAP). Baraka, a playwright and poet, is also credited with leading the Black Arts Movement during the 1960s and 1970s (Warren, 1990).During this period, numerous people attended poetry readings, street theaters, and art workshops.

The purpose of the Kawaida doctrine was to provide identity, purpose, and direction for African Americans cultural nationalist activists. According to Karenga (2008), Kawaida is "a communitarian African philosophy created in the context of the African American liberation struggle and developed as an ongoing synthesis of the best of African thought and practice in constant exchange with the world" (p. 3).These principles were derived, in part, from the teachings of Malcolm X (Joseph, 2006; Woodard, 1999; X, 1990).The philosophy has seven dual emphases – (1) philosophy and practice; (2) culture and community; (3) tradition and reason; (4) dialog and recovery; (5) language and logic; (6) critique and corrective; and, (7) synthesis and exchange within the world (Karenga, 2008, p. 1).

Kwanzaa, an African American holiday, was created in 1967. The Nguzo Saba, the seven principles of Blackness, is part of the Kawaida Doctrine. The principles of the Nguzo Saba are:

1. Umoja (Unity) – To develop and maintain unity in the family, community, nation, and race.
2. Kujichagulia (Self Determination) – To define ourselves and speak for ourselves instead of being defined and spoken for by others.
3. Ujima (Collective Work and Responsibility) – To make our brothers' and sisters' problems our problems and to solve them together.
4. Ujamaa (Cooperative Economics) – To develop our own stores, shops, and other businesses and to profit together from them.
5. Nia (Purpose) – To make as our collective vocation the building and developing of our community.

6. Kuumba (Creativity) – To always do as much as we can in the way that we can to restore our people to their traditional greatness.

7. Imani (Faith) – To believe with all our hearts in our parents, our teachers, our leaders, and the righteousness and victory of our struggle (Karenga, 2008, p. 2).

Although members of US, CFUN, and CAP were the major followers of the tenets of Kawaida, they were not alone. The doctrine and principles guided the way of life of activists in many groups that identified with cultural nationalism (Joseph, 1999; Karenga, 2008). Today, Kwanzaa is observed by millions of African Americans throughout the United States (Woodard, 1999).

The Black Power Movement and Pan-Africanism.

Pan-Africanism is a cultural and intellectual movement that has a history going back to slavery and colonialism (Carmichael, 1971; Warren, 1990). In 1900, H. Sylvester Williams promoted the idea of pan-Africanism during a meeting he organized of Africans from Africa and the diaspora. However, W.E.B. Du Bois is credited with being the "Father of Pan-Africanism" primarily because Dubois continued to promote pan- Africanism after the death of Williams in 1911 (Warren, 1990). Several African American leaders, such as Du Bois and Garvey, promoted the expatriation of African Americans to Africa. Other leaders, such as Baraka (aka LeRoi Jones) and Karenga did not.

According to Carmichael (1971), pan-Africanism is the belief that all African people, wherever they are, are one and belong to the African nation (p. 221). Many African leaders on the continent of Africa and in the diaspora were and are proponents of pan- Africanism. Some noteworthy individuals were W. E. B. Du Bois, Henry Sylvester Williams, George Padmore, Marcus Garvey, Patrice Lumumba, Malcolm X, Ahmed Sekou Toure, Kwame Nkrumah, Amiri Baraka, and Maulana Karenga. According to Carmichael (1971), Black nationalism is African nationalism. Pan-Africanism is the highest aspiration of African nationalism. Black power means African power; therefore, "The African's power base is his homeland – Mother Africa. In order to achieve African power, Mother Africa must be strong. To be strong, she must be unified" (p. 224- 225).Pan-Africanism was a major tenet of those in the Black Power Movement.

The role of COINTELPRO in the Black Power Movement.

COINTELPRO (Ball, 2013; Federal Bureau of Investigation (FBI) Counter Intelligence Program (COINTELPRO), 2013; Glick, 1989) was an external variable that played a significant role in the change process. It was an effort of government officials to maintain the status quo by controlling what they considered were radical groups that endangered the country. In this case, its targets were idealistic students who wanted to change injustices in the world so they could realize the American dream. COINTELPRO had a devastating impact on individuals and organizations that it targeted. It has had a long lasting effect and individuals who were targeted continue to be suspicious of individuals and institutions; and, believe in conspiracy theories today. Development and use of critical thinking skills became a matter of survival for them. This effect contributed to the resistance the researcher encountered when conducting this research.

Because of advocacy efforts, the domestic spying program was outlawed in the 1970s. However, many Black Power activists consider the Patriot Act (ACLU, 2013; ARPS, 2013) to be a resurrection of COINTELPRO. This belief and the current National Security Administration (NSA) spying scandal have served to fuel the continuation of suspicion and mistrust of government.

African American Activism and Higher Education

African American activism related to higher education can be traced back to the emancipation of Blacks (Du Bois, 1903). The first post-secondary schools for Blacks emerged shortly before the Civil War. Three schools were established in border states. Thirteen schools were established between 1864 and 1869. Nine additional schools opened between 1870 and 1880. Five schools were established after 1881 and four schools were established with agricultural funds after passage of the Morrell Land Grant Act in 1890 (Du Bois, 1903; Rudolph, 1990). African American scholars debated the type and quality of education needed by African Americans to transition them from the institution of slavery to full citizenship. Booker T. Washington (1903), who founded the Tuskegee Institute, advocated for an industrial education that would teach Blacks trades and technical skills. He purported that this type of education would give them the skills they needed for employment. Du Bois (1903) stressed the need for a liberal arts education that would produce Black critical thinkers. Not trusting Whites to educate Blacks, Du Bois advocated for the development of African American scholars who would teach other African Americans. This tenet became known as the —Talented Tenth. Du Bois' position was supported by Carter G. Woodson (1933) who stated that Blacks were being mis-educated by Whites. Woodson further stated that Black teachers who are educated by Whites mis-educate other Blacks. Woodson's arguments were repeated by Black Power activists during the 1960s and 1970s when they advocated for changes in curricula and the formation of Black studies departments.

With a few exceptions, the vast majority of educational institutions from elementary to higher education were segregated until 1954. In 1954, the Supreme Court ruled that segregated schools were unconstitutional. In 1956, Autherine Lucy was one of the first Black students to enter a White higher education institution. The school that she attended, the University of Alabama, later suspended her for her own safety. The school remained segregated until 1963. One outcome of the advocacy of civil rights organizations and the death of President Kennedy was passage of the Higher Education Act in 1965. This Act provided financial aid, which enabled all students who, regardless of income, desired an advanced degree to attend higher education institutions (U. S. Department of Education, 2008).

Current Scholarship on the Effect of Black Power Activism on Higher Education

The researcher reviewed books and articles that have recently been published by Black Power scholars and found that none of the books focused specifically on contributions to higher education. These publications included books such as *Up Against The Wall: Violence in the Making and Unmaking of the Black Panther Party* by Austin (2006), *Stokely Speaks: Black Power Back to Pan-Africanism* by Carmichael (1971), *In Struggle: SNCC and the Black Awakenings of the 1960s* by Carson (1981), *The Deacons for Defense: Armed Resistance and the Civil Rights Movement* by Hill (2004), *Black Liberation in Conservative America* by Marable (1997), *By Any Means Necessary: The Life and Legacy of Malcolm X* by Marable (1992), *Black Power: The Politics of Liberation* by Ture and Hamilton (1992), *Radio Free Dixie: Robert F. Williams & the Roots of Black Power* by Tyson (1999), *Negroes with Guns* by Williams (1998), *A Nation within a Nation: Amiri Baraka (LeRoi Jones) & Black Power Politics* by Woodard (1999), and *Malcolm X on Afro-American History* by Malcolm X (1990). In reviewing the literature, the books and journals focused on their work in communities. None of the materials reviewed, specifically, focused on advocacy efforts for changes in higher education.

Several scholarly articles provided hints of the influence of African American activism on higher education. In response to student efforts to change a university history course to include multicultural content at the University of California in Berkley, California, Bennett (1988) gave a passionate argument for maintaining Western civilization as the foundation of history courses. He argued that Western culture was superior to other cultures and should remain the core of these courses. Hirsch (1983) responded by pursuing the development of cultural literacy in school curriculum on the primary and secondary levels. Both articles failed to examine the context, rationale, and players that promoted the changes.

In their article, Chang, Altbach, and Lomotey (2005) discussed the challenges of race in higher education. They concluded that race is a changing manifestation that continues to elude resolution. Throughout higher education literature, race and African American activism are grouped with discussions on student protest but the literature does not report outcomes resulting from the activism. From October 8–10, 1969, the American Council of Education analyzed the causes and possible responses to student unrest at its 52nd annual meeting that was held in Washington, DC. Background papers from the conference illustrated the views of university scholars on options for responding to student unrest (curriculum change, Black student unions, and Black studies departments).

In one paper, *Racial Pressures on Urban Institutions,* Samuel Proctor, Professor of Education at Rutgers State University, stated:

1. University catalogues and menus of courses at conventional colleges and universities reveal a bias in favor of the understanding and appreciation of Western European, Anglo-Saxon, Germanic, French, and Mediterranean cultures;
2. Governance of universities is in the hands of an appointed (by the governor) or a self-perpetuating board of trustees;

3. The facilities, costs, calendar, and the organization of the school year (including when food services are closed) indicate that students must have a fairly substantial home base of support;

4. The procedures for students to achieve success and "honors" rest heavily on the early accumulation of facts and a healthy memory; and

5. A walk through the campus will show that, in spite of pretensions of freedom, the university follows the mores of the community at its worst (Procter, pp. 25-27). In another paper, *Racial Minorities and Curriculum Change*, W. Todd Furniss,

Director of the Commission on Academic Affairs at the American Council on Education, framed five general rationales that motivated demands for Black studies programs. The rationales were:

1. Correcting American history by a more adequate recognition of the past and present experience of 25 million Black citizens.

2. Hastening integration by improving the understanding of Blacks by nonBlacks.

3. Hastening integration by preparing Black students to take part in the American society with pride and self-confidence.

4. Preparing Black students to understand and work for a Black community.

5. Providing Black students with a sense of "power" (p. 1).

In a third paper, *Faculty Response to Racial Tensions*, Amtai Etzioni (1969), presented four issues for consideration by university faculty. They included admission of students from disadvantaged backgrounds, compensatory education for those admitted without full qualifications, specialization in ethnic studies, and separate facilities for the social life of students of a minority group (p. 108). He concluded that the shortest route toward a pluralistic integrated society was the creation of Black social centers in addition to other existing ethnic ones within the limits of universal shared core values. In summary, the papers presented at the Conference indicated a consensus that something had to be done to improve campus life for Black students within certain limits.

In Defense of Themselves: The Black Student Struggle for Success and Recognition at Predominantly White Colleges and Universities, Williamson (1999) provided in-depth information about the struggles of Black students attending predominately-White colleges and universities (PWCU). Williamson conducted a literature review and interviewed African American students who attended higher education institutions during the 1960s and 1970s on their experiences at PWCUs. The study, which presented the student perspective, clearly connected the development of Black student unions, Black studies departments, and Black cultural centers with the Black Power Movement. These centers, also called Black houses (p. 15), were meeting places for Black students and Black nonstudents from the surrounding community. Many of these nonstudents were community activists. Black Power leaders frequently gave lectures at the centers and encouraged students to organize for changes on campus.

Critical Race Theory, Racial Microaggressions, and Campus Racial Climate: the Experiences of African American Students is a study that was conducted by Solorzano, Ceja, and Yosso (2000) on how race, racism and their micro-level forms affected structures, processes, and discourses in the collegiate environment. They studied race and racism inside and outside of the classroom setting. The elements of critical race theory (CRT) were the foci of their study. For the study, they cited Banks' (1995) definition of race. Race was defined as —a socially constructed phenomenon created to differentiate racial groups and to show the superiority or dominance of one race – in particular, Whites – over others. Lorde's (1992) and Marable's (1992) definitions of racism were cited. Lorde defined racism as "the belief in the inherent superiority of one race over all others and thereby, the right to dominance" (p. 496). Marable defined racism as "a system of ignorance, exploitation, and power used to oppress African Americans, Latinos, Asians, Pacifica Islanders, American Indians, and other people on the basis of ethnicity, culture, mannerisms, and color" (p. 5).

The five elements of CRT that comprised the focus of their study included:

(a) the centrality of race and racism and their intersectionality with other forms of subordination, (b) the challenge to dominant ideology, (c) the commitment to social justice, (d) the centrality of experimental knowledge, and (e) the transdisciplinary perspective (p. 63). The researchers studied the following four questions: (1) How do African American students experience racial microaggressions? (2) What impact do these racial microaggressions have on African American students? (3) How do African American students respond to racial microaggressions? (4) How do racial microaggressions affect the collegiate racial environment (p. 63)? They found that at elite undergraduate universities where educational conditions may appear to be equal, inequality and discrimination still exist and the cumulative effects of racial microaggressions can be devastating.

Critical race theory researchers use stories of those directly impacted to explain their realities. Some of the stories presented in the study included a) a male students difficulty getting into study groups because of a belief that he could not be Black and still be intelligent, "I don't want to work with you because you're Black," b) stereotype threats (e.g., an assumption that Black students are there because of affirmative action), c) being closely watched because of the fear of theft, and d) having to depart from social functions out of the back door instead of the front door as other students. The study clearly illuminated the devastating effects of microaggressions.

In 2006, Joseph published two books on the Black Power Movement. One book, *Waiting 'til the Midnight Hour*, was a narrative history. The other book, *The Black Power Movement: Rethinking the Civil Rights – Black Power Era*, was a collection of essays about varying aspects of the Black Power Movement. Although information on the impact of the Black Power Movement on higher education appeared in each book, higher education was not the focus of either book.

The History of Black Student Unions

The experiences of Black student activists with Black power activists provided inspiration for the students to organize Black student unions. Initially, students joined diverse community groups and selected some over others. Some students joined the National Association for the Advancement of Colored People (NAACP) but found that the organization's mission did not reflect their reality and dropped out (Williamson, 1999). Many African American students experienced racial hostility, alienation, stark class differences, and isolation on predominantly White college campuses. They felt they needed an organization of their own on campus. The notions of developing a power base and safe zones for their academic survival resonated. The first Black student union was established in 1966 at San Francisco State College (Joseph, 2006; Williamson, 1999).

Similar organizations emerged at PWCUs across the country. Organizations, such as the Student Organization of Black Unity (SOBU), the Student Nonviolent Coordinating Committee (SNCC), and the Congress of African People (CAP) played major roles in organizing Black student unions on college campuses. Memberships in the organizations were modest until the assassination of Martin Luther King, Jr. in 1968.After his death, they experienced rapid growth. There were numerous Black student unions during the 1970s and many continue to exist today.

Black student unions and cultural nationalism.

As stated previously, one of the goals of cultural nationalist organizations was to develop parallel Black institutions to serve the African American community (Woodard, 1999). One of the areas of prolific development was education. Freedom schools, also known as independent Black schools, became numerous. Most cultural nationalist organizations operated a school as a component of its structure. These schools became a training ground for Black educators (Baraka, 1997; Karenga, 2008).

Cultural nationalist organizations also led study circles for activists and college students. Books on African and African American history were read and discussed, and visiting scholars lectured on African and African American history and politics. Black college and university students were invited to participate in the circles to enhance their knowledge and to encourage them to take their knowledge and skills back to the Black community after they completed their education. Members of the study circles studied enriched African history, which was defined by Robinson, Battle, & Robinson, Jr. (1987) as cultural and anthropological history (p. 26). According to Robinson et al., the values flowing from studying enriched African history are:

1. the heightening of abstract and mathematical intelligence;
2. an increase in creativity in all areas but particularly in science, literature, and music;
3. an increase in physical energies, mental health, and a joy of living;
4. love for African adults and children individually and collectively;
5. a loss of hatred for Whites; and
6. the production of a society-wide aura of positive psychic energy that fosters Black intellectual and spiritual development (p. 27).

These values were embraced by African American students because they addressed the frustrations they were experiencing on PWCU campuses.

The studying of enriched African history also strengthens the "cultural glue" (Robinson et al., p. 28) of African Americans. Cultural clue, which exists within all groups, is defined as binding the members of a group together to achieve group protection, group dignity and honor, group material enrichment, group political power, group financial power, group physical and mental health, positive group recognition, and group educational achievement (p. 28). The ingredients of cultural glue of African Americans are:

1. Knowledge of a common African homeland;
2. Appreciation and honor for that homeland;
3. Appreciation and honor of heroes and heroines of that homeland;
4. Practice of traditions that deepen appreciation of the homeland;
5. Appreciation of the language of the homeland;
6. Appreciation of the music of the homeland;
7. Belief in a mystique concerning the people of the homeland; and,
8. Continual exposure to drama portraying the beauty, grandeur, and sophistication of the culture of the homeland (pp. 27–28).

According to the authors, history is to the human race as memory is to the individual. Memory "lifts humans out of an eternity of unconnected moments to create a sense of continuity and unity with their past" (Newsweek, February 1983 as cited by Robinson et al., 1987, p. 30). It is this setting that laid the groundwork for the development of Black student unions.

Exum summarized the benefits of Black student unions. Exum (1985, as cited by Williamson) stated there are six critical services that Black student unions provide for Black students. They:

1. meet social, psychological, and academic needs that were not being met through traditional university mechanisms;
2. provide a safe forum for the exploration of identity issues;
3. enable the development of collective Black student values and ideological beliefs;
4. help to develop a sense of collective competence and ability;
5. enable collective action and behavior on issues relevant to Black students; and
6. provide a training ground for the development of political organization, participation, and leadership (p. 10).

A number of the services listed mirror the benefits of attending the study circles held by Black Power activists.

Black student unions and revolutionary nationalism.

According to Williamson (1999), Exum stated that Black student unions had many commonalities. In *Faculty Response to Racial Tensions*, Etzioni (1969) presented, as a typical list, the demands of Black students at the University of Wisconsin:

1. An autonomous Black studies department controlled by Black students and faculty which would enable students to receive a BA in Black studies;
2. A Black chairman of the Black studies department who would be approved by a committee of Black students and faculty;
3. That at least 500 Black students be admitted to the university next fall;
4. That 20 teachers be allocated for the initiation of the Black studies department with the approval of Black students;

5. That amnesty, described as no reprisal or chastisement, be given all students who participate in boycotts or other such actions in reference to our demands;

6. That a Black co-director of the Students Financial Aids Office (scholarships, loans, etc.) be appointed with the approval of Black students;

7. That Black counselors be hired by the Student Financial Aids Office with the approval of Black students;

8. That scholarships be provided for all athletes up until the time they receive their degree. Some athletes have to go for a fifth year;

9. That the existing Black courses be transferred to the Black studies department;

10. That it be established that Black students with the Black faculty have the power to hire and fire all administrators and teachers who are involved in anything related to Black students;

11. That it be established that control of the Black cultural center be in the hands of Black students;

12. That all expelled Oshkosh (State University) students who wish to attend the University be admitted immediately; and

13. That proof as defined by Black students that the above demands have been met be given to Black students by the administration (p. 109).

These demands were considered typical. They were in the platform presented by Heath (1976). When compared side by side, the ten-point platform of Black student unions (Heath, 1976) was similar to the ten-point platform of the Black Panther Party (Austin, 2006). The striking similarity leads one to conclude that the platforms of Black student unions were derived from the platform of the Black Panther Party.

Table 1

Comparison of Black Student Union and Black Panther Party Platforms

Black student union (February 1969)	Black panther party (October 1966)
1. We want freedom. We want power to determine the destiny of our school.	1. We want freedom. We want power to determine the destiny of our Black community.
2. We want full enrollment in the schools for our people.	2. We want full employment for our people.
3. We want an end to the robbery of the White man of our Black community.	3. We want an end to the robbery of the White man of our Black Community.
4. We want decent educational facilities, fit for the use of students.	4. We want decent housing, fit for shelter of human beings.

5. We want an education for our people that teach us how to survive in the present day society.

5. We want education for our people that exposes the true nature of this decadent American society. We want education that teaches us our true history and our role in the present-day society.

6. We want racist teachers to be excluded and restricted from all public schools.

6. We want all black men to be exempt from military service.

7. We want an immediate end to police brutality and murder of black people. We want all police and special agents to be excluded and restricted from school premises.

7. We want an immediate end to **police brutality** and **murder** of black people.

8. We want all students that have been exempt, expelled, or suspended from school to be reinstated.

8. We want freedom for all Black men held in federal, state, county, and city prisons, and jails.

9. We want all students when brought to trial to be tried in student court by a jury of their peer group or students of their school.

9. We want all black people when brought to trial to be tried in court by a jury of their peer group or people from their black communities as defined by the Constitution of the United States.

10. We want power, enrollment, equipment, education, teachers, justice, and peace.

10. We want land, bread, housing, education, clothing, justice, and peace. And, as our major political objective, a United Nations supervised plebiscite to be held throughout the Black colony in which only Black colonial subjects will be allowed to participate for the purpose of determining the will of Black people as to their national destiny.

Note: **From** *Up against the wall: Violence in the making and unmaking of the Black panther party* **(p. 353), by C. J. Austin, 2006, Fayetteville, AR: University of Arkansas Press and** *Mutiny does happen lightly: The literature of the American resistance to the Vietnam war* (pp. 1-3), by G. L. Heath, 1976, Metuchen, NJ: Scarecrow Press.

Rituals, dress, and practices of members of Black student unions.

In addition to embracing and emulating the philosophy of the revolutionary nationalists, members of Black student unions also emulated the dress and practices of cultural nationalists (Joseph, 2006;Procter, 1969; Williamson, 1999; Woodard, 1999).They wore traditional African clothing and natural hairstyles (Afros and braids), learned to speak traditional African languages (Kiswahili), learned traditional African dances and songs, held study circles, promoted African American holidays, and changed their names from European to African names. The students in many Black student unions submerged themselves in African thought and practice, following the tenets of the Nguzo Saba and the Kawaida Doctrine (Karenga, 2008).

History of Black Studies Courses at Higher Education Institutions

According to Joseph (2006), Black studies departments were the institutionalization of Black Power in higher education. The teaching of African and African American courses can be traced back to the early 1900sfollowing the founding of the Association for the Study of Negro Life and History (ASNLH) in 1915 by Carter G. Woodson (Okafor, 1999). In 1919, Carter G Woodson released a report on African American courses that were being taught at PWCUs (Okafor, 1999). The report stated that a course was offered at Ohio State University, Nebraska University, Stanford University, University of Oklahoma, University of Missouri, University of Chicago, University of Minnesota, and Harvard University. William Leo Hansberry was a major proponent of Black studies. In 1922, he joined the staff at Howard University to teach a series of courses called *Negro Civilizations of Ancient Africa.* He succeeded in establishing an African Civilization Section within the college's history department (Robinson et al., 1987). These events marked the beginning of the emergence of Black studies departments.

The emergence and growth of Black studies departments.

The typical platform of Black student unions above shows that Black student activists consistently demanded the creation of Black studies programs on higher education campuses. These demands emanated from their discontent, frustrations, and enhanced social and political awareness - Black consciousness derived from the Black Power Movement (Norment, Jr., 2007). In 1969, as a result of a strike of student activists at San Francisco State University that was led by students in a newly formed Black student union, the Division of Ethnic Studies and departments of Black, Asian, Chicano, and Native American studies were established. These were considered the first of their kind. The university's Black student union wrote a position paper entitled *The Justification for African American Studies.* The paper was subsequently used to promote the establishment of Black studies departments at more than 60 universities (Okafor, 1999).

Colon (1980 as cited by Williamson) stated that the purpose of Black studies departments was:

1. Corrective: to counter distortions, misperceptions, and fallacies surrounding Black people;

2. Descriptive: to accurately depict the past and present events constituting the Black experience; and

3. Prescriptive: to educate Black students who would eventually uplift the race (p. 12).

According to Norment, Jr. (2007), African American studies have "changed the face of the higher education system, along with the ways in which research is conducted to deal with issues concerning African Americans" (p. 45). It has strengthened African American leadership; elevated discourse on the historical and contemporary experiences of African Americans; provided space for Black students to be mentored, recognized, and supported; and, it has presented people of African descent with alternative ways of viewing the world based on traditional African beliefs and values (known as an African- centered worldview). The discipline also opened the door for university support for other ethnic-specific minority groups, facilities, and activities.

By the late 1960s, there was mainstream university support for Black studies departments. By 1974, at least 1,300 colleges and universities offered at least one course in African American studies and approximately 800 higher education institutions had full-scale African American studies programs. By the mid-1990s, due to limited funding, the number of Black studies departments dwindled to 375 (Okafor, 1999).

Literature Gap and Summary

The influence of the Black Power Movement on the development of Black student unions and Black studies departments is apparent when examining the philosophical tenets promulgated in Black student unions and in the curricula of Black studies departments. The Black Power Movement's notion of separatism to facilitate meaningful integration was embraced by both groups, Black student unions and Black studies departments, which institutionalized one of the tenets of Black Power. The first Black studies department at the San Francisco State University was created in response to advocacy efforts of a coalition organized by students in the Black student union (Norment, Jr., 2007). The link between the emergence of Black studies departments and the advocacy of Black students is clear.

The authors of texts on the history of American higher education had limited knowledge of African American activism because, with the exception of the Civil Rights Movement, the activities of the Black Power Movement were not documented by those who were part of it (Carson, 1981; Joseph, 2006; Ture & Hamilton, 1992; Woodard, 1999).Recently, a number of books and articles on African American activism have been published but the information has not been integrated into curricula or used as major texts. This has caused unevenness in the coverage of the contributions of African Americans to higher education in courses on the history of American higher education. This study can contribute to knowledge on the role of the Black Power Movement in changes made in higher education from 1960 – 1980 and may inform higher education curriculum for an accurate representation and inclusion of African Americans as contributors to higher education.

The model of Nigrescence developed by Cross (Cross & Fhagen-Smith, 2005) explains identity formation of African American people relative to racism. This model and definitions of race are currently being taught in student development courses. In addition to the effect of racism on the identity formation of African Americans, African American culture should be taught. Because Africans Americans were born and raised in the United States, there has been a failure of mainstream society to recognize that African Americans have a culture that is distinct from other American population groups (Hilliard, 1989; Robinson et al., 1987). Often, African American culture is omitted in cultural competency courses. Their focus is usually on foreign nationals and immigrants.

The term, diversity, has also served to expand the definition of culture to include other groups such as women and homosexuals. For this reason, there has been tension between the concepts of cultural competency and diversity among African American scholars (West, 2001). Clarification of definitions is needed as well as enhancement of curricula in this area.

In this chapter, the researcher provided a brief history of the issue, information on the scholarship that currently exists on the Black Power Movement, primary sources that were used for the project, the conceptual frameworks, and offered tentative conclusions based on review of the literature. The next chapter provides details of the research methodology.

CHAPTER III

METHODOLOGY

The purpose of this historical study is to analyze the contributions of the Black Power Movement to higher education during the period of 1960–1980through the voices of African American leaders, faculty, and students. The researcher focuses on two changes in higher education – the emergence of Black student organizations and Black studies departments. This information was obtained through a review of the literature and interviews of African American leaders, faculty, and students who were active in the Black Power Movement. Following is the (a) recapitulation of the research questions, (b) research design, (c) conceptual frameworks, (d) description of the population and sampling procedures, (e) instrumentation, (f) data collection and handling, (g) data analysis, (h) trustworthiness, (i) researcher subjectivity statement, and (j) ethical issues.

Recapitulation of Research Questions

The general research question was, "What effect did the Black Power Movement have on changes in higher education from 1960 – 1980?" The following sub-questions were answered:

1. What role did it play in the development of Black student organizations, particularly Black student unions?
2. What role did it play in the development of Black studies departments?
3. What does the San Francisco State University experience in the development of a Black student union and a Black studies department suggest about the Black Power Movement and higher education?
4. What other important cases provide information on the effect of the Black Power Movement on changes in higher education?

Research Design

This is a historical book. Busha and Harter's (1980) steps for historical research methods were followed. This researcher identified the idea, topic, or research question; conducted a background literature review; and, determined that historiography would be the data collection process. This researcher refined the background literature review, identified and located primary and secondary data sources, confirmed the authenticity and accuracy of source materials; analyzed the data; and, developed a narrative exposition of the findings (p. 91).

A historical analysis of African American activism during the period of 1960- 1980 relative to changes in higher education is presented. Data was collected through a literature search, interviews with representatives from selected organizations in the Black Power Movement, a study of the first Black student union and Black studies department at San Francisco State University, and personal testimony. Sources for the study included primary documents and materials from the National Archives, the Library of Congress, Moreland Springarn Research Center at Howard University, the Center for Research in Black Culture, the University of Pennsylvania, the University of San Francisco, and archival documents of organizations that participated in the movement.

Three populations – African American leaders, students, and faculty – were interviewed on three topics –African American activism, Black student organizations, and Black studies departments. Interviews were conducted with leaders of the Black Power Movement, students, and former faculty at San Francisco State University (SFSU).

The activities of the Black Power Movement were presented through the voices of activists of the period. Ten African American organizational leaders were interviewed on their personal experiences, and the structure and activities of their organizations during 1960–1980. The interviews were 45–90 minutes in duration. Survey instruments were used to guide the interviews.

The effect of the Black Power Movement on changes in higher education was traced from the period of initial activism to institutionalization. These interviews were semi-structured. The researcher investigated the sequence of events leading to the emergence of Black student unions and Black studies departments at higher education institutions.

Conceptual Frameworks

The conceptual frameworks for this research are Lewin's model of change, which emanated from group dynamics and action research (1948), and critical race theory (CRT), which emanated from theories and movements, such as the Black Power Movement, critical legal Studies, Marxist criticism, and radical feminism (Delgado & Stefancic, 2006). A summary of each follows.

Theory of change.

Lewin was a psychologist who developed the theory in 1939 before the field of organizational development emerged. He described the change process in terms of force fields. There are forces that resist change and forces that promote change.

Organizational or group stability is achieved when social equilibrium is maintained between the forces. Social habits and groups standards are examples of forces that resist change. Group decision-making is a method employed to modify these group-based habits. The impetus to change is triggered by external environmental forces. The preferred way to reestablish equilibrium with the least amount of conflict is change. This process is called the unfreezing-movement-refreezing process. When stress or dissatisfaction forces become stronger than the forces resisting change, unfreezing occurs. Unfreezing allows movement to occur and changes in policy and/or practice are made. The institutionalization of the changes leads to reestablishment of the equilibrium, which is refreezing.

Critical race theory (CRT).

This theory emerged in the mid-1970s from Derrick Bell and Allan Freeman, who were law professors. They were later were joined by a number of scholars such as Richard Delgado, who has authored several books on the topic (WiseGeek.com, 2013).

Critical race theory initially examined race relations regarding laws passed because of successful advocacy efforts of the Civil Rights Movement in the 1960s and 1970s. Legal professionals were concerned about the slow pace of racial reform in the United States and the erosion of civil rights victories. Many educators have now embraced the theory to increase their understanding of classroom dynamics, school discipline, achievement testing, and curriculum bias (Ladson-Billings, 1998).

According to CRT scholars, the 14th Amendment in the Constitution can only remedy blatant forms of discrimination, which are called macroaggressions. Daily, people of color also cope with micro-aggressions, which are just as hurtful. These microaggressions include differential treatment of Whites over people of color (also known as White privilege), which is rarely addressed. Microaggressions are subtle insults directed at people of color sometimes automatically or unconsciously (Solorzano, Ceja, & Yosso; 2000, p.60). To explain this phenomenon, CRT scholars encourage people of color to share their stories to name their realities and articulate their experiences.

In *Critical Race Theory: An Introduction* (2012), Delgado and Stefancic presented the basic tenets of CRT:

1. Racism is ordinary, not aberrational,
2. Our system of white-over-color ascendency serves important purposes, both psychic and material (p. 1).

A third tenet holds that race and racism are socially constructed products of social and race relations. A fourth tenet that has emerged is the belief that White is normal or the standard against which people of color are judged. Policies and practices are developed and implemented based on a colorblind philosophy, which are based on the standard.

This creates the social construct of people of color being considered "the other." The terms race and racism were defined by Banks, Lorde, and Marable (Solorzano, Ceja, and Yosso; 2000). Banks defined race as "a socially constructed phenomenon created to differentiate racial groups and to show the superiority or dominance of one race – in particular, Whites – over others." Lorde defined racism as "the belief in the inherent superiority of one race over all others and thereby, the right to dominance" (p. 496). Marable expanded Lorde's definition and defined racism as "a system of ignorance, exploitation, and power used to oppress African Americans, Latinos, Asians, Pacifica Islanders, American Indians, and other people on the basis of ethnicity, culture, mannerisms, and color" (p. 5).

31

Lewin's theory of change model, the tenets of critical race theory, and the responses of participants explain the phenomenon of student activism in the Black Power Movement on college campuses. Unfreezing was triggered by passage of the Higher Education Act of 1965 (U. S. Department of Education, 2008), the subsequent sharp increase in enrollment of first generation and minority students at predominantly White colleges and universities (PWCU), the frustration of these new students after arrival on campus, and student unrest. Movement occurred as faculty on campuses considered ways to address grievances. Refreezing occurred through the institutionalization of entities such as Black student organizations and Black studies departments. This process reestablished a calm learning environment on campus. Critical race theory explained African American students feeling like outsiders, their discontent with curriculum (the call for Black Studies departments), and their need to form academic and social counter spaces (Black student unions) for validation and to survive in a hostile environment. Together, these theories provide clarity on the dynamics of activism on higher education campuses relative to African American activism during the 1960s and 1970s.

Population and Sampling

The population that was studied are African Americans who were activists in the Black Power Movement from 1960-1980, students who were members of Black student unions, and faculty at Black studies departments. With the exception of their personal experiences related to events, the focus of this study is on events and activities during the period, not the personal lives of the individual activists. The questions on the survey instruments maintained this focus.

Participant selection.

The focus of the study was the responses of Black Power leaders, students, and faculty. Ten African American leaders, two students, and one faculty member from San Francisco State University were interviewed. The total number of key informants interviewed was13 persons.

Sampling strategy.

Purposive sampling was used to select individuals who were interviewed by stratifying representation of Black Power organizations, Black student unions, and Black studies departments. Persons interviewed included five African Americans leaders of organizations that were part of the Cultural Nationalist Movement; five African American leaders of organizations that were part of the Revolutionary Nationalist Movement; one student who was a member of the Black student organization at San Francisco State University; one student who was a member of the Black student union at Howard University; and, one former faculty in the Black studies department at SFSU. Ten leaders, two students, and one faculty were interviewed.

The sampling method was selected because the target populations have special knowledge about the topic. The African American leaders are former heads of organizations or were in the top tier of the organizations' hierarchies. They have knowledge of their organization's structure and activities, the relationship of their organization with other organizations, key personalities that affected events, and the successes and challenges they faced. Students who were interviewed are or were members of a Black student union and have first-hand knowledge of the organization.

The faculty member that was interviewed had special knowledge of the Black Student Union and Black Studies Department at San Francisco State University.

Table 2					
Research Matrix for Interviews					
Category	African American activists				
	Cultural nationalist movement	Revolutionary nationalist movement	Black student union	Black studies department	Total
African	5	5			10
American					
Leaders					
Faculty				1	1
Students			1	1	2
Totals	5	5	1	2	13

Because the leaders interviewed were active in the 1960s and 1970s, many were age 50 and above. Several of the individuals who were identified as potential interviewees have become prominent in electoral politics and higher education. The individuals interviewed live and/or work on the east coast, mid-east, and west coast of the United States.

Instrumentation

Interview procedures.

Semi-structured interviews were the primary tool used for gathering data. Two survey instruments were used. One survey instrument gathered data from African American leaders and a second survey instrument gathered information from students and faculty. Interviews with students and faculty were conducted to enable the sharing of rich thick data and to allow for their varying degrees of involvement and levels of knowledge. During the interviews, faculty and students were asked to share their knowledge on the beginning of the Black student union and/or Black studies department. Because of the semi-structure nature of the interviews, the interviews ranged from 45 to 90 minutes.

Interview protocols.

The survey for African American leaders was designed and piloted by the researcher to meet the requirements of a course. The findings of the research were shared with the professor and presented at an Educational Symposium for Research and Innovations (ESRI) conference. The questions were framed to stimulate discussion.

Methodology included face-to-face interviews and interviews over the telephone. Five leaders were interviewed. Based on the experience and for the purposes of this study, some questions were revised for greater clarity and five questions were added.

The instrument for faculty and students was a five-question interview protocol.

Questions included:

1. What memories do you have of the establishment of the Black student union and/or the Black studies department at your university? Are there any popular stories you would like to share?
2. What was the impetus for their establishment?
3. Were there any particular events that were important?
4. Who were the key people who participated in the effort? Who were the key students? Who were the key community leaders? Who were the key faculty?
5. Are there any records available that would be helpful in understanding how they emerged?

A 14-question interview protocol was used for interviews with African American leaders. The questions in the survey were framed to solicit information on their perception of the Black Power Movement, their organization's structure and activities, and if their organization had any contact with higher education institutions and/or students. A question was included in the protocol to identify other knowledgeable activists and other higher education institutions for interviews. The instrument contains the following questions:

1. What are your memories of the Black Power Movement during this period?
2. Please share any information you have on the goals of the Black Power Conference of 1967 that took place in Newark, New Jersey.
3. Were you active with any organizations and, if so, what organization(s), in what capacity, and for what period of time?
4. What global events influenced the formation and activities of your organization?
5. What were the strengths and challenges of the organization?
6. What were the accomplishments of the organization?
7. What do you know about COINTELPRO?
8. What is the current status of the organization?

9. How did the activities of your organization affect colleges and universities on campuses and in the community?
10. Did your organization's activities affect the development of Black student organizations and, if so, how?
11. Did your organization's activities affect the development of Black studies departments at higher education institutions and, if so, how?
12. Are you aware of any activities, programs, or benefits to higher education resulting from the efforts of your organization or other organizations in the Black Power Movement during the period from 1960 – 1980? Do they still exist today?
13. Are there other persons you feel would provide helpful information on this topic?
14. I am collecting information on the sequence of events leading to the development of the first Black student union and the first Black studies department at San Francisco State University. Are there experiences at other college or universities that you feel would be informative?

Table 3

Cross Walk Table (Relation of Research Questions to Instrument Items)

Interview questions for African American leaders	Research questions				
	1	2	3	4	5
1. What are your memories of the Black Power Movement during this period?	X				
2. Please share any information you have on the goals of the Black Power Conference of 1967 that took place in Newark, New Jersey.	X				
3. Were you active with any organization and, if so, what organization, in what capacity, and for what period time?	X				
4. What global events influenced the formation and activities of your organization?	X				
5. What were the strengths and challenges of the organization?	X				
6. What were the accomplishments of the organization?	X				
7. What do you know about COINTELPRO?	X				
8. What is the current status of the organization?	X				
9. How did the activities of the organization affect colleges and universities on campuses and in the community?		X	X		
10. Did your organization's activities affect the development of Black student organizations? How?		X			

Interview questions					
11. Did your organization's activities affect the evelopment of Black studies departments at higher education institutions? How?			X		
12. Are you aware of any activities, programs, or other benefits to higher education that resulted from the efforts of your organization or other organizations from 1960 – 1980? Do they still exist today?	X	X	X		X
13. Are there other persons you feel would provide helpful information on this topic?					X
14. I am collecting information on the sequence of events leading to the development of the first Black student union and the first Black studies department at San Francisco State University. Are you aware of events at other colleges or universities that you believe would be helpful for this study?					X

Table 4

Interview Questions for Students and Faculty

Interview questions	Research questions				
	_1_	_2_	_3_	_4_	_5_
1. What memories do you have of the establishment of the Black student union and/or the Black studies department? Are there any popular stories you would like to share?	X	X	X	X	X
2. What was the impetus for their establishment?		X	X	X	X
3. Were there any particular events that were important?	X	X	X	X	X
4. Who were the key people who participated in the effort? Who were the key students? Who were the key community leaders? Who were the key faculty?	X	X	X	X	X
5. Are there any records available that would be helpful in understanding how the Black student union or the Black studies department began?	X	X	X	X	X

The Xs in the tables above indicate the research question that was answered.

Questions 1, 2, 3, 4, 5, 6, 7, and 8 on the survey instrument for African American leaders provide information on the nature and activities of organizations in the Black Power movement. Questions 9, 10, and 12 provide information on the organizations' involvement with Black student unions and questions 9, 11, and 12 provide information on their involvement with Black studies departments.

Question 13 provides information on other persons who could be interviewed. Question 14 identified the experiences at other higher education institutions that could be informative on the topic.

In the survey questions for students and faculty, questions 3 and 4 provide information on the involvement of African American activists with Black student unions and Black studies departments. Questions 1, 2, 4, and 5 provide information on the Black student union and the Black studies department.

Table 5

Data Collection Strategies

Strategies	Research questions				
	1	2	3	4	5
Interviews	X	X	X	X	X
Survey	X	X	X	X	X
Member Checks	X	X	X	X	X
Review of Primary Data	X	X	X	X	X
Review of Literature	X	X	X	X	X
Personal Testimony	X	X			
Review by Readers	X	X	X	X	X

With the exception of personal testimony, data was collected to answer the main research question and the four supporting questions. The personal testimony does not provide extensive information on Black studies departments because the researcher had limited experience with them. The interviews and data gathering process were triangulated to provide multiple avenues to answer each question.

Data Collection and Handling

Interviews were conducted between March 2011 and May2013. Selected leaders of Black Power organizations were interviewed using the interview instrument. A letter requesting an interview was sent to each person identified. Agreement to be interviewed was secured by telephone or e-mail following correspondence. After agreement, each person signed a consent form. The survey instrument was sent to the interviewee before the interview took place. The location of the interview was chosen by the person interviewed. Each interview was taped by the researcher and professionally transcribed. The data was analyzed and coded to reveal themes. Information received during interviews was verified and additional information sought from books, on-line databases, and the archival records of libraries that have extensive repositories on African American activism, such as the Library of Congress, Howard University, and San Francisco State University.

Former faculty at San Francisco State University was interviewed and an interview of a student leader from San Francisco State University was included in the data. Answers sought included their knowledge of the establishment of the Black student union and/or Black studies department, the major players in the effort, why they joined the organization, challenges, and accomplishments. The information provided during all interviews was compared with each other and with the information from archives, online databases, journals, and books.

Data collection process.

The following chart depicts the data collection process.

Table 6

Data Collection Process

Data collection process	African American activism	Black student unions		Black studies departments	
		PWCU	HBCU	PWCU	HBCU
Interviews	X	X		X	
Survey	X	X		X	
Member Checks	X	X		X	
Review of Primary Data	X	X	X	X	X
Review of Literature	X	X	X	X	X
Personal Testimony	X	X			
Review by Readers	X	X	X	X	X

Note: PWCU = Predominately White College and University

HBCU = Predominately Black College and University

Data was collected in accordance with the following steps.

Steps

1. Identified up to 15 African American organizational leaders for interviews to ensure there are enough individuals for 10 leaders to be interviewed;
2. Separated organizations by type into Cultural Nationalist or Revolutionary Nationalist;
3. Sent correspondence to the individuals selected and followed up with telephone calls;
4. Sent additional correspondence and made additional telephone calls until up to 15 people agreed to be interviewed
5. Sent a copy of the survey instrument with the correspondence;
6. Obtained signed consent forms from all who agreed to be interviewed;
7. Scheduled interviews
8. Replaced any individuals who cancelled their interview or became unavailable for other reasons;
9. Interviewed 10 African American activists based on the chart above;
10. Taped all interviews;
11. Transcribed each interview;
12. Shared transcriptions with persons interviewed to ensure accuracy;
13. Made revisions based on feedback;
14. Reviewed primary records on the evolvement of the Black student union (BSU) at San Francisco State University (SFSU) from advocacy to establishment;
15. Reviewed primary and secondary data on the current status of the BSU;
16. Reviewed primary and secondary records on the evolvement of SFSU Black studies department from advocacy to establishment;
17. Interviewed one faculty who had knowledge of the history of the department;
18. Reviewed data on the current status of the department;
19. Compared the information provided for accuracy of the responses;
20. Researched data on student protests, Black student unions and Black studies departments at PWCUs and HBCUs in the National Archives, the Library of Congress, Howard University, other selected libraries and on-line data bases;
21. Researched primary and secondary data on student protests, Black student unions and Black studies departments at PWCUs and HBCUs from archival records of selected higher education institutions, print media and databases;
22. Made/obtained copies when possible;
23. Recorded/summarized findings at every step of the process. Maintained a journal of initial findings and gaps in process;
24. Grouped like and disparate information.
25. Stored data in encrypted files.

Procedures for analyzing the data.

Because this is historical research, the researcher focused on analyzing information from interviews and documents for new information, discerning patterns, and verifying facts. The constant comparative method (Lichtman, 2006) compared the relationship between cultural nationalism and higher education, revolutionary nationalism and higher education, the relationship between the Black Power Movement and Black student unions, and the relationship between the Black Power Movement and Black studies departments. Data gathered from interviews was coded, categorized, analyzed for themes using Atlas TI software following the six-step process outlined by Lichtman (2006).

Step 1: Initial coding. Going from the responses to some central ideas of the responses.
Step 2: Revisiting initial coding.
Step 3: Developing an initial list of categories or central ideas.
Step 4: Modifying the initial list based on additional rereading.
Step 5: Revisiting categories and subcategories.
Step 6: Moving from categories to concepts (p. 168).

A journal of observations and impressions was maintained. Notes and copies of print data was consolidated and summarized. Member checks provided clarification and accuracy.

Trustworthiness

To ensure trustworthiness, multiple modalities were used to collect and analyze data. The researcher used external criticism of data for authenticity and provenance and internal criticism for historical reliability (Garraghan, 1946). External criticism includes higher criticism and lower criticism. Higher criticism examines when the source was written/unwritten, where it was produced, who authored it, and if there are any pre-existing materials used as the basis of its production. Lower criticism is also known as textual criticism. It examines the original form of the material. Internal criticism considers the credibility of the contents of the source. This level of criticism includes eyewitness testimony and oral tradition.

Data from interviews was compared to each other and to written data. The evolution of events and documents of Black student unions and Black studies departments was compared with the activities, events, and documents of the Black Power Movement. The information obtained during interviews was audio taped and professionally transcribed verbatim. Before analysis, member checks were done by having the persons interviewed review the transcriptions for accuracy. Reflection, bracketing, and triangulation were used to control potential bias (Denzin & Lincoln, 2000). For credibility, Dr. Andrew Zimmerman, who is a historian, reviewed the data, analysis, and findings.

Subjectivity statement.

I am an African American female who was active in the cultural nationalist movement, participated in forming a Black student union when attending a predominantly White undergraduate school, and was chief executive officer of an African-centered school. These experiences have affected my worldview. Reflection was used to control bias. My personal testimony follows.

I grew up in New Jersey in a small African American rural community that was an enclave of White suburbia. Children from my neighborhood were bused to White schools. When compared to the life circumstances of my neighbors, my family was considered pretty well off. However, when we went to school in the White neighborhood, stark differences in social economic status of African Americans and Whites were apparent in housing and life style. The injustice of the inequities was validated when I was age 10 by the late Congressman Adam Clayton Powell who talked about economic disparities faced by African Americans and said there was no such thing as a Negro because Negroland did not exist. According to him, all people are connected to land and the term, Negro, was demeaning. He was the first person I remember who called Black people African Americans. At age 13, I moved from New Jersey to New Haven, Connecticut where I attended a high school that was 40% African American. It was a very different nurturing environment for me.

I entered Southern Connecticut State College (SCSC) in 1964. Again, I was in a White environment. Out of about 7,000 students, 35 were people of color. Of the 35 students, about 25 were African American and two of them were trying to pass for White. One of the few extracurricular activities that engaged us was membership in an International Club. As the literature indicates, during the early 1960s, there was a lot of political activity; however, my focus remained on achieving in school. I did not participate in the 1963 March on Washington because I thought it was too dangerous.

My activism was triggered when I was a sophomore and decided to take all of the chemicals out of my hair and wear it natural. This was a practical not a political decision. The responses of Whites and some African Americans made me indignant. The message was that they thought I was a nice person and somehow I had betrayed them. My right to make a decision about my personal look was challenged and I began to realize that displaying my Blackness was a threat. I also began to look at the textbooks used and messages conveyed in my classes. The need for a Black student union (BSU) that would provide a supportive environment for African American students became apparent. I participated in establishing a BSU at SCSC. At the time, African American students at other higher education campuses across the Country were also establishing Black student unions. The reasons for establishing these organizations had little to do with the Civil Rights Movement. The primary impetus was to create a supportive environment for African American students on White campuses.

I graduated from SCSC in 1968 and went to work as a school social worker. In 1969, I heard about a conference that was being convened in Atlanta, Georgia. In 1970, I traveled to Atlanta, Georgia to attend the Congress of African People. The experience changed my life. There were approximately 3,000 people, many of them higher education students, attending the event. There, I was introduced to cultural nationalism. Conference participants learned about African culture, traditional African dress, the problems experienced by African Americans, and what we needed to do to rebuild the community. The conference focused on eleven institutional areas: economics, education, criminal justice, political liberation, social development, religion, media, self-defense, health, technology, and science. A council was formed for each area. I joined the Social Welfare Council, which was chaired by Amina Baraka, the wife of Amiri Baraka (aka LeRoi Jones). Mr. Baraka's organization, called Committee for Unified New Ark (CFUN), was based in Newark, New Jersey. CFUN was modeled after a cultural nationalist organization in Los

Angeles, California that was founded by Dr. Maulana Karenga, the US Organization. I continued to live and work in New Haven but traveled to New Jersey to attend classes every other weekend. My role was to organize African Americans in New Haven. We formed a group (cadre) in New Haven and began the work. The operating principles were work and study. We met daily early in the morning to plan our day, exercise, and study. We organized study groups throughout the city and met periodically with other groups from other organizations, such as the Black Panther Party, one of the Black student unions, or one of the Black labor unions when there was an issue or objective that was of mutual interest (such as launching a breakfast program in one of the schools).

We were not involved in illegal activities; however, I was among those targeted by the federal government's Counter Intelligence Program (COINTELPRO). Two incidents exemplify this issue. In 1971, I hosted a meeting of the Social Welfare Council at my home in New Haven. Amina Baraka came to the meeting. Shortly before the meeting, a camera was installed on a telephone pole across the street from my house.

Minutes after the arrival of my guests, my telephone service and electricity were cut off. The meeting was held anyway using candles. After it ended, my telephone service and electricity were restored. After Kenneth Gibson was elected Mayor, I moved to Newark, New Jersey for a short time. I became a member of CFUN but left after three months when they attempted to sever my ties with my family. I then lived with my brother and worked as a teacher at the Chad School, an independent Black school. One day, while I was at work, the FBI visited my home and spoke to my brother. They informed him that I was active in the African American community and provided details of my activities.

Fortunately, my brother recognized that the visit was an effort to intimidate me and asked them to leave saying, "If you know that much about her, you know that right now she is teaching at a school. Get out of my house." During this same period, several of my friends reported similar events.

In 1973, I was recruited from Chad School to work at the New Ark School, which opened in 1970 following the rebellion there. The mission of the school was to identify indigenous leaders and develop their leadership skills. The school was an African- centered organization that operated an adult education program, an early learning center, an after school program, a summer camp, a continuing education program, and a residential treatment program. It was a site for training college interns and seminars on institutional racism were conducted for corporate personnel of Bell Laboratories. Public school teachers taught adults in the school's evening program. A number of these same individuals pursued advanced degrees in higher education. I left the school in 1983 and relocated to the Washington, DC area where I worked for two national health organizations, pursued an advanced degree, and administered three community-based human service organizations. The New Ark School later closed in 1987 due to a lack of funds.

Ethical considerations.

Written consent was obtained from all persons who were interviewed. All data obtained from interviews is maintained in encrypted files and in a locked box that is only available to the researcher. The confidentiality and privacy of all persons interviewed is being honored. Since this topic focuses on organizations, policies, and practices, when appropriate, permission to disclose identities may be requested in the future.

Summary

In Chapter III, the researcher presented the research questions, the research design, a description of the population and sampling procedures, the instrumentation, data collection and handling, data analysis, trustworthiness, a subjectivity statement, ethical considerations, and the timeline for the project. This research is a historical study that will help to fill the knowledge gap on the Black Power Movement and its relationship to changes in higher education. Population sampling was purposive to obtain information from individuals who have special knowledge on the topic. Through semi-structured interviews and a review of primary and secondary documents, the researcher investigated the activities of Black Power organizations relative to the establishment of Black student unions and Black studies departments at higher education institutions from the perspectives of Black Power activists, higher education faculty, and higher education students. Triangulation, bracketing, and reflection were used to ensure trustworthiness. For accuracy, Dr. Andrew Zimmerman and Dr. Komozi Woodard, who are historians, reviewed the data and analyses.

CHAPTER IV

RESULTS

The purpose of this chapter is to review the data gathering process and present an analysis of the findings of this study based on the responses of participants to five research questions that were presented in Chapter I, the characteristics of the population sampled, and contributions by organization. A summary of the history and status of the African American Black Power organizations researched will be provided. The history of the development of the Black Student Union (BSU) and Black Studies Program at San Francisco State College (SFSC) will be presented. Correlations between the responses given during the interviews and literature reviewed will be analyzed.

Analysis of Findings by Research Question

The general question researched was, "What effect did the Black Power Movement have on changes in higher education from 1960-1980?" The four supporting research questions were:

1. What role did the Black Power Movement play in the development of Black student organizations, particularly Black student unions?
2. What role did the Black Power Movement play in the development of Black studies departments?
3. What does the San Francisco State University experience in the development of a Black student union and Black studies department suggest about the Black Power Movement and higher education?
4. What other important cases provide information on the effect of the Black Power Movement on changes in higher education?

Responses to the questions on the survey instruments were cross-walked with the research questions as depicted in Table 1.

Table 7					
Crosswalk of Interview Questions with Research Questions					
Research Questions	General Question	Question 2	Question 3	Question 4	Question 5
Survey of African American Leaders	1, 2, 3, 4, 5, 6, 7, 8	9, 10, 12	9, 11, 12	13	13, 14
Survey of Faculty and Staff	1, 2, 3, 4, 5	2, 3	2, 3	1, 2, 3, 4, 5	

Responses to questions 1, 2, 3, 4, 5, 6, 7, and 8 on the survey instrument for African American leaders provided information on the general research question, depicting the nature and activities of organizations in the Black Power movement. Responses to questions 9, 10, and 12 provided information on research question number 2, the organizations' involvement with Black student unions. Responses to questions 9, 11, and 12 provided information on research question number 3, involvement of the organizations with Black studies departments. Responses to question 13 provided information on research question number 4, the San Francisco State University case and persons who are authoritative on the topic. Responses to question 14 provided information on research question number 5, experiences at other higher education institutions that merit further study.

Responses of students and faculty to survey questions 1, 2, 3, 4, and 5 provided information on research question 3, the San Francisco State College experience relative to the emergence of the first Black student union and Black studies department in the country. Much of the information on San Francisco State University's experience was obtained from a comprehensive archival collection at SFSU and an oral interview with a leading student activist that was conducted in 2007 and published in 2009 (Rogers, 2009).

Black Power Movement Organizations Included in the Study

Interviews conducted with African American leaders ranged from 45 – 90 minutes. Of those interviewed, a number of participants would not sign consent forms until after the interview was completed, transcribed, and the content was reviewed by them. To maintain confidentiality and ensure a more accurate description of the inner workings of the organizations and the course of events of the period, the interviews were not limited to the top leaders of the organizations. A collective of individuals led the majority of Black Power organizations. The persons interviewed were part of the collectives at high levels in the organizations.

Participant Profiles

The participants interviewed were placed in one of four categories: African American leaders who were cultural nationalists, African American leaders who were revolutionary nationalists, African American faculty, and African American students. The number of interviews conducted is depicted by category in the following table.

Table 8

Number of Interviews by Category

Category	Number of Interviews
African American Leaders – CN	6
African American Leaders – RN	4
Faculty	1
Students	2
Total Number of Interviews	13

Current and former leaders of 10 Black Power organizations were interviewed, six organizations that identify/ied as cultural nationalist (CN) and four organizations that identify/ied as revolutionary nationalist (RN). For the purposes of this study, cultural nationalist organizations are defined as groups whose mission is to re-educate the Black masses, restore the link between African Americans and Africans in continental Africa, and create independent Black institutions (Joseph, 2006). Organizations that self-identify as revolutionary nationalist groups embrace a socialist ideology and focus on defending African Americans against police brutality and what was viewed as police occupation in African American communities (Ture & Hamilton, 1992). One former faculty from San Francisco State University was interviewed regarding the history of the first Black Student Union and the first Black Studies Department in the country. One student who graduated from Howard University was interviewed. No interviews were conducted with former students of San Francisco State University because of their unwillingness; however, an excerpt of an interview conducted in 2007 with James Garrett, one of the student founders of the Black Student Union at San Francisco State University, is presented.

Characteristics of Research Participants

Information obtained through a review of the literature, interviews, and testimony provided rich information about the histories of the development of Black student unions and the emergence

47

of Black Studies departments, and showed how one entity developed from the other. What is clear from the data is the Black Power Movement, particularly on campuses, was student-driven. An often-overlooked fact is many of the members of Black Power activist groups during that period were college students – often first- generation college students. One participant interviewed noted that many of the well- known activists, such as Huey Newton, Bobby Seale, and Stokely Carmichael, were students. During the course of the study, the researcher found that the majority of respondents were at some point college students. As one person interviewed stated, Black Power activists wore many hats, serving multiple roles. This assertion was supported when examining the responses of the participants to the research questions.

The responses to the survey questions for African American leaders also provided information on African American student experiences while enrolled in college. Table 4 below graphically depicts the multiple roles of participants.

Table 9

Roles of Participants by Organization: 1960-1980

	Roles			
<u>Organization</u>	<u>Organizational Leader</u>	<u>Student</u>	<u>Faculty</u>	<u>Total</u>
Black Panther Party	X	X	X	3
Black Youth Organization	X	X		2
Committee for Unified New Ark	X	X		2
Congress of African People	X		X	2
National Assn of Black Social Workers	X	X		2
Republic of New Afrika	X	X		2
Revolutionary Action Movement	X	X		2
ROOTS Activity Learning Center	X	X		2

Student Nonviolent Coordinating Committee	X	X		2
Student/Youth Organization for Black Unity	X	X		2
Total	10	9	2	21

As the table above indicates, 100% of the respondents functioned in more than one role in the Black Power Movement. Of the 10 participants who were African American leaders, nine were also students during the period studied.

An interesting finding is the number of African American professors interviewed who were once student activists. When seeking leaders for interviews, the researcher found that many were professors at higher education institutions. Two of the leaders interviewed were also faculty at a university during the period studied. After the period, three additional participants became faculty; therefore, fifty percent of the participants interviewed were faculty members. These individuals transitioned from student activism to advancing higher education curricula from inside higher education institutions. A number of them are currently researchers and prolific writers. So, as one participant stated, for them, the process has continued.

Themes Emanating from the Interviews

Several themes emerged among the participants interviewed. These included discontent with the conditions in African American communities, feelings of hostility and rejection by faculty and other students on higher education campuses, feelings of betrayal emanating from the realization that they had been mis-educated, academic challenges, the need to maintain a connection with people in their communities, experiences with COINTELPRO, infiltration of their organizations by agent provocateurs, and a search for the truth. A sense of injustice was a common thread that propelled their activism.

Most of the persons interviewed were over age 50. When interviewed, they talked about their anger and outrage but indicated that they had addressed the rage some time ago, appreciating the complexity of the dynamics that were occurring at the time. However, they continued to carry with them scars from microaggressions and their experiences with COINTELPRO. Most were skeptical and suspicious, and some believed in conspiracy theories.

The leaders interviewed represented the full era of 1960 – 1980, pioneers and new leaders that emerged later in the period. Three of the leaders interviewed were students during the 1960s and emerged as leaders after 1970. These new leaders articulated a different experience than the pioneering activists.

Organizational Profiles

Thirteen organizations were studied - seven organizations that identified as cultural nationalist and six organizations that identified as revolutionary nationalist. The following chart gives the names of the organizations by category.

Table 10

Organizations Included in the Study

Cultural Nationalist Organizations	Revolutionary Nationalist Organizations
The Black Youth Organization	The Black Panther Party
The Committee for Unified New Ark	The Nation of Islam
The Congress of African People	The Republic of New Africa
The National Association of Black Social Workers	The Revolutionary Action Movement
The New Ark School	The Student Nonviolent Coordinating Committee
ROOTS Activity Learning Center	The Student Organization for Black Unity
The US Organization	

Leaders of each organization in the table above were interviewed except leaders of the Nation of Islam (NOI), the US Organization (US), and the Student Organization for Black Unity (SOBU). Two organizations, the Nation of Islam and the Revolutionary Action Movement, were included in the study because of their connection to Malcolm X, who was the major spokesperson and inspiration for the Black Power Movement. The US organization was studied because of the significance of Dr. Maulana Karenga and the US Organization in the cultural nationalist wing of the Black Power Movement. The Student Organization for Black Unity was studied because it organized a network of Black student organizations on college campuses that was part of the Black Power thrust but were not Black student unions.

Contributions of the Organizations Studied

Table 11
Contributions of Participants by Organization: 1960-1980

Organization	Black Student Unions	Black Studies Departments	Increase in Black Faculty	Other Contributions
Black Panther Party	D	D	D	D
Black Youth Organization	N	I	N	I
Committee for Unified New Ark	D	D	D	D
Congress of African People	A	D	D	D
National Assn of Black Social Workers	I	I	D	D
Republic of New Afrika	N	N	N	N
Revolutionary Action Movement	D	D	D	D
ROOTS Activity Learning Center	N	N	N	N
Student Nonviolent Coordinating Committee	D	D	D	D
Student/Youth Organization for Black Unity	N	D	N	D

Note: D = Direct Contributions; I = Indirect Contributions; N = No Contributions

Responses of the participants demonstrate that the contributions to higher education of the organizations studied varied and were realized at different levels of intensity. Table 9 depicts the contributions of Black Power organizations by organization and type of contribution relative to Black student unions, Black Studies departments, an increase in Black faculty, and other contributions. The other contributions category included development of other Black student organizations; revision of curricula; and, an increase in Black professional groups, Black researchers, and Black authors. Types of contributions were coded as D for direct contributions, I for indirect contributions, A for organizations contributing in an advisory manner, and N for organizations that did not contribute in these areas.

Of the 10 organizations, eight directly or indirectly contributed to the emergence of Black student unions and/or Black studies programs on college campuses. Only two organizations, the Republic of New Afrika and the ROOTS Activity Learning Center did not contribute to the effort. The Republic of New Afrika focused on international affairs and the ROOTS Activity Learning Center, which was established in the late 1970s after many of the advocacy efforts were well underway, was active in the Anti-apartheid and Free Nelson Mandela movements. The Black Panther Party, the Committee for Unified New Ark, the Revolutionary Action Movement, and the Student Nonviolent Coordinating Committee directly contributed to the development of Black student unions and Black Studies programs, an increase in the number of Black faculty at higher education institutions, and the development of other Black student groups. The Congress of African People played an advisory role. The literature review showed that the US organization also played a pivotal role. Participants attributed major credit for these accomplishments to the Student Nonviolent Coordinating Committee. A summary of each organization studied and the responses of participants by organizational type and research question follow.

Cultural Nationalist Organizations Included in the Study

The Black Youth Organization (BYO).

The Black Youth Organization was established by college students in 1967 as an outcome of a summer tutoring and mentoring project in Newark, New Jersey. College students provided tutorial services for high school students in reading and mathematics. The students who provided the services found their mentees in great need academically. This experience was the impetus for establishing an organization called the Black Youth Organization with a primary mission of developing and operating an independent Black school. In the fall of 1968, the group opened the school with an initial enrollment of 70 children. They named the school after Chad, a country in Africa, because Chad is physically located in the heart of Africa.

Representatives from the Black Youth Organization attended a Black Power Conference held in Newark, New Jersey in 1967. After listening to the discussion at the meeting, they determined that the activities planned would lead to the death, injury, and/or imprisonment of a number of activists. Based on this assessment, they decided to work underground as an organization and focus their time and energy strictly on education. The Black Youth Organization had two divisions: the Chad School and a shadow group called the House of August. The Black Youth Organization was a coed group; however, the House of August was an all-male group. The purposes of the House of August were to protect the faculty and students of the Chad School, and develop and implement economic projects to provide funding for the school. Because the House of August division functioned primarily underground, there is little information on this group in the literature. Consequently, most of the information provided in this summary is based on the experience of the researcher, who was a teacher and parent at the school, and the testimony from a former leader of the Black Youth Organization.

The Black Youth Organization had a president, secretary, and board of directors.

Leon Moore was president of the Black Youth Organization and the administrator of Chad School. Economic projects that were developed and operated by the House of August included a music store located in Liberia, Africa; an African art store in the United States; a printing press called Pyramid Press; and, a construction company called the August Construction Company. The printing press produced African-centered curriculum materials for the school and provided printing services for the public. The construction company renovated houses.

The Chad School was an African-centered tuition-based school that offered classes for African American children from three to 12 years of age. To teach at the Chad School, applicants had to successfully complete a high school equivalency examination and attend rigorous teacher training classes conducted by Mr. Moore, who was considered the sage of the organization. Throughout its existence, the school was recognized for its educational excellence. Students that graduated from Chad went on to be top performers at area high schools and most attended and received degrees from higher education institutions. Because of Chad's reputation, over the years, annual enrollment grew to 400 students.

The Chad School, as an institution, embraced and reflected the philosophy of Black Power. All of its students, teachers, and board members were African American. To ensure non-interference from the government, the Black Youth Organization refused to pursue or accept government grants for the school. In the early 2000s, the organization decided to allow White people to join its board of directors. The new board of directors attempted to change the cultural nationalist focus of the school and its policy on accepting grants. Staff and volunteers who had worked at the school since its formation objected to the changes. They organized another board of directors that was comprised of African Americans who had a history of being active and supportive of the school. A power struggle ensued between the two boards. This struggle exacerbated operation and funding problems. The school closed in 2005.

The Committee for Unified NewArk (CFUN).

The United Brothers was an organization that emerged in 1967 in Newark, New Jersey. The initial purpose of the organization was to transform the political system in Newark. In 1968, the United Brothers changed its name to the Committee for Unified NewArk and later, in 1972, to the Congress of African People (Woodard, 1999). In 1967, the organization established an organizational unit for women called United Sisters. The Committee for Unified NewArk was led by the late Amiri Baraka (also known as LeRoi Jones), who became its spiritual leader with the title, Imamu, and his wife, Amina Baraka, who was given the title, Bibi. Other officers included a chief community organizer, a key political officer, a chief economic officer, and a political advisor. The men in the collective secured strategic leadership positions in public agencies across the city of Newark. The United Sisters formalized its division, with Amina Baraka as its recognized leader, and worked side-by-side with the men. In 1967, the United Sisters established the African Free School, an African-centered school for the children of its members (Baraka, 1997).

During the 1960s, Baraka became a protégé of Maulana Karenga from the US Organization, which was located in Los Angeles, California. Under Baraka's leadership, the Committee for Unified NewArk members embraced the cultural nationalist theory and practice (known as Kawaida) promulgated by Karenga. Kawaida, a Kiswahili term that means "tradition and reason,‖ was the driving force of the organization (DiscovertheNetworks, 2013, p. 1). The US Organization became known as the cultural giant of the West coast and the Committee for Unified NewArk had a similar image on the East coast. Activists from all over the country commuted to their sites to attend weekly classes about manhood, womanhood, Kiswahili, Kawaida, the Nguzo Saba, politics, community organizing, and African-centered axioms and practices that flowed out of the US Organization. The men and women in the organizations wore traditional African clothing, had natural hairstyles, decorated their homes in African cultural themes, and conversed in Kiswahili in an effort to recapture traditional African values, reclaim traditional practices, and reconnect African Americans to their homeland in Africa. The Kawaida Doctrine provided the philosophical framework for this effort. In 1972, the Committee for Unified NewArk was subsumed under the Congress of African People.

The Congress of African People (CAP).

In 1970, following a series of Black Power conferences, a Congress of African People convention was held in Atlanta, Georgia. Over 3,000 activists attended. The focus of the convention was developing a Black agenda to build Black institutions. There were 11 workgroups. Each focused on an institutional area: economics, education, criminal justice, political liberation, social development, religion, media, self-defense, health, technology, and science. Each workgroup was charged with following up on the decisions made during the convention by organizing similar groups across the country. Organizational representatives agreed to work together in operational unity even if they did not agree on all issues under the banner, —unity without uniformity. Hayward Henry (aka Mtangulizi Sanyika) was elected the first chair of the Congress of African People in 1970. In 1972, Baraka emerged as the organization's national spokesperson and key organizer. One of the outcomes of the convention was the decision to build a Black Political Party. In March 1972, a National Black Political Convention was held in Gary, Indiana. This initial meeting was followed by other conventions in Little Rock, Arkansas and New Orleans, Louisiana. The conventions had mixed results because of ideological differences.

Because of these differences, there was disagreement over the elements of the platform. Under the leadership of Baraka, the ideology of the Committee for Unified New Ark became a dominant force in the Congress of African People. In 1972, Baraka merged the Committee for Unified NewArk under the Congress of African People; however, in 1976, Amiri and Amina Baraka abandoned cultural nationalism and embraced communism as their political philosophy. These changes caused dissension in the cultural nationalist network and marked the beginning of the demise of the Congress of African People nationally and the Committee for Unified NewArk locally. In May 1976, the Committee for Unified NewArk (and the Congress of African People) was transformed from a Black Power organization to a Marxist-Leninist organization called the Revolutionary Communist League (Woodard, 2001).

The National Association of Black Social Workers (NABSW).

The National Association for Black Social Workers (NABSW) is a membership association for professional and lay social workers who are devoted to the upliftment of African Americans. It is an African-centered cultural nationalist organization that was created in 1966 by the late Cenie Jomo Williams and a small group of social workers from New York after they severed ties with the

Council on Social Work Education in protest of a perceived failure of the organization to address the unique concerns of African Americans. Currently, the National Association for Black Social Workers has 49 regular and 25 student chapters across the country. The 25 student chapters are located on the campuses of higher education institutions at schools of social work. The association provides education and training for social workers; participates in political discourses on issues that affect African Americans; and, provides education, training, mentoring, and scholarships for social work students.

The National Association for Black Social Workers' national office is located in Washington, DC. It is managed by an eight-member executive committee of elected officials who are supported by a staff of four people. It has a steering committee that includes the executive committee, committee chairs, and chapter representatives. Many of the members of the steering committee are professors at higher education institutions. The leader interviewed told this researcher, "The Steering Committee runs the Organization."

The National Association for Black Social Workers has 15 committees and four task forces. Major program activities include an African-centered Social Work Academy and a Sankofa Mentoring Project. Past presidents of the association belong to a council of sages that advises the sitting president. The organization uses ceremonies, rituals, and symbols extensively. Examples are conducting spiritual awakenings, pouring libations to honor the ancestors – the deceased founder, past presidents, family members, and s/heroes, reading a pledge at the beginning of each general session, reciting an oath, singing the Black National Anthem, holding processionals of dignitaries preceding major ceremonies such as the Opening Session and Harambee Ceremony.

The functions of the presidency include supervising staff at the national office, making decisions on national policy matters, appointing committee chairs, serving as the national spokesperson, chairing the executive committee, and serving as the organization's spiritual leader. The most important functions of the presidency are to strengthen the organization, maintain unity, and develop innovative programs. The organization's current stated priorities include documenting the history and programs of the association by overseeing the writing of two books - one on the history of the organization and past presidents; and, another which describes spiritual awakenings; fostering intergenerational pairing; and, raising the public profile of the association by strengthening media relations, increasing public policy activities, and increasing membership.

Conflict resolution, fund development, and engaging young professionals are the major challenges of the organization. Because of the voluntary nature of the organization's leadership and the strong passions connected to the organization's mission, often there are divergent views on methods for accomplishing objectives. To maintain its independence, early in its existence, the leadership of the National Association for Black Social Workers decided not to pursue or receive government grants. Because of this decision, fund development has continued to present major challenges. Currently, the major sources of the association's revenues are membership dues, workplace giving, and conference registration fees.

A number of members of the association's steering committee are pioneers who have served in various leadership positions of the organization for many years. The organization's surviving founding members are still active in the Association. Because the leaders of the association are aging out, the current president views the preparation of new leadership as critical for the organization's continuity and longevity (National Association for Black Social Workers Program, 2007).

The New Ark School (NAS).

The New Ark School was a grassroots community organization that opened its doors in 1968 following the 1967 rebellion and Black Power Conference in Newark, New Jersey. The location of the school was the Central Ward in Newark, where the rebellion occurred. In that area, there was a concentration of high-rise 17-story apartments for low-income residents called "projects." The majority of the adult residents in the apartments were high school dropouts. Crime was a significant problem in the area. It was so severe that, because of safety concerns, law enforcement officers often refused to enter the dwellings when in pursuit of someone who had just committed a crime. The New Ark School emerged out of a movement to gain community control of the public schools and social services agencies that served their community, and to reduce the violence in the area. The mission of the school was to identify and mentor indigenous leaders so they would have a greater voice in their community.

The creation and expansion of program services at the school were driven by the needs of the population served. All programs services were provided free to residents. The first program the school offered was a high school equivalency (GED) program for high school dropouts. Many of the students that attended the classes were parents. They frequently missed classes because they did not have anyone to watch their children or funds to pay a childcare provider. To address the issue of childcare, the school established an early childhood learning center for their children. Because a significant number of students who enrolled in the high school equivalency program did not read at a high school equivalency (7th grade) level, they had difficulty completing the program.

To address this problem, an adult basic education program for adults that functioned at a 5th grade reading level was established. Students, who needed it, could then begin in the ABE program, transition to the GED program, and graduate by successfully taking the GED test. The early childhood learning program that was created for their children was expanded to include all income-eligible children in the neighborhood because of the great need for childcare in the area. The childcare program subsequently expanded to include a primary school and a before and after school program for school age children. The after school program served a number of students who were referred to the program by the public schools because of behavioral problems. This program became a day camp program that had residential components during the summer months. The school expanded and opened a residential treatment facility for teenage youth who had been diagnosed as socially maladjusted or emotionally disturbed. The majority of the youth were referred by a youth center, which was a prison for adjudicated youth. The two remaining initiatives of the school were continuing education classes for adults such as photography classes, martial arts, African dance, and nutrition classes; and, community education such as an annual Marcus Garvey festival to enhance awareness in Newark.

Based on its development and expansion, it is apparent that the New Ark School responded to Black needs in Newark from the 1960s to the 1980s.

Many of the independent Black schools that emerged during the period were managed by umbrella organizations (such as the Chad School by the Black Youth Organization and the African Free School by the Committee for Unified NewArk). This was not true for the New Ark School. The school, however, was led by Black Power activists who established an informal cadre. The co-leaders of the School were Robert Dixon and Kennedy Wilson. Other members of the cadre included Juanita Wilson, Jeannette Robinson, Kinaya Sokoya, and John Wilson. Kennedy Wilson and Robert Dixon were responsible for development; Jeannette Robinson oversaw the administrative and development functions of the School; Juanita Wilson and Kinaya Sokoya were responsible for program development and implementation, and John Wilson was in charge of property and procurement. Four of the individuals above - Kennedy Wilson, Robert Dixon, Jeannette Robinson, and Kinaya Sokoya served as executive director during the life of the school. One by one, members of the cadre resigned to pursue other interests (e.g. higher education). It was difficult to find replacements that had the same passion and commitment to the school. The last person in the cadre left the school in 1982. Unfortunately, the individuals who followed them were unable to manage the grants that were the life-blood of the school and, in 1987, the school closed due to lack of funding (Sokoya, 2013).

ROOTS Activity Learning Center (RALC).

ROOTS Activity Learning Center opened in October 1977 as an outcome of the founder's goals and experiences while a student at Central State University (then College), a historically Black higher education institution. The groundwork for the development of the school began there. The school opened as an infant care and early childhood learning center that served infants and children from six months to kindergarten. Since 1977, classes at the school expanded to serve children from birth through eighth grade. The structure of the school, which is tuition-based, is an infant center, a preschool, a primary school, and a middle school. Classes are multi-level so each student has the same teacher for three years and older students can mentor younger students. The teaching staff is African Americans who have either a degree or, minimally, certification. All staff receives year-round training, which becomes more intensive during the summer months.

The school curriculum is rigorous and African-centered. Students are taught Kiswahili and the center's philosophy embraces the principles of the Nguzo Saba, the African value system that promulgates the seven principles of umoja (unity), kugichagulia (self-determination), ujima (collective work and responsibility), ujamaa (cooperative economics), nia (purpose), kuumba (creativity), and imani (faith). The stated mission of the ROOTS Activity Learning Center is to promote and secure the connection of Mother Africa within its children; prepare students to break the chains of psychological conditioning that attempt to keep them powerless in all phases of society; provide students with a strong African-centered learning environment; guide students towards academic excellence, exemplary character, and social responsibility; and, encourage success leading to self-reliance and economic, social, and political contributions to society (ROOT Activity Learning Center.org., 2013).

Standardized tests, which are administered at the beginning and the end of each school year, are used as tools to gauge where students are academically, facilitate the development of individual educational plans, and evaluate the progress made during the school year. During the summer months, the school operates a summer day camp. New students who participate in the camp are given priority for enrollment in the school in the fall. The school operates a rites of passage program for students in its middle school called the Young Lions and Black Madonnas. Most of the school's graduates enroll in local parochial high schools. Since its establishment, the school has been recognized for its educational excellence. Several of its students have had perfect SAT scores. In 1999, the administrator opened a public charter school using the same curriculum (ROOTS Activity Learning Center, 2013). The school continues to serve students in the Washington DC metropolitan area.

The Student/Youth Organization for Black Unity (SOBU/YOBU).

The Student Organization for Black Unity was formed by the Student Nonviolent Coordinating Committee (SNCC) in May 1969 at North Carolina A&T College (Student Nonviolent Coordinating Committee, 2013). Founders included Nelson Johnson, Tim Thomas, Milton Coleman, John McClendon, Mark Smith, Alvin Evans, Victor Bond, and Jerry Walker. In August 1972, the name of the organization was changed to the Youth Organization for Black Unity (YOBU) to expand its membership to youth beyond college (Woodard, 2013).The organization's stated ideology, which is described in a 36-page paper, was Pan Africanism. The Youth Organization for Black Unity's priorities were to advocate for the release of incarcerated African Americans, which they considered political prisoners; educate students and other activists through publication of a bi-weekly newsletter called "The African World;" support Black education by promoting and supporting independent Black schools and historically Black colleges and universities; redefine Black education on college campuses; and, inform Black students about the geography and politics (e.g. liberation struggles) of Africa (Johnson, 1972).

Events sponsored and/or organized by the Youth Organization for Black Unity included organizing and sponsoring an African Liberation Day celebration in Washington, DC on May 19, 1972 in celebration of Malcolm X's birthday, sponsoring a Southern African Week, and operating a Pan-African Medical Program. It issued articles on the pan-Africanism of Malcolm X and issued a report on the United Nations. From its founding in 1969 to 1972, the then Student Organization for Black Unity focused its organizational efforts on internal development. Chapters were established on higher education campuses across the country, however, the researcher could not find literature on how many chapters existed or where they were located. In 1972, the Youth Organization for Black Unity began to reach out to other student groups to form cadres across the country. The literature on this organization as a national entity is sketchy.

Some of the colleges and universities where it had a presence, such as the University of Texas and Harvard, have information on the specific group on their campus in their archives. Although there is evidence that the organization was in existence during the 1980s, it is not known if it continues to exist today.

The US Organization (US).

The US organization is located in Los Angeles, California. It was co-founded by Maulana Karenga and Hakim Jamal on September 7, 1965 following the revolt in Watts, California (Brown, 2003). Due to a disagreement on strategy, Jamal left the US organization in 1966 and formed another organization called the Malcolm X Foundation. Karenga then became the driving force of US. His vision was to promote African American cultural unity through service, struggle, and institution-building (US Organization, 2013). In the quotation below, Karenga explained the influence of Malcolm X on the formation of the US Organization.

"Malcolm was the major African American thinker that influenced me in terms of nationalism and Pan-Africanism. As you know, towards the end, when Malcolm is expanding his concept of Islam, and of nationalism, he stresses Pan-Africanism in a particular way. And, he agrees that, and this is where we have the whole idea of a cultural revolution and the need for revolution …we need a cultural revolution. He argues that we must return to Africa culturally and spiritually, even if we can't go physically. And so that's a tremendous impact on US" (Halisi, 1972, pp. 27-31).

During the 1960s and 1970s, the US Organization became recognized by Black Power organizations as the leading cultural nationalist organization in the United States. The list of accomplishments of the US Organization is lengthy. Kwanzaa, an African American holiday that occurs in late December, was one of the earliest successes of the US Organization. Through Kwanzaa, the US Organization promoted a Black value system (Nguzo Saba). The first Kwanzaa celebration was held in December 1966. US was also responsible for the establishment and/or development of the Black Congress in Los Angeles, PACO (a Black Federation in Dayton, Ohio), another Black Federation in San Diego, and the Committee for Unified NewArk in Newark, New Jersey. It co- founded initiatives such as the Brotherhood Crusade, the Mafundi Institute, the Community Alert Patrol, the Watts Health Foundation, the Young Lions (Simba Wachanga) youth group, and the Ujima Housing Project. US also claims credit for having a significant role in the development of the Black Studies discipline and the formation of Black student unions on college campuses (The US Organization, 2013).

The Organization continues its work today. With the exception of a short hiatus from 1971-1975, the US Organization has been active since 1965. Currently it operates an African American Cultural Center (a cultural school for children), the Kawaida Institute of Pan-African Studies, a men's group (Senu Society), a women's group (Senut Society), and a monthly study circle. It is also active in an extensive network. On its website (US Organization, 2013), the US Organization lists the following seven future objectives. It will continue to sustain and promote African culture by providing models of excellence and paradigms of possibilities; expanding political education; training social change agents; organizing and mobilizing people around their own interests; expanding participation in cooperative projects; continuing to be a reference and resource center; and, rebuilding and expanding the liberation movement (US Organization, 2013).

Revolutionary Nationalist Organizations Included in the Study

The Black Panther Party (BPP).

The Black Panther Party for Self Defense (BPP) was not one organization but a coalition of organizations that grew out of local circumstances (Williams, 1998). The Lowndes County Freedom Organization, which was an Alabama-based group that used violence to retaliate against the barbarity perpetrated against Black people by the Ku Klux Klan, was the original Black Panther Party. It was organized by members of the Student Nonviolent Coordinating Committee and local residents following a freedom ride for a voter registration campaign. In 1966, Huey Newton and Bobby Seale founded the national office of the Panther Party in Oakland, California.

Between 1966 and 1982, there were more than 32 chapters and 100 affiliates across the United States and abroad (Austin, 2006). The chapters differed based on cultural and regional influences. These differences were reflected in their ideology, methodology, and activities; however, the network of organizations (chapters, affiliates) ideologically embraced Marxism and advocated for the needs of the "lumpenprolateriat" (the masses of people) (Williams, 1998, p. 65).

The Black Panthers recruited many of its members from colleges and universities. To expand their membership, leaders of the Black Panther Party gave presentations on college and university campuses. In Illinois, for example, the Chicago Police Department files listed the following higher education institutions as campuses where there was Panther Party activity: Chicago State University, Crane Junior College (now Malcolm X College), Illinois Institute of Technology, Northeastern Illinois University, Northwestern University, Roosevelt University, Southern Illinois University in Carbondale, University of Illinois at Chicago Circle, University of Illinois at Urbana-Champaign, Wilbert Wright Junior College, and Woodrow Wilson Junior College (now Kennedy-King College). In 1968, African American college students in Chicago organized students at college campuses across Illinois and formed the Congress of Black College Students (Williams, 1998).

In some states, activist groups were formed at higher education institutions and the activism of students flowed from the colleges to high schools. In Illinois, however, student activism began in the high schools and expanded to college and university campuses. The primary focus of college students was changing the curriculum while the advocacy efforts of high school students focused on community control of public schools. Support flowed both ways. University students helped high school students advocate for community control and high school students helped college students advocate for curriculum change.

The national office of the Black Panther Party network was located in Oakland, California. A majority of the chapters across the country replicated the operational structure of the national office. A collective called the Central Committee led the organization. The Committee was comprised of six people called ministers, three field lieutenants, and a chair. In some chapters, ministers were called deputy ministers; however, the responsibilities of their positions were the same. There was a Minister of Information, Minister of Communication, Minister of Defense, Minister of Culture, Minister of Labor, and Minister of Finance. Each minister was in charge of a cadre.

Huey P. Newton was the National Chairman.

The overall mission of the Black Panther Party was to defend the Black community from police oppression and brutality. In 1971, after an initial focus on self- defense and arms, the organization decided to de-emphasize the military aspects of the Party and focus on the development and implementation of survival programs, community organizing, coalition-building, and electoral politics. The survival programs included a free breakfast program for public school children, medical research health clinics, a public awareness campaign on sickle cell anemia, free food for low-income families, free busing to prisons, free childcare centers, free clothing, a free ambulance service, and an emergency heating program.

The Party networked with diverse groups to combat racism. Some of the groups had White members and/or White leadership. The names of some of the organizations were Students for a Democratic Society, the Weathermen, the American Indian Movement, and the Puerto Rican

Young Lords (Austin, 2006). The governments of North Viet Nam, China, Palestine, and Algeria also supported the Black Panther Party.

Relative to electoral politics, a number of Panther Party members ran for elected office, several successfully (e.g. Bobby Rush, Bobby Seale). Some of the former members of the Party continue to serve as elected officials.

In 1968, then Director of the Federal Bureau of Investigation (FBI), J. Edgar Hoover, proclaimed that the Black Panther Party was the most dangerous group in America and began a public and covert campaign to destroy the organization. This initiative, which was established to destroy dissident groups, was called the "Counter Intelligence Program" (COINTELPRO) (Williams, 1998, p. 173). The activities of the Black Panther Party were monitored by law enforcement agencies across the country. In Chicago, the Red Squad (the intelligence arm of the Chicago Police Department), the FBI, and local media joined forces to discredit the Illinois Black Panther Party. During its existence, the Black Panther Party was the target of 223 out of 295 Black nationalist COINTELPRO activities (Stanford, 1986, p. 189). According to Williams (1998),

> "The FBI's secret war against the Panthers exhausted all of COINTELPRO's methods, including a media offensive, silencing the Panther newspaper, attacking the free breakfast for children program, preventing coalitions, neutralizing Panther supporters, exacerbating intergroup/intraparty tensions, infiltrating the organization, sponsoring raids and pretext arrests, encouraging malicious prosecutions, and even assassinating Panthers" (p. 173).

The word "assassinating" referred to the case of the late Fred Hampton, who was Chair of the Illinois Black Panther Party. In 1969, police killed Hampton during a raid of his apartment. The Hampton family subsequently filed a wrongful death suit against law officials and, in 1978, the court found the FBI, Cook County government, and the city of Chicago guilty of abuse of power and misconduct (Williams, 1998, pp. 215-216). In 1983, the Hampton family was awarded a $1.85 million settlement.

The Black Panther Party officially closed in 1982. The legacy of the Black Panther Party can be summarized into three areas – survival programs, formation of the original Rainbow Coalition, and the martyrdom of Fred Hampton. The most popular of the survival programs was the free breakfast program for schoolchildren. This program, which was adopted and institutionalized by public school systems across the country, continues today. Government also replicated the Panther Party's community health centers. The Panther Party established the original Rainbow Coalition predating Jesse Jackson's organization. The coalition is recognized as being responsible for the election of the first Black mayor (Harold Washington) in Chicago. The name, Fred Hampton, continues to be a catalyst for community organizing and development in Illinois.

The Nation of Islam (NOI).

Although the Nation of Islam (NOI) was established in 1930 by Wallace D. Muhammad, long before the activism of the 1960s and 1970s, because of Malcolm X (aka El Hajj Malik El Shabazz), it played a significant role in the Black Power Movement. Elijah Muhammad became the leader of the Nation of Islam in 1934. In 1952, Elijah Muhammad appointed Malcolm X as the national spokesperson for the Nation of Islam. During the 1960s, Malcolm X served as a counterpoint to Rev. Dr. Martin Luther King, Jr.'s philosophy of non-violence and promoted the right to self-defense. After the expulsion of Malcolm X from the Nation of Islam and his subsequent death, Louis Farrakhan became the national spokesperson and is the recognized leader of the Nation of Islam today.

The stated mission of the Nation of Islam is "to improve the spiritual, mental, social, and economic condition of African Americans in the United States and all of humanity" (Nation of Islam, 2013, p. 1).After 1946, Elijah Muhammad pursued the priorities of increasing membership, establishing a separate state for African Americans, adopting a religion based on the worship of Allah, and promoting African Americans as the chosen people (Nation of Islam, 2013). Malcolm X promoted these priorities when he was appointed the national spokesperson for the organization in the 1952. In February 1964, he was expelled from the Nation of Islam because of controversial statements he made after the assassination of President John Kennedy and allegations he made against Elijah Muhammad. After he left the Nation of Islam, he created the Organization of African American Unity. Through this organization, he planned to take the plight of African Americans to the United Nations. He was assassinated in February 1965.

Malcolm X's prominence increased after his death. During his life, he had given many speeches, which were transcribed, and had written several books and articles. His speeches and writings were studied and analyzed by young people who became activists in the Black Power Movement. Two different interpretations emerged from their analyses, one promoting self-defense another calling for a cultural revolution. The cultural nationalists of the Black Power Movement embraced the need for a cultural revolution and the revolutionary nationalists embraced the need for self-defense.

The Nation of Islam's platform explains what its members want and what they believe. There are 10 items that explain what they want and 12 items that explain what they believe. The items in the platform address the social and economic needs of African Americans as well as spiritual development, and align with the platforms and/or manifestos of other Black Power organizations. For example, a summary of the first four items listed under "What the Muslims Want" are:

1. Freedom
2. Equal Justice under the Law
3. Equality of Opportunity
4. Establishment of a separate country for African Americans (Nation of Islam, 2013).

The two platforms are attached.

During the 1960s and 1970s, the Nation of Islam claimed a membership of 500,000 and had 75 Nation of Islam centers across the country. Currently, there are 10,000 to 50,000 members in the organization with 130 Nation of Islam temples in the United States, Ghana, London, Paris, and the Caribbean Islands. The organization has undergone numerous changes since its establishment in 1930 but continues to pursue its mission today.

The Revolutionary Action Movement (RAM).

Undergraduate students at Central State University in Ohio established the Revolutionary Action Movement in 1962. Its stated purpose was "to educate African Americans on the economic, political, and cultural basis of the racial situation in the United States and the world; to develop unity with Africans in the United States and the world; and, to unite and organize African American students to become active in the African American liberation struggle" (Stanford, 1986, p. 204). In 1961, a group of Central State University students formed an organization called Challenge. In the fall of 1961, it decided to take over the student government at the university to politicize the students on campus. Their members ran successful campaigns and were elected to all of the offices. After the election, Challenge determined that its mission had been accomplished and decided to dissolve the organization. It formed a new organization called the Revolutionary Action Movement and its leaders became leaders of the new organization. The purpose of this national centralized organization was to coordinate the Black Power Movement.

The impetus for organizing the Revolutionary Action Movement was discontent with organizations in the Civil Rights Movement (e.g., the National Association for the Advancement of Colored People {NAACP}, the Student Nonviolent Coordinating Committee {SNCC}, the Urban League, and the Congress of Racial Equality {CORE}). The students disagreed with the use of non-violence as a strategy for liberation and searched for a group that would involve itself in confrontational direct action. As individuals, the students had previously joined one or more of the civil rights groups and were dissatisfied. An example is one student who went from the National Association for the Advancement of Colored People to the Congress of Racial Equality to the Revolutionary Action Movement looking for a home. The students considered the aforementioned groups bourgeois and timid, seeking reform, rather than revolution.

From 1963-1964, the Revolutionary Action Movement organized local community groups for voter registration campaigns, conducted economic boycotts, advocated for jobs, and protested police brutality. In July 1964, student leaders formalized the Revolutionary Action Movement and developed a 12-point program that outlined its goals and objectives. These objectives included development of:

1. A national black student organization movement,
2. Ideology (freedom) schools,
3. Rifle clubs,
4. A liberation army,
5. Training centers,
6. An underground vanguard,
7. "Liberation unions" for black workers,
8. Block organizations (called cells),
9. A separate country (nation within a nation; government in exile),
10. A war fund,
11. Black farmers co-operatives, and
12. An army of the Black unemployed (Ahmed, 2008, pp. 1- 2).

The students planned to accomplish these objectives on three levels. The first level included organizing secret cells in cities. The cells would be the political bases for the organization and would provide financial support for activists to serve as full-time roving field organizers. The second level was establishing local chapters across the country and the third level was recruiting secret members who would fund the organization.

After Malcolm X left the Nation of Islam, he secretly joined the Revolutionary Action Movement and publicly established another organization, the Organization of African American Unity. Through the Organization of African American Unity, he planned to change the philosophy of civil rights organizations, moving them from civil rights to human rights; and, to internationalize the movement. The Organization of African American Unity and the Revolutionary Action Movement worked together. The Organization of African American Unity was the public organization and the Revolutionary Action Movement coordinating the Black Liberation Front underground.

The structure of the Revolutionary Action Movement was multi-faceted and intentionally confusing. A number of local student groups around the country adopted the name of the Revolutionary Action Movement. In 1964, the following officers were elected and installed:

- International Spokesman: Malcolm X

- International Chairman: Robert Williams

- National Field Chairman: Max Stanford

- Executive Chairman: Donald Freeman

- Ideological Chairman: James Boggs

- Executive Secretary: Grace Boggs

- Treasurers: Milton Henry and Paul Brooks (Naison, 1978, p. 37).

In 1965, James and Grace Boggs resigned their positions. New officers were elected and the organization decided to keep their names secret. These officers formed a secret central coordinating committee called the Soul Circle.

After 1965, Revolutionary Action Movement members led and participated in numerous demonstrations and protests but did not use the name of the Revolutionary Action Movement in the efforts. It closed all of its offices and published its materials anonymously to maintain secrecy. The organization created a code of ethics for cadres and rules for safekeeping secrets to maintain discipline and secrecy. These documents are attached. See Appendix Q. Three membership categories were established: professionals, full-time field organizers, and general members. All persons who desired to join the organization had to complete training on ideology, politics, and activism.

During its existence, the Revolutionary Action Movement organized study groups that met weekly. Participants in these study groups were recruited for membership in the cells. It conducted free weekly Black history classes in northern Philadelphia for community members and organized three types of cells. Area cells were organized in cities, work units were established in factories, and political units were established to infiltrate civil rights organizations. The Revolutionary Action

Movement established local student chapters on college campuses on both historically Black college campuses across the country and at predominantly White college campuses in the North; and, organized a youth self-defense section of ex-gang members that was initially called the Black Guards and later the Black Liberation Army. The Revolutionary Action Movement also helped to establish the Black Panther Party, the Republic of New Africa, the League of Revolutionary Black Workers, and the All African People's Revolutionary Party. It radicalized the Student Nonviolent Coordinating Committee and led and/or participated in numerous protests. In 1967, the FBI called Max Stanford, a Revolutionary Action Movement leader, "the most dangerous man" in America. He was subsequently imprisoned (Stanford, 2013, p. 2). Because of problems with COINTELPRO, the national central committee dissolved the Revolutionary Action Movement in 1968.

The Republic of New Afrika (RNA).

Two brothers who were protégés of Malcolm X established the Republic of New Afrika in 1968: Milton Henry (aka Imari Obadele) and Richard Henry (aka Imari Abubakari Obadele). In 1968, they formed the Malcolm X Society and collaborated with another organization, the Group on Advanced Leadership, to organize a conference of 500 participants in Detroit, Michigan (RNA, 2013). At the conference, called the "Black Government Conference," they declared African Americans free and formed a provisional government (PG-RNA). At the conference, 100 of the attendees signed a declaration of independence and a manifesto.

The Republic of New Afrika had three major goals:

1. Create an independent African American majority country on what they termed was subjugated land. This included the states of Mississippi, Louisiana, Alabama, Georgia, and South Carolina; and, in majority Black counties adjacent to the states in the surrounding states of Arkansas, Texas, North Carolina, Tennessee, and Florida;
2. Advocate for payment of $400 billion in reparations by the US government for the injustices of slavery; and,
3. Advocate for a referendum to give all Black people the opportunity to determine their citizenship because they were not given the opportunity to state their choice after slavery ended.

A People's Revolutionary Leadership Council was established to build New Communities and manage the new country. The following individuals were elected to office:

- First President: Robert F. Williams
- First Vice President: Gaidi Obadele (Milton Henry)
- Second Vice President: Betty Shabazz
- Minister of Information: Imari Obadele (Richard Henry)
- Minister of Health and Welfare: Queen Mother Moore
- Minister of Education: Herman Ferguson

- Minister of State and Foreign Affairs: William Grant

- Minister of Defense: Jalil Al Amin (H. Rap Brown)

- Co-Ministers of Culture: Imamu Amiri Baraka (LeRoi Jones); Maulana Karenga, and Baba Adefunmi (added later)

- Minister of Justice: Joan Franklin

- Minister of Finance: Raymond Willis

- Special Ambassador: Muhammad Ahmed (Maxwell Stanford) (RNA, 2013, p. 2).

The individuals listed above were already popular leaders among African Americans and several were leaders of their own organizations.

The leaders of the Republic of New Afrika realized that their organization would be controversial because of its goals. In preparation for anticipated encounters with law enforcement, they received training in weaponry and organized a militia for self-defense. Their activities were scrutinized by the FBI's COINTELPRO initiative and the Detroit Police Department. The Republic of New Afrika was involved in two well-known violent confrontations with law enforcement during which three police officers were killed. A number of the Republic of New Afrika activists were killed and the rest were jailed. The imprisonment of most of the organization's leaders left the organization without leadership and its popularity among African Americans significantly declined.

By 1980, all of the jailed leaders were released from prison. The Republic of New Afrika continues to advocate for reparations for African Americans. Although the organization does not publicize the number of members in its group, it boasts a membership of between 5,000 and 10,000 people today.

The Student Nonviolent Coordinating Committee (SNCC).

The Southern Christian Leadership Conference established the Student Nonviolent Coordinating Committee in April 1960. Ella Baker, at the suggestion of Rev. Dr. Martin Luther King, Jr., was the primary organizer (The Student Nonviolent Coordinating Committee, 2013). This student movement was one of a few Black Power organizations that changed its philosophy from being a civil rights organization, embracing the strategy of non-violence, to a Black Power organization that embraced the strategy of self-defense. The change in philosophy resulted from the violence student activists experienced during voter registration drives in the South. From 1960-1966, the group was a civil rights organization. From 1966-1971, it was a Black power organization.

In April 1960, the Southern Christian Leadership Conference held a conference at Shaw University to organize students (The Student Nonviolent Coordinating Committee, 2013). One hundred and twenty six students who were activists at sit-in centers in 12 southern states and students at 19 northern colleges attended the conference. The establishment of the Student Nonviolent Coordinating Committee was an outcome of the conference. Marion Barry was elected its first chair. From 1960 to 1966, members of the Student Nonviolent Coordinating Committee were active in the civil rights movement. It participated in sit-ins, freedom rides, voter registration drives, the 1963 March on Washington, and formed the Mississippi Freedom Democratic Party to challenge the then all White State Democratic Party.

In 1965, a crisis in philosophy (civil rights v. Black power) caused the organization to split into two factions (the Student Nonviolent Coordinating Committee, 2013) and White members were expelled from the organization. The transformation of SNCC from civil rights to Black power is reflected in its leadership:

Civil Rights era:
- Marion Barry, first Chairman, 1960-1961

- Charles McDew, second Chairman, 1961-1963

- John Lewis, third Chairman, 1963-1966

Black Power era:
- Stokely Carmichael, fourth Chairman, 1966-1967

- H. Rap Brown, fifth Chairman, 1967-1969.

The cry for "Black Power" with a raised fist originated from the Student Nonviolent Coordinating Committee in 1966 in Greenwood, Mississippi. Although Carmichael popularized the term, it was actually Mukasa (aka Willie Ricks), another member of the Student Nonviolent Coordinating Committee, who cried "Black Power" when the Student Nonviolent Coordinating Committee was completing a march from Memphis, Tennessee to Jackson, Mississippi. James Meredith organized the march to encourage voter registration. During the march, Meredith was shot by a sniper and hospitalized. Black leaders showed up the next day to complete the march and during the march, Mukasa cried "Black Power." When queried about the meaning of Black Power, Carmichael responded,

> "We have to do what every group in the country did – we gotta take over the community where we outnumber people so we can have decent jobs" (History Learning Site, 2013, p. 2).

The Student Nonviolent Coordinating Committee was instrumental in establishing the Black Panther Party. In 1964, the organization helped form the Lowndes County (Alabama) Freedom Organization, which was the original Black Panther Party. In 1967, Stokely Carmichael left the Student Nonviolent Coordinating Committee to join the Black Panther Party. H. Rap Brown, who, in 1969, changed the name of the organization to the Student National Coordinating Committee (The Student Nonviolent Coordinating Committee, 2013), succeeded him. In 1969, Brown also resigned and joined the Black Panther Party as its Minister of Justice. When the Student Nonviolent Coordinating Committee changed its philosophy from civil rights to Black power, the government placed it under surveillance as part of its COINTELPRO initiative. In 1967, the Department of Defense stated:

> "SNCC can no longer be considered a civil rights group. It has become a racist organization with Black supremacy ideals and an expressed hatred for Whites.

It employs violent and militant measures that may be defined as extreme when compared to those of more moderate groups" (The Student Nonviolent Coordinating Committee, 2013, p. 6).

Because of a loss of funding and COINTELPRO, the Student Nonviolent Coordinating Committee closed its doors in 1971.

The Black Power organizations described above pursued a wide spectrum of activities ranging from confrontational direct action to Black healing and institution building. Some were externally focused on local, national, and international issues relative to racism and oppression. Others focused on the internal needs of African Americans, designing activities and programs to heal African Americans emotionally and spiritually from the ravages of slavery, and, through education, to develop future African American leaders. Throughout the literature, there is documentation that, regardless of their focus, the activities of the organizations were monitored by the criminal justice system through COINTELPRO (FBI files, Republic of New Africa website). This information was confirmed in the interviews with African American leaders.

Cross-Organizational Analysis of the Findings of the Study

As stated in Chapter I, the paradigm of inquiry for this research is social constructivism, specifically critical race theory (CRT), which is a part of the paradigm. The social constructivist perspective is based on three assumptions: reality is constructed and is a social invention, knowledge is socially and culturally constructed, and learning is a social process (Kim, 2001). Humans are part of a constructed environment and the environment is part of the individual (Kim, 2001). In accordance with critical theory in the Stanford Encyclopedia of Philosophy (2005), the researcher explained problems with current social reality (African American history), identified actors to effect changes (authors and faculty), and provided achievable goals for social transformation (student development practices, curricula and andragogy). The goal of the researcher is to erode ignorance and give voice to the disenfranchised, in this case Black Power Movement activists. The researcher was a Black Power activist (see subjectivity statement on page 64) and, through this study, is reconstructing history to give voice to African American activists who endured violence, imprisonment, and deferred pursuit of their educational goals to help eliminate oppression and to improve the educational experience of the African American students who would follow them.

The conceptual frameworks used for this analysis were Lewin's theory of change (Lewin, 1948) and critical race theory, which was developed by Bell and Freeman (Delgado & Stephancic, 2006). Because the FBI's Counter Intelligence Program (COINTELPRO) played a significant role in the activism of the Black Power Movement, its impact will also be presented.

Analysis of Findings Based on Lewin's Theory of Change

According to Lewin (1948), behavior is a function of the person and the environment; or $B=f[P, E]$. Lewin's theory of change is a theory of opposing forces, which involves a process of unfreezing, movement, and refreezing. In order to maintain stability, there must be equilibrium between the opposing forces. Movement occurs when the equilibrium between the forces is disrupted. Refreezing occurs when equilibrium is reestablished.

In this case, freezing is represented by the established social norms of society and higher education institutions, which maintain tradition. Movement occurred when four environmental factors disrupted the equilibrium of the opposing forces. This included the passage of two federal laws, one law that ended discrimination based on race and another law that increased access to higher education; the cry for "Black Power"; and, the unrest that occurred when first-generation African American college students experienced microaggressions on college campuses.

The Civil Rights Act, which made discrimination based on race illegal, became law in 1964 (National Archives and Records Administration, 2013). The Higher Education Act, which made higher education affordable for all who were qualified and wished to attend college, was passed in 1965 (U. S. Department of Education, 2008). After passage of the laws, many first-generation African American students enrolled in predominately-White colleges and universities across the country. On the campuses, they experienced culture shock, hostility, and isolation. Due to ongoing racial discrimination, violence perpetrated against African American activists, and economic oppression in African American communities; in 1966, Black activists launched a cry for Black Power (Student Nonviolent Coordinating Committee, 2013). Many of the activists that joined the Black Power Movement were college students. These four events came together to form a perfect storm that led to demands for changes in higher education policy and curricula.

Following passage of the Higher Education Act, higher education faculty did not anticipate or made any provisions to address the needs of the new population of students. According to Williamson (1999), there was a sentiment articulated by faculty that the students should be grateful for the opportunity to attend college. The cultural conflict and cognitive dissonance experienced by the students were not anticipated. Students found themselves isolated in a strange world where they had to contend with microaggressions on a daily basis. The cry for Black Power by community activists resonated with Black college students because of their negative experiences on campuses and the disruptions (rebellions) at home. The students decided to introduce and implement the Black Power concept on college campuses. They formed Black student groups as counter spaces to strengthen their cultural glue (Robinson et al., 1987) and get the support they needed in the campus environment. Their goals were to complete their studies and graduate. The students advocated for changes in higher education policy and curricula by organizing demonstrations, participating in rebellions, and taking over administration buildings.

In response to the disruptions, higher education administrations made changes to address the concerns articulated. Black student unions were accepted and supported.

African American and Africana studies departments were established. More African American professors were hired. Curricular changes were made. Dress codes were relaxed to allow for more diversity. These efforts served to reduce the number of microaggressions African American students had to endure and to re-establish social equilibrium on campuses, which represents the refreezing phase of Lewin's theory.

Based on Lewin's theory, the cry for Black Power is one of a number of actions that could be considered movement in a series of freezing-movement-refreezing cycles. These cycles go back to the institution of slavery in the United States (Robinson et. al., 1987). The savagery of slavery led to revolts of those who were enslaved, abolition of the institution of slavery, and the Civil War. Refreezing occurred after declaration of the Emancipation Proclamation, which officially ended slavery, and the repeal of oppressive laws during what is called the Reconstruction Period (Robinson et al., 1987). These events represent one change cycle.

Although slavery officially ended, racism continued. There was a backlash by segments of the White population, who were dissatisfied with the new way of life during Reconstruction. They worked for change through passage of the Black Codes, which were laws that restricted the movement and rights of formerly enslaved African Americans, and by forming an organization called the Ku Klux Klan to terrorize African Americans. Civil rights activism emanated from advocacy efforts to repeal the Black Codes, fight the Ku Klux Klan, and address the economic depression and oppressive conditions that led to explosions in cities and in African American communities. The cry for Black Power emanated from the frustration of activists with the non-violent and integration strategies employed by the Civil Rights Movement in the face of the violence perpetrated on Blacks by the White dominant society. Passage of the Civil Rights Act, the Voting Rights Act, the Higher Education Act, and the emergence of a strong federal government to enforce and ensure full rights and equal opportunities for all citizens served to restore equilibrium in the system. This sequence of events represents another cycle in Lewin's theory. However, these actions also triggered another cycle on college campuses.

Analysis of Findings Based on the Critical Race Theory

As stated, critical race theory (CRT) was developed in the mid-1970s by Derrick Bell and Allan Freeman, who were law professors. They were later joined by a number of scholars such as Richard Delgado, who has authored several books on the topic (WiseGeek.com, 2013). Many educators have now embraced the theory to increase their understanding of classroom dynamics, school discipline, achievement testing, and curriculum bias.

The tenets of critical race theory and the findings of the study help to explain the phenomenon of student activism on college campuses during the Black Power Movement. They explain African American students feeling like outsiders, their discontent with curriculum (the call for Black studies departments), and their need to form academic and social counter spaces (Black student unions) to survive Ina hostile environment.

When first-generation African American students arrived on college campuses, they felt isolated in a hostile environment. They were the other. As stated in Chapter I, many of the students lived in socially and economically depressed segregated communities where there was a lack of opportunity, high unemployment, and violence.

Poor education was a norm in these communities. Families who lived there viewed higher education as an elusive dream that was out of their reach. High school graduation was the common goal. These conditions led to advocacy for equal opportunity, rebellions in cities across the country, and the call for Black Power.

Despite these conditions, many African American youth were able to overcome the challenges of their environment, practice healthy life styles, and academically achieve. After the barriers to higher education were removed and qualified African American students were able to afford a college education, they enrolled in large numbers to predominately-White colleges and universities. This was a new experience for them. However, instead of being welcomed, they were met with perceived resentment, hostility, and the realization of stark class differences. A new set of challenges had emerged.

In addition to culture, the communities from which they came represented a different social class than traditional college students, particularly privileged and legacy students. Legacy students come from wealthy families who have a long intergenerational history of attending exclusive higher education institutions (Grove, 2014; Shulman & Bowen, 2001). Their parents, grandparents, and other family members have a tradition of attending and/or funding these institutions. This gives them special status at the institutions they attend. African American students' reality of the world was different.

They did not have the wealth of these students, such as material paraphernalia (clothing and expensive cars) and the ability to travel abroad. They were unfamiliar with the culture of the wealthy. Although these African American students came from low- income communities, they lived in communities with others who had a similar income status, so social class was not an issue. They became more conscious class differences after they arrived on college campuses.

Language plays an important role in critical race theory. The language used in the Black Power Movement is one example of race as a social construction for liberation.

Two of the participants who were interviewed discussed a debate that was taking place during the period among African American leaders regarding an acceptable label for Black people who were born in the United States. In this case, the goal was to enhance identity and increase self-esteem among Blacks. At the time, the label being used to describe the population was Negro. There was consensus among African American leaders that Negro was no longer an acceptable term. The 1903 Encyclopedia Britannica defined the term, Negro, as a person or group without history, culture, a mind, heart, or soul. In the *Black Image in the White Mind* by Fredrickson (1971), Negroes were presented as descendants of the gardener of the Garden of Eden, who raped Eve. This mythology provided a rationale for attacks, mutilations, and lynching. The labels that were considered to replace the term, Negro, were Black, and African American.

Most leaders of Black power organizations insisted on changing the label from Negro to African American. By changing the construct, the Black Power Movement changed Black identity from a Black person being a Negro with a limited history of oppression and no connection to a land mass to a people with a rich heritage, a connection to the peoples of Africa, the right to group life, culture, intellectual development, and spiritual power (Dubois, 1903). The initiatives of organizations in the Black Power Movement challenged the construct of White culture being the standard with a monopoly in honor, history, culture, intellectual development, and spiritual salvation. This Black intellectual and cultural movement created symbols of self-respect, self-determination, and self-respect. It enhanced the identity and self-esteem of African Americans and was part of the impetus for the cry for shared power. Among other things, the Black Power Movement reconstructed the identity of African Americans as being part of the Black race. Most African Americans, including African American college students, embraced this change in identity.

Many predominately-White higher education institutions have a "sink or swim" rugged individualism philosophy. Upon enrollment to college, students are considered instant adults and personal responsibility is stressed. African American students viewed this philosophy, which is Eurocentric and incongruent with the cultural and affiliation needs of African Americans (Robinson et al., 1987), as a form rejection. African American students and culture were judged, frequently negatively judged, according to a White standard. During that period, the extra-curricular activities and events on campuses were designed for White students. There were few African American outlets or role models. This environment fostered feelings of alienation and anger among African American students and the feeling that they were the other.

On predominately-White higher education campuses, the content and andragogy in classes often portrayed African Americans negatively and, in many instances, the contributions of Africans and African Americans to society were totally omitted. These microaggressions created academic challenges, isolation, and cultural shock. Conditions were better at historically Black colleges and universities (HBCU) because many of the faculty at the institutions came from the same communities as the African American students and understood the culture. However, the curricula at HBCUs mirrored the curricula at the predominately-White institutions in which Whites are the standard (Woodson, 1933). This issue led to advocacy for changes in curricula at both HBCUs and predominately-White colleges and universities. Advocacy efforts for changes in curricula at HBCUs included inclusion of courses on African American and African culture and history, and promotion of the link between African Americans and continental Africa.

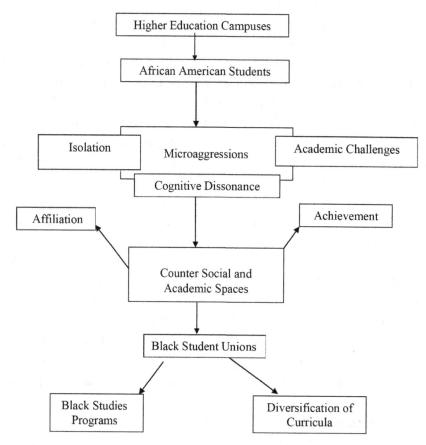

Figure 1: First-generation African American students on college campuses.

Figure 1 is an analysis based on critical race theory that graphically depicts the strategies employed by African American students to succeed in what they perceived was a hostile environment. Affiliation and achievement needs were addressed by the formation of social and academic counter spaces, Black student unions and other Black student organizations. In addition to providing social support for the survival of their members, these organizations also provided study groups to help them succeed academically. Issues around the lack of representation and inclusion in the curricula emerged out of the study groups. Many students also attended study groups that were being held in African American communities and were exposed to literature on traditional African culture and African American heroes that were not available on college campuses. A number of student groups began to study this literature independently. The activism for changes in curricula to include Africana studies emerged from discussions in these groups.

Analysis of Responses of African American Leaders by Research Question

An analysis of the responses of African American leaders is presented below by research question. Response to the general question will be answered through analysis of the four supporting research questions, questions 2-4.The analysis of research questions 2 and 3 regarding Black Power organizations follow. The analysis of research questions 4 and 5 regarding the San Francisco State University experience will be presented following the timeline on the development of the Black studies department at San Francisco State College.

2. Role of the Black Power Movement in the development of Black student organizations, particularly Black student unions.

The responses of participants and the information in the literature are highly congruent on the role of the Black Power Movement in the development of Black student unions. The consensus of the participants interviewed was that the Black Power Movement was pivotal in the development of Black student groups. It was not only the driving force for Black student unions, but also was responsible for the formation of other student groups and achievements as well. Some of the participants interviewed had first- hand experience in organizing student groups on their campuses. Other participants played an advisory role.

According to one participant, Black Power represented a paradigm shift in the Black community.

> We had gone through integration and it really didn't work – the way things evolved
> in the general Civil Rights Movement – integration and non-violence. Black Power
> was the big cry nationally. It was a turning point. When Black Power hit in 1966,
> the students coming back to campus wanted to bring Black Power back to campus.
> All over the country, they tended to do that.

The Student Nonviolent Coordinating Committee (SNCC), which transformed itself from a civil rights organization to a Black power organization, emerged as one of the leading student organizations that established student groups in the Black community. According to the SNCC participant,

Nineteen sixty-six was when we made the cry of Black Power. …Every household was divided on the question of Black Power. Where some people were against Black Power, you had someone in that household that supported Black Power. So, Black Power became a very intense debate in the African community.

The Student Nonviolent Coordinating Committee is also recognized for establishing a number of Black student unions (BSU), SNCC chapters, and other student groups on college campuses including the Student Organization for Black Unity (SOBU), which was renamed the Youth Organization for Black Unity (YOBU). According to a participant,

We began to demand Blackness and set up Black Power chapters at all of the Black schools and asked the kids at the White schools to do the same thing. In doing so, they began to demand more from the schools and put together Black Studies programs and all those things.

Another participant described the difference between Black student unions (BSU) and the Student Organization for Black Unity/Youth Organization for Black Unity (SOBU, YOBU).

…SOBU (later YOBU) had a distinct ideological worldview, a pan-African worldview. BSUs were diverse organizations. They (BSUs) were united fronts with different tendencies and they focused their energy primarily on campus questions. SOBU had an ideological position and it focused its energy on global questions as well.

A number of students belonged to both groups. There was a myriad of Black Power student groups on campuses. One student stated that she belonged to different campus groups. She stated that the Black student union at her campus emerged in 1967. Before that, the predominant groups for Black students were Black history organizations and Black study groups. The study group to which she belonged was called the *Nkrumahs*, in honor of Kwame Nkrumah. Members of the group studied all of the works of Kwame Nkrumah and Karl Marx.

A leader from the National Association of Black Social Workers stated,

We have student chapters all over the place. Internationally, we have student groups in South Africa and Nova Scotia… and the Caribbean. The purposes of the groups are activism and mentoring young Black social work students to be more effective in serving people in African American communities.

Only one of the participants interviewed was, at one point active, in the Civil Rights Movement. The messaging of the Civil Rights Movement did not resonate with the other activists that were interviewed. One of the reasons they got involved in the Black Power Movement were the microaggressions they endured as students on a daily basis, being judged using a White standard, and being portrayed negatively in course literature. These aggressions mirrored what African Americans were experiencing and Black Power activists were articulating in African American communities across the country. The hostile environment they encountered on college campuses and the need for support propelled them into activism. Further, they were unwilling to give up their Black identity as a condition of being educated. The more they learned, the more they realized they had been mis-educated and they disliked how they were being portrayed as a race.

These macroaggressions and microaggressions led to a sense of betrayal and anger. Following are several quotations from participants that describe their experiences, which reflect a resistance to microaggressions and their decision to form counter spaces for support.

Malcolm X was the one who inspired me because he was talking about what I was experiencing (miseducation and microaggressions). King's message was too weak.

I was so upset with Rutgers. I thought it was the most racist experience I ever had (microaggressions). There were five full time African American students among 104 graduate students. When I got my degree, I put it in a drawer.

I think (because) of the impact of racism and the violence against Black people, we had to come together (counter spaces).

I went to Regina High School from 1970-1973. I was influenced by the Black Panther Party. I used to hang out with them. I was always drawn to the Black Panther Party Movement as opposed to the Civil Rights Movement. I came up in the era of the 60s, well really the 70s, and we were reading the *Autobiography of Malcolm X*. It had an impact on me even before reading *Manchild in the Promised Land* and looking through a pictorial history of the Negro in America…when I saw a picture of 14-year-old Emmet Till, who was murdered. His murder happened the same year or the next year after my birth so it really had an impact on me (microaggression). So, for whatever reasons I was drawn more towards Black Power.

I have very strong memories of the Black Power Movement. In 1963, three or four girls were bound and killed in Birmingham, Alabama. I remember very clearly that Martin Luther King said that no matter what they do, we're going to keep on loving them. I remember my friends and me, I was about 12 years old at the time, had just witnessed something disgusting. We said, —Keep on loving them? They killed those four little girls that very Sunday I had been in my family's Baptist church. I was the same age as those girls that had been killed and I identified with them (microaggression). I just thought that Dr. King's response was so weak. But when my mother's friend said that she had gone to see a man named Malcolm X speak at the Nation of Islam temple in Chicago and he said that Black people should get their own army and should go down South and protect our churches and protect our people from being abused by the Klan and these racists, I said right then that whenever that army started, I want to be in their army. I didn't care if they just let me stir grits or carry water; I want to be in that army (counter space).They're protecting Black people from the Klan and having our little kids blown up. So, that was my first concept that there was actually a different way {of thinking} than Martin Luther King's.

Young Black African Americans, for the most part in the North, were knocked down with the Dr. King stuff. We respected him, but letting White people spit on you and kick you and you just keep singing and talking about you gonna keep loving them and all that, most of the young people and teenagers in the North, were just disgusted by that (microaggression). We didn't support him. So, when Stokely Carmichael says, "Black Power", and we heard about Malcolm X, as 15 and 16-year old, that is what we identified with.

I was in college during my years at CFUN (Committee for Unified NewArk). When we learned that CFUN was forming a Congress of African People, we decided to form a Congress of African Students, a parallel organization (counter space). It was not known but the Ku Klux Klan was attacking students in Pennsylvania. We organized the student group at Dickerson College in Pennsylvania and developed a statewide newspaper.

The sentiments conveyed in the statements above correspond with the information in the literature (Biondi, 2012; Joseph, 2006; Williamson, 1999; and Solorzano, Ceja, and Yosso, 2000). Students were personally experiencing hostility on college campuses and many of them came from communities where there was widespread discontent. They felt compelled to act to change the injustices they saw and experienced.

3. Role of the Black Power Movement in the development of Black studies departments.

Among the participants interviewed, there was consensus that the establishment of Black studies departments resulted from the advocacy of Black student unions.

College campuses were learning communities, so the focus of the Black student groups was relevant teaching of African American students. As one participant stated:

It was clear that part of what was happening during that whole period was a shift in our consciousness and our understanding that we had been deceived. That was a widespread sense back then…we had not properly taught our own history and culture …and we needed to be taught.

Another participant stated,

Black students had come back to campus in 1966…and they were concerned about what they were being taught (White standard). They were getting bad grades by comparison. They organized as a group and out of the group came other notions and criticisms of the classes (microaggression). They disrupted classes and wanted to learn about their own.

He continued, stating,

Even White students wanted to learn about the Black thing. They were curious about Black people then because Blackness was in the air. Black Power was the thing. It was exciting to the White students too. They were more receptive to Blackness than they are now.

The establishment of Black Studies was a natural outcome from Black student unions, which were organized for mutual support (counter spaces) and a need to learn more about themselves. What began as Black history and Black study groups developed, with advocacy, to Black studies departments.

Frequently, the Civil Rights Movement is given credit for changes on college campuses. Several participants disputed that belief, stating that civil rights leaders did not support Black student groups and Black studies programs because they viewed them as separatist programs, which were contrary to their mission of integration. The participant from SNCC articulated the hostility of civil rights leaders to Black student groups and Black studies.

> We had to defeat the civil rights leaders on the question of Black Power. We had to fight them. They condemned us – SNCC. They joined the government against us.

According to another participant,

> I remember when the battle started for an African American and African studies department at that university, and I know it was students with big Afros and all that who were protesting and sitting there, and who had never crossed (paths with) Dr. King.

Another participant stated,

> I'll never forget when we pressed for Black education in schools and the NAACP denounced it as separatist.

Another participant stated,

> …look at the movement that took place on Howard University's campus, where you got E. Franklin Frazier and all of them arguing against Black studies saying,

> "You see, you got to assimilate. You don't need Black studies."

Civil rights leaders had difficulty advocating for integration and Black studies at the same time. Based on these statements and the literature, one can conclude that the Black Power Movement, not the Civil Rights Movement, was responsible for the establishment of Black student unions and Black studies departments.

The Case of San Francisco State College

Emergence of the First Black Student Union

The first Black Student Union (BSU) and Black Studies department were established at the San Francisco State University (SFSU), then San Francisco State College. The literature documents the linkage on the emergence of both entities. The

Black studies program came out of the demands of students in the Black student union and its network of individuals and organizations. A student activist, James Garrett, was one of the key leaders in forming the BSU at San Francisco State College. This researcher was unable to interview Mr. Garrett; however, Dr. Ibram Rogers, who was then a doctoral candidate at Temple University, interviewed James Garrett in 2007 (Rogers, 2009). The interview, entitled *Remembering the Black Campus Movement: An Oral History Interview with James P. Garrett*, was published in the Journal of Pan- African Studies (2009). In his introductory remarks, Dr. Rogers described the sequence of events leading to the establishment of the Black student union and Black studies program at SFSU.

> During that first semester at San Francisco State, the nation's first BSU was founded under Garrett's tutelage. This BSU focused on gaining power and university resources to advance the Black campus community, and the nearby Black communities. Soon he would build this organization into one of the most powerful and influential organizations during the Black Campus Movement. That year, Garrett also conjured up the idea for the discipline of Black Studies—an idea that soon circulated throughout the nation, as it became the major demand of newly organized BSUs during the Black Campus Movement. In the spring of 1967, Garrett wrote and submitted to the faculty at San Francisco State the first conceptual proposal for a Black Studies department (Rogers, 2009, p. 31).

An excerpt of the interview with Mr. Garrett that captures his perspective on the rationale and sequence of events leading to the formation of the BSU and the Black Studies program at San Francisco State College is presented below.

Ibram Rogers (IR): Explain to me the events surrounding the founding of the Black Student Union at San Francisco State in 1966.

James P. Garrett (JG):

> There was already in existence an organization called the Negro Student Association that had been started some years ago through people like Willie Brown and others who were in the group that predated our activities. But, let me go back just in terms of my own work.
>
> I had been taught by Bob Moses and others in SNCC. And, based on readings I had been doing on Fanon, Mao Tse-tung, and others, they said you have to do a study of the area. So, I did a study, kind of a city study and a college study of the San Francisco Bay area. During that time, there were several people, who were my colleagues in SNCC, who came out because they knew that I was going to the campus to organize. I didn't go to the campus to be a student. We went to the campus for two reasons. One is to avoid being called in the military, which we weren't going to go. SNCC people had taken a position that they weren't going to go.
>
> So we did a study, a historical study on modern history—that is a 20thcentury historical study of San Francisco and the founding of the state college system and the master plan. And, it was based on that study and the communications that I had with a

number of people who were involved in community work, poverty program work with CORE and others, that when I came onto the campus, I was pretty well armed.

So it wasn't any active genius when I called for the change...from Negro Student Association to Black Student Union. I called for it in March [of 1966]. Finally, about seven or eight of us met in April of 1966 to formalize what became the Black Student Union. Marianna Waddy, Jo Ann Mitchell, Benny Stewart, Jerry Varnado and a couple of others and myself came together to form this and I became the chair.

IR: Why did you decide to call for a name change?

JG:

Because of the national consciousness. What we were coming out, at least what I was coming out of, was a combination of factors: the need to organize as opposed to simply mobilize and protest, which we were learning from our experience in SNCC. I had been involved in SNCC since the early 60s. And, the second reason was the rise of consciousness from the uprisings that were taking place. I had just left LA and had been in the middle of what people call _the Watts riot 'and what we call[ed] _the Los Angeles uprising' because it took place all over Los Angeles in 1965. So there was a national consciousness that was developing and consolidating and the use of that consciousness distilled into the notion of Black or Blackness or the validity of Blackness. And the idea was to politicize this growing consciousness into a formation of a union because of the connection we thought we had with the union movement. That it is not simply an alliance or an association, but a union. It is a coming together of a broad base of people. So, Black student and union all had meaning that was connected. Blackness was the new consciousness or the consolidation of a consciousness that came from Malcolm X, and from Martin King, Jr. in his latter days, as personifications.

SNCC had moved from defining themselves from Negroes to Blacks. All of these things were coming into being at that time. The Los Angeles uprising was the crystallizing force, at least personally for me.

IR: What was going to be the role of the new Black Student Union?

JG:

The goal was to restructure San Francisco State as a model for acting as a resource base to serve the Black community. So, the whole thing was to take the school, to take it over literally or the pivotal areas of the school, such that whatever resources it had could be used to benefit or ameliorate the Black community, which we saw as a revolutionary force in the United States.

So, the concept of the Black student union was to include everybody who considered themselves Black whether they were students, faculty, security people, buildings and grounds, landscapers, gardeners, maids who worked in the dorms; we didn't care where they were and who they were. If they were Black, then they were members of the Black Student Union. So we didn't have a membership fee, you were a member by definition. Africans on the campus were members by definition. People from Puerto Rico or

Nicaragua, if they considered themselves to have African blood they were members of the Black Student Union. So that was one thing, to consolidate everybody under that banner. Then we moved to include all the fraternities and sororities, all the people who were excluded from sororities or fraternities because of color or whatever, we would include them. We moved to include the athletes who were in some cases isolated from all of these folks. We moved to pull in the cultural people: poets, writers. There were a number of people that we tried to pull in.

Then, we wanted to link the San Francisco community with our organization. We moved to take over the tutorial program. In those days, a lot of White students were involved in the tutorial program and they were paid work- study money to do tutoring; and, they did a lot of them in our community. What we did is take the tutorial program and transform it into a tutoring program where Whites were being tutored by Whites, Asians by Asians, Black by Blacks, and Latinos by Latinos; and then, we cross fertilized them by sending groups from various constituencies to work with others.

We moved to take over the student government. We did not move to become president. We moved to take over the finances of the student government. Then we moved to the administration to take over the pool of funds that came through work-study. We moved to take over the alumni so we found people who had graduated and sent them to the alumni organization because that alumni association gave parties and raised money. One of my main roles was to build a relationship with the guy who was the president of the school and was very much of a liberal and who wanted to open space for people of color. And, it basically got to a point in which [San Francisco State President] John [Summerskill] didn't make policy decisions unless he consulted with me.

We laid out a whole process for dealing with taking over the school. But we fell into a hole. The hole was people did not have a consolidated worldview. I wrote a document called the "Justification for Black Studies" in the late fall of 1966. That became the piece that was used to organize Black Studies. The reason I wrote the document was that we had people that we were placing in all these positions that did not have national consciousness. They had Negro consciousness, or petty bourgeois consciousness, middle class consciousness, personal independent individual aggrandizement consciousness, but they didn't have collective consciousness. So Black Studies became a means to consolidate that certain type of consciousness, by giving everybody at least a generalized understanding of African, Black history at the global level, and the politics that we needed to follow in order to come to grips with sovereignty and collective ownership.

I was very much a socialist, very much probably a Marxist, and I tried to fuse that with what was my own growing national consciousness. So that document became the justification for Black Studies, it became the basis for creating the curriculum.

IR: How and why did the San Francisco State BSU become so powerful with so much influence?

JG:

We went out and found the Danny Glovers. We went out in the street and found Danny Glover. Danny Glover wasn't in school. He was on the street corner when I found him. We began to recruit large numbers of students and demanded that the state colleges and private institutions increase the number of Black students because we needed a critical mass. You can't build a movement unless you have critical mass of somebody. The second thing was to organize the masses around whatever kind of worldview you have.

In the two years that we did our organizing from the spring of 1966 to the spring of 1968, we had gone from about 150 students to 600 students. By the fall of 1968, there were 900 Black students at San Francisco State. At the same time at other campuses, there were quantum leaps in the number of students coming to the campus owing to the generally liberal concept of recruitment. At that time, the second or third biggest industry in the country was education. And, it was a growing institution. And so, that was a place that was an industry; and, the more potential products in that industry the better. So, it was to the benefit of faculty, administrators, etc., to bring people on to the campus.

Our main tactic was conversion. We also used coercion. We did. We threw a racist professor out of a second-story window. That's true. We got into a fight with some of the members of *The Gator*, which was the campus newspaper. That's true. We ended up in pitch battles with some of the people in the athletics department. That's true. We didn't use coercive tactics against our constituents, against students. Many of them were on work-study. We controlled the work- study money. In order for them to get jobs, they had to go through us. So if that's called coercion, then yes, but physical coercion—no. We didn't have to demand that anybody be a member of the Black Student Union. You were member of the Black Student Union just by virtue of being Black on campus (Rogers, 2009, pp. 31-36).

Establishment of a Black Studies Department at San Francisco State College

In collaboration with a broad coalition, the Black Student Union fought for the establishment of Black Studies at San Francisco State. The struggle led to a strike, which lasted for five months, from November 1968-March 1969. SFSU maintains extensive archives on the events, activities, key players, and outcomes of the strike leading to the establishment of the department, which was only one of the outcomes of the effort (San Francisco State University, 2013).

Following is one of the documents in the archival collection (San Francisco State University, 2013) that memorializes the chronology of activities and events that led to the establishment of the Black Studies department at San Francisco State University. The document includes a timeline for the strike, the demands that emanated from the strike, and the outcome of the advocacy effort. Presentation of this data is important for a historical study because it shows the multi-faceted complex nature of the effort and provides details for further study. At the time, SFSU had a predominantly White student population. To achieve establishment of a Black studies department, the Black Student Union had to form a coalition with many groups. The results were establishment of centers of learning for diverse populations. James Garrett, founding member of the Black Student Union at SFSU, described the effort:

So, we brought people onto the campus and we had to organize those people in various ways. We tried to lay the example of organizing. In many cases by the time other campuses started demanding Black Studies, we had made our initial demands. They had only mobilized people. They hadn't organized. Our beginning was at a different historical stage. We started to organize in the spring of 1966, while they started to organize in the spring of 1968. In that two years we had built an organization that included a Third World Liberation Front. We built a Latinos Student Union, a Philippine organization, and an Asian Student Organization. Our thing was to take over the college campus. Other people saw the Black Student Union because it was the vanguard, because it was the leader, and that's all you have to have to organize. We thought that you had to organize everybody, including the 18,000 White students that were on campus. And, we did. We took over the leadership of SDS [Students for a Democratic Society].

We took over the leadership of the Progressive Labor Party. We took everything that we could. I don't mean by violence. You take it over by asserting your leadership and your mottos, by winning battles, and by winning over people (Rogers, 2009, p. 36).

Timeline for the Establishment of the Black Studies Program

A timeline that presents the struggles from beginning to the end follows.

September 1966

Dr. John Summerskill is appointed seventh President, San Francisco State College. He is young, liberal, and has the reputation of being able to get along with faculty, administration, and students.

May 2, 1967.

Sixty students "sit in" in Dr. Summerskill's office, protesting the college practice of providing students' academic standing to the selective service office.

June 22, 1967.

Students and faculty picket campus administrative offices to protest Chancellor Glenn Dumke's directive to the campus to continue supplying academic standing records to the selective service office.

June 22, 1967.

A "major corporation" (the Carnegie Corporation of New York) invites San Francisco State College to apply for funds to develop programs for teaching black history, art, and culture on campus. This information is divulged during a discussion of Black Student Union activities on campus in the spring 1967 semester.

November 6, 1967.

Several black students attack James Vaszko, editor of the Gater the campus newspaper. Mr. Vaszko had stated in an editorial that he had written to the Carnegie Corporation asking them to cease any plans they might have had to grant money to the college's "service programs", which included Black Student Union sponsored programs.

November 11, 1967.

Six of the black students who attacked James Vaszko are booked on felony charges.

The Gater, November 7, 1967

November 17, 1967.

The Black Students Union members hold a press conference and discuss their programs, which have been designed to awaken and develop black awareness and consciousness.

November 18, 1967.

San Francisco State College's Board of Appeals and Review holds closed hearing on the suspension of students accused of assaulting Vaszko. Sympathetic students picket outside.

November 29, 1967.

Dr. Summerskill appoints ten faculty members to a committee to investigate the causes of campus tension, which resulted in the Vaszko attack.

December 2, 1967.

Two writers for the campus literary paper, Open Process, are suspended after publishing a poem, which uses offensive language and contains sexual connotations. Four hundred and fifty students protest and attack Summerskill's "liberalism" and the Vietnam War.

December 6, 1967.

Students protest over suspension of the Black students in the Vaszko incident and break into the administration building. Summerskill closes the campus rather than calling in the police.

December 10, 1967.

Dr. Walcott Beatty, Chairman of the Academic Senate, says that campus demonstrations and disturbances will not end because of the causes, including Vietnam and racial tension. He says, "The campus is a microcosm of society."

February 22, 1968.

Dr. Summerskill hands in his resignation, effective in September, even though the Trustees of the California State College system have given him a vote of confidence. *February 29, 1968.*

Three hundred high school and junior college minority students come to the campus to ask for waivers of admission requirements for the fall semester. Dean of Admissions Charles Stone says that he does not have power to grant waivers. Sociology professor Juan Martinez is influential in inviting the students.

March 1968.

Black Panther Minister of Defense Bobby Seale speaks in the main auditorium at San Francisco State and tells the audience (mainly white students) that the only power Blacks have is with a gun.

March 23, 1968.

The Third World Liberation Front (a coalition of the Black Student Union, the Latin American Student Organization, the Filipino-American Student Organization, and El Renacimiento, a Mexican American student organization) occupies the YMCA office on campus, and moves YMCA staff out.

March 26, 1968.

Several San Francisco State College student leaders call on State Superintendent of Schools Max Rafferty to protest campus activities of the Black Student Union and the hiring by the student government of Black playwright LeRoi Jones, who was a visiting professor in the spring, 1968 semester.

March 31, 1968.

Summerskill tells the Third World Liberation Front to move out of the occupied offices. Professor Juan Martinez has not been re-hired for the following year, and this factor complicates the eviction process.

May 21, 1968.

Police are called in to remove students from the Administration Building after a nine- hour sit-in. Approximately 400 students were protesting: (1) An end to Air Force ROTC on campus, (2) Retention of Juan Martinez, (3) Programs to admit 400 ghetto students in the fall semester, and (4) The hiring of nine minority faculty members to help the minority students. Twenty-six persons are arrested.

May 23, 1968.

Students again protest for campus reform. Demonstrations are led by Students for a Democratic Society and the Third World Liberation Front.

May 24, 1968.

Chancellor Glenn Dumke asks Dr. Summerskill to resign immediately.

June 1, 1968.

Dr. Robert Smith becomes President, San Francisco State College. He is a professor of education.

September 10, 1968.

George Mason Murray is rehired as a teaching assistant. He was a graduate student in English, and was hired to teach special introductory English classes for 400 special students who were admitted to the college.

September 18, 1968.

President Robert Smith announces the creation of a Black Studies Department. Dr. Nathan Hare is named Acting Chair.

September 26, 1968.

California State College trustees vote to ask Dr. Smith to reassign Black Panther George Mason Murray to a non-teaching position. At a Fresno State College rally, he allegedly had stated that, "We are slaves and the only way to become free is to kill all the slave masters". At San Francisco State College, he allegedly had said that Black students should bring guns to campus to protect themselves from White racist administrators. President Smith refuses.

October 24, 1968.

Chancellor Dumke orders President Smith to suspend Murray temporarily.

October 31, 1968.

Chancellor Dumke orders President Smith to suspend Murray after Smith refuses to carry out the trustees' request. President Smith delays. The Black Students Union threatens a strike on November 6, and presents their 15 demands.

November 1, 1968.

President Smith suspends George Murray.

November 6, 1968.

Student strike begins. Strike is led by Black Student Union and Third World Liberation Front members, as a protest for a larger Black studies program and for the reinstatement of George Murray. Most students attend classes. Police are called in after students march on the Administration Building.

November 13, 1968.

The campus is closed after a week of confrontations between students and police. During the week, there has been widespread minor damage by striking students all over the campus. Some faculty members are considering striking.

November 14, 1968.

At a faculty meeting in the Main Auditorium, Dr. S. I. Hayakawa, Professor of English, speaks on racism. He urges the faculty to support Dr. Smith. President Smith appeals to Dr. Dumke to reinstate George Murray. The Academic Senate debates the issues, and requests Chancellor Dumke's resignation.

November 15, 1968.

The faculty meets to consider the problems. Dr. Smith asks the faculty and administration to consider plans under which the campus could be reopened.

November 18, 1968.

Governor Ronald Reagan wants the campus reopened. The trustees order Dr. Smith to reopen the campus immediately. President Smith wants the students to return for discussion, not formal classes. A faculty grievance committee says that George Murray was suspended without due process.

November 19, 1968.

The faculty does not want to reopen the campus, but want to have a convocation to discuss the issues.

November 20, 1968.

Approximately 10% of the students return to campus for departmental discussions. Few classes are held. The convocation begins.

November 26, 1968.

Convocation continues. Black Student Union leaders confront the faculty panel and President Smith at the convocation. BSU leader Jerry Varnardo calls President Smith a 'pig,' and is booed by the audience. President Smith resigns. Dr. S. I. Hayakawa is named Acting President. His first official act is to close the campus.

December 2, 1968.

Campus is reopened. Sound truck incident occurs. Striking students position sound truck at corner of 19th and Holloway Avenues to urge other students to continue the strike.
Hayakawa climbs on the truck and tries to disconnect the speakers. A crowd pulls his tam o'shanter from his head. He allegedly yells, "You're fired!" to noted author Kay Boyle, and she calls him "Hayakawa Eichmann" in return.

December 10, 1968.

Ronald Haughton, University of Michigan professor and labor arbitrator is called in to mediate the strike. Mayor Joseph Alioto has also organized a citizen's committee to help settle the strike.

December 11, 1968.

The campus American Federation of Teachers local seeks strike sanction from the San Francisco Labor Council. More than 50 AFT members have set up an informational picket line around the campus, urging the trustees to negotiate with the students.

December 13, 1968.

School is closed for the Christmas holidays one week early. Campus offices remain open.

December 15, 1968.

Trustees meet with AFT representatives to hear their grievances. Mayor Alioto's citizen's committee works on mediation efforts.

January 4, 1969.

Acting President Hayakawa bans meetings and gatherings on the central campus, says no unauthorized persons will be allowed to set foot on campus, and states that picketing must be limited to the perimeters of the campus.

January 6, 1969.

Campus reopens. The San Francisco State College local of the American Federation of Teachers goes out on strike, and puts a picket line around the campus. About 350 teachers are involved. They wanted educational reforms, removal of police from the campus, agreement to student demands, and a collective bargaining contract for the California State College teachers.

January 8, 1969.

Judge Edward O'Day of the San Francisco Superior Court orders the AFT teachers to call off their strike. The strike continues.

January 19-20, 1969.

Striking students, including some student library workers, initiate a "book-in" in the library. They take books off the shelves and bring them to the circulation desk, leaving them there in order to clog library operations.

February 3, 1969

Acting President Hayakawa speaks before a Subcommittee of the House Education Committee concerning campus unrest.

February 4, 1969

Judge Henry Rolph of San Francisco Superior Court orders the San Francisco State AFT local to end the strike. The strike continues.

February 24, 1969

The San Francisco State AFT local announces a tentative strike settlement.

February 29, 1969

Black Studies Department Chair Nathan Hare and English instructor George Murray are not rehired for the following year. The strike continues.

March 5, 1969

Timothy Peebles, San Francisco State freshman, sets off a bomb in the Creative Arts building at night. It explodes in his hand, and his hands and face are injured.

March 20, 1969.

An agreement is signed between "representatives of the Third World Liberation Front, the Black Student Union, and the members of the Select Committee concerning the resolution of the fifteen demands and other issues arising from the student strike at San Francisco State College.

March 21, 1969.

Strike ends (San Francisco State University, 2013).

The timeline above clearly shows how the coalition advocated for the formation of a Black studies department. The results exceeded their expectations. Three major groups submitted demands that were granted. Following is a list of strike demands as put forth by the Black Student Union (BSU), the Third World Liberation Front (TWLF), and the American Federation of Teachers, Local 1352 Union AFT).These demands were listed in the same SFSU archival document (San Francisco State University, 2013).

Ten Black Student Union Demands

1. That all Black Studies courses being taught through various other departments be immediately made part of the Black Studies Department, and that all the instructors in this department receive full-time pay.
2. That Dr. Nathan Hare, Chairman of the Black Studies Department, receive a full professorship and a comparable salary according to his qualifications.
3. That there be a Department of Black Studies which will grant a Bachelor's Degree in Black Studies; that the Black Studies Department, the chairman, faculty and staff have the sole power to hire faculty and control and determine the destiny of its department.
4. That all unused slots for Black students from fall, 1968 under the Special Admissions Program be filled in spring, 1969.
5. That all Black students wishing to be admitted in fall, 1969.
6. That twenty (20) full-time teaching positions be allocated to the Department of Black Studies.
7. That Dr. Helen Bedesem be replaced from the position of Financial Aids Officer, and that a Black person be hired to direct it, that Third World people have the power to determine how it will be administered.
8. That no disciplinary action will be administered in any way to any students, workers, teachers, or administrators during and after the strike as a consequence of their participation in the strike.
9. That the California State College Trustees not be allowed to dissolve the Black programs on or off the San Francisco State College campus.
10. That George Murray maintain his teaching position on campus for the 1968-69 academic year.

Five Third World Liberation Front (TWLF) Demands

1. That a school of Ethnic Studies for the ethnic groups involved in the Third World be set up with the students in each particular ethnic organization having the authority and control of the hiring and retention of any faculty member, director and administrator, as well as the curriculum in a specific area study.
2. That fifty (50) faculty positions be appropriated to the School of Ethnic Studies, 20 of which would be for the Black Studies Program.
3. That in the Spring Semester, the college fulfill its commitment to the non-White students in admitting those that apply.
4. That to the fall of 1969, all applications of non-White students accepted.
5. That George Murray, and any other faculty person chosen by non-White people as their teacher, be retained in their position.

Strike Issues of the San Francisco State College AFT, Local 1352

1. *Strike Issues Directed to the President and Administration of San Francisco State College:*

   A. Negotiation of and adoption of comprehensive rules and regulations governing:

      1. Grievance procedures related to faculty affairs.
      2. Personnel decisions (hiring, firing, tenure, promotion, demotion, suspension, lay-off).
      3. Conditions under which pay can be reduced or docked.
      4. Sick leave and other fringe benefits.
      5. Unit and class load assignments for full and part-time faculty.
      6. Stipulation of prerogatives and delineation of authority at various administrative levels.
      7. Guidelines and standards for professional perquisites (sabbaticals, travel, research leaves).
      8. Faculty involvement in decisions on academic matters (curriculum selection, assignment of faculty and staff, grading, graduation requirements, determination of calendar, admission requirements).
      9. Faculty involvement in decisions governing all local administrative matters (office space, parking).
      10. Recovery of faculty positions bootlegged for administrative purposes.

   B. Protection of Constitutional Rights

      1. Amnesty for all faculty, students, and staff who have been suspended or have been subject to other disciplinary action and/or arrested, and withdrawal of outstanding warrants as a result of activity to end racism at San Francisco State College.
      2. No disciplinary action for exercising constitutionally protected rights.

   C. Black Student Union and Third World Liberation Front grievances must be resolved and implementation assured.

   D. All agreements on the above to be reduced to a written contract.

2. *Strike Issues Directed to the Trustees of the California State Colleges:*

   All agreements made with the local administrations under (1) above shall be binding upon and accepted by the Trustees.

   E. Sufficient funds shall be provided from current reserve and emergency funds to:

      1. Maintain the present faculty positions (this will prevent the lay-off of 100-125 faculty in the Spring Semester, 1969).
      2. Gain new positions to replace those given by various departments and schools to staff a Black Studies Department and a School of Ethnic Studies.
      3. Protect the revised workloads presently scheduled in many departments for spring, 1969, and assure the same for everyone who requests it.

F. Rescission of the ten disciplinary rules passed by the Trustees on November 26, 1968.

G. Approval of the Student Union plan presented by the Associated Students at San Francisco State College.

H. Cancellation of proposed changes in Title 5 that would take away student control of student body funds.

I. Recognition of college constitution that emerges from the Constitutional Convention called by the Academic Senate at San Francisco State College.

3. Strike Issues Directed to the Governor and the Legislature:

A. That a special joint committee of the California State Assembly and Senate be appointed to conduct negotiations with the State College Board of Trustees and the Union to agree on systematic and continuing financing for the proposals under I and II above to provide the necessary increases in salary required to maintain a qualified faculty at San Francisco State College.

B. That when the special Legislative Committee, the Board of Trustees, and the Union have reached agreement, the Committee report to the next session of the Legislature so that necessary monies may be provided to put the agreement into effect.

Analysis of Findings of the San Francisco State College Experience

An analysis on the findings of the San Francisco State College case by research question follows. The sub-research questions that will be analyzed are questions 4 and 5.

4. Implications of the San Francisco State University experience in the development of a Black student union and a Black studies department relative to the link between the Black Power Movement and changes in higher education.

The experience of San Francisco State University (then SFSC) was repeated on college campuses, PWCUs and HBCUs, across the country. SFSU established the first Black student union and Black studies department, and the experience had a ripple effect on the establishment of groups and departments on other campuses. As stated earlier, after the cry for Black Power in 1966, college students from all over the country wanted to bring the Black Power Movement to campuses. Because students at SFSU were the first group to be successful, the strategies and materials developed for that struggle provided a prototype for the establishment of Black student groups and departments on other campuses.

One of the interesting findings was the diversity of activists at SFSU who advocated for a Black Studies department. The campus had a predominantly White student population, which joined with others to advocate for a Black studies department. The Black Student Union had already emerged from a group called the Negro Student roup. In order for a Black or African Studies department to become a reality at SFSU, it was necessary to call a five-month strike.

Those involved in the strike included students; faculty; local, state, and national elected and appointed officials; a union; community groups, namely the Black Panther Party; and, individuals. White students played essential roles in the strike and were arrested along with other activists.

According to a participant, lead activists included members of the Black Student Union, members of Students for a Democratic Society (SDS), left-wing Whites, Latino students from the Third World Liberation Front, a woman who would become president of the National Organization of Women, members (students and community representatives) of the Black Panther Party, and members of the American Federation of Teachers. Because of the broad-based activism, the establishment of a Black studies department was only one of the accomplishments of the strike. Other accomplishments included the right for students to hire and fire teachers and establishment of a School for Ethnic Studies that included an Asian Studies department, a Native American department, and a Latino department in addition to the Black Studies department. The initiative is a testament to what can be achieved by a broad-based coalition with divergent interests. SFSU maintains an extensive archive on the strike that led to the establishment of their Black Studies Department.

5. Other important cases on the effect of the Black Power Movement on changes in higher education.

There are a number of cases on the effect of the Black Power Movement on college campuses. Each experience had similar themes relative to resistance along with unique differences. Universities cited by participants included the rebellion at Fisk University following the first Black Power conference for students. The rebellion was a reaction to a Black man being beaten by the police in a community adjacent to Fisk University while the conference was taking place. Other cases include the Orangeburg massacre at Texas Southern University; Tennessee State University, which was the site of a rebellion following the one at Fisk University; and Harvard University, which established the second Black studies department in the country. A struggle occurred at Northwestern University when students demanded Black studies. Students at Sarah Lawrence College demanded the hiring of Black professors to an all-White faculty.

Central State University responded to the demand for Black studies by calling in the National Guard. Administrative buildings were taken over on a number of college campuses, most notably Cornell University and Columbia University. Martha Biondi (2012) wrote a book called *The Black Revolution on Campus*. In it, she described a number of the rebellions that occurred on college campuses and the conditions that gave impetus to activism. She focused on experiences at Northwestern University and the University of California in Los Angeles. These cases, which are not exhaustive, provide insight into the development of Black student groups, development of Black studies departments, an increase in the number of African American faculty and/or researchers, the importance of cultural responsiveness for a diverse population of students, and curriculum changes.

As the SFSU experience showed, achievement of Black studies led to other accomplishments such as the establishment of Asian studies, Native American studies, and Latino studies. Curricula offerings at many colleges and universities have now expanded to include world studies, women studies, and gay studies, among others. Some universities have included information on the

Black experience in sociology and psychology courses. This diversity in curricula and personnel emanated from the advocacy of the Black Power Movement for Black studies departments at higher education institutions.

After the establishment of the Black Student Union and Black studies department at San Francisco State College, Black student unions and Black Studies departments emerged on the campuses of many other higher education institutions. The strategies employed by the students at San Francisco State College and the documents developed became prototypes for the development of Black Student unions and Black Studies departments across the country.

Summary

In this chapter, the history and status of the Black power organizations included in the study were summarized. The responses of participants interviewed were analyzed based on the research questions and were cross-referenced with the findings of the literature review. Themes in the responses were identified. The role of Black power organizations in the establishment of Black student unions and Black studies programs was presented. Also presented was information on the emergence of the first Black student union and Black studies department at San Francisco State College. Included in the chapter are excerpts of a published interview of James Garrett, one of the primary founders of the Black Student Union at San Francisco State College, a timetable of strike events in the struggle for the creation of a Black studies department at San Francisco State College, a list of demands presented to the administration, and the outcomes of the struggle for establishment of a Black studies department. The data were analyzed based on Lewin's theory of change and critical race theory. The analysis included the rationale for activism by African American students and coping strategies they employed to survive and achieve on college campuses. In the next chapter, the book process and findings will be summarized and the implications for further research will be presented.

CHAPTER V

INTERPRETATIONS, CONCLUSIONS, AND RECOMMENDATIONS

The purpose of this research is to increase knowledge to understand the relationship between the Black Power Movement and changes in higher education between 1960 and 1980. The general question researched was, —What effect did the Black Power Movement have on changes in higher education from 1960 – 1980? This research question was divided into four supporting research questions. An analysis by research question is presented below.

1. The Effect of the Black Power Movement on Changes in Higher Education from 1960-1980

In the early 1960s, several events occurred that affected higher education campuses across the country. In 1962, American cities began to go up in flames because of horrendous conditions (Finkel, 2013). Leaders of the Civil Rights Movement responded to the crisis by leading non-violent marches and demonstrations to end the despair in African American communities and to create equal opportunity for African Americans. Their efforts were televised across the country. On television screens in their homes, Americans saw non-violent activists being beaten, shot, chained, and hosed with water by local officials; and, bitten by dogs. In 1964, because of advocacy efforts of the Civil Rights Movement, the Civil Rights Act of 1964 was passed (National Archives & Records Administration, 2008). This landmark legislation outlawed discrimination based on race, ethnicity, religion, and gender. As part of the war on poverty, in 1965, the federal government passed the Higher Education Act (U. S. Department of Education, 2008). The purpose of the legislation was to increase access to post-secondary education for young people from families with limited income who desired to attend college by removing financial barriers. An influx of first-generation African American students onto predominately-White college campuses followed. In 1966, during a march in Birmingham, Alabama, Mukasa (Willie Ricks) of the Student Nonviolent Coordinating Committee gave the cry for Black Power (Ture & Hamilton, 1992). Collectively, these events changed higher education campuses and curriculum for the next two decades.

First-generation African American students enrolled in higher education institutions optimistic about their futures and the possibility of upward mobility. The influx of these students onto college campuses necessitated changes in policies and curricula that were in place prior to their arrival because they brought with them a different set of needs, perspectives, experiences, and challenges. The communities from which they came represented a different reality from traditional college students. Their reality of the world was different. The need for changes to address the realities of African American students was not recognized or operationalized by higher education institutions, however. On arrival on campus, African American students found what they perceived as hostility from faculty and traditional students, unexpected wealth, and a foreign culture. They were judged and treated according to a White standard, which was considered colorblind. The communities from which they came represented a different social class than traditional college students, particularly legacy students (Grove, 2014). Their reality of the world was different. They did not have the material paraphernalia, such as clothing and expensive cars, or the wealth of traditional students. They were unfamiliar with the culture of the wealthy.

Because of the failure of higher education institutions to recognize the different cultural perspectives and needs of African American students, the students experienced microaggressions on a daily basis. These microaggressions led to disillusionment, anger, and the decision to demand more support and changes in what they were being taught. One of the responses to the constant affronts and the need for support was the emergence of social counter spaces, Black student groups. Subsequently, the students called for a more representative education, which resulted in the establishment of Black studies departments and departments to study the cultures of other groups such as women, Native Americans, Latinos, and Asians. Their demands also promoted the hire of more African American faculty and researchers. The influx of African American students changed the environment on college campuses; however, life on campuses also changed them. Many of them are now college faculty, researchers, authors, corporate heads, and leaders in all walks of society.

2. The Role of the Black Power Movement in the Development of Black Student Organizations, Particularly Black Student Unions

The findings from the data clearly demonstrate that the Black Power Movement on college campuses was a student driven movement that was responsible for the development of counter spaces on college campuses called Black student unions and other student organizations. Following the cry for Black Power, Black students joined with community activists to make changes in African American communities and on college campuses. Through encouragement of leaders of Black Power organizations, they brought the Black Power Movement to college campuses. The formation of Black student unions and Black studies departments required intense advocacy with higher education administrations. Students protested and took over university buildings to demand changes on campuses all over the country. In some cases, when there was violence, law enforcement was called in to restore order, students were arrested, and some were expelled from school (Biondi, 2012; Columbia University, 2007; Rogers, 2009).

After first-generation African American students arrived on campuses, they found that in campus life, once again, like in the general society, they were more like observers than participants (Solorzano, Ceja, & Yosso, 2000; Williamson, 1999). There was little in place on campuses with a White standard to validate their worldview and, because they were first-generation students, help from members of their families was limited. They simply did not know what to expect. Resources to help them adjust to campus life were scarce. These conditions led the students to advocate for changes to ensure their survival and validate their worldview.

The newly arrived African American students needed academic and social support. They were disenchanted and angry about the daily psychological assaults they were enduring on campuses. During the same period, advocacy efforts were becoming more intense in their home communities. Many of them had heard of or were active in Civil Rights organizations, but the message of these organizations, of employing non- violent strategies for change in the face of violence, did not resonate with them (Ture & Hamilton, 1992). However, the cry for Black Power, which validated their right to self- defense, did. In 1966, the students decided to bring Black Power to their college campuses (Rogers, 2009). Black Power leaders encouraged them to form Black support groups to address their specific needs (Stanford, 1986; Student Nonviolent Coordinating Committee, 2013). Following their advice, the students formed Black student unions and Black study groups for academic support and stimulation, and social support.

Through contact with leaders of the Black Power Movement, the students' racial identities and place in the world were reconstructed. Their contact with cultural nationalists led to a redefinition of their identity as descendants of Africa and recognition that ancient Africans had a rich history of making significant contributions to the world (Brown, 2003; Karenga, 2008; Joseph, 2006). Their contact with cultural nationalist and revolutionary nationalist leaders led to a redefinition of and/or embracing of the concept of self-determination and their right as a people to share power (Carson, 1981; Marable, 1997; Karenga, 2013). They formed study groups to learn about their African heritage, the freedom struggles in the United States, and the freedom struggles in continental Africa and the African Diaspora (Lang, 2001; Warren, 1990; Williamson, 1999). To reconnect with Africa, many students studied African history and traditional African religions; changed their clothing to traditional African garb; wore natural hairstyles; learned about and practiced African folklore and traditions, including speaking Kiswahili; and, observed African-centered holidays such as Kwanzaa (Karenga, 2013; Woodard, 1999). Their experiences in the "Black is Beautiful" aspect of cultural nationalism transformed their identities from being Negro or Black to African American, where they were connected to land and a people (Biondi, 2012; Warren, 1990).

3. The Role of the Black Power Movement in the Development of Black Studies Departments

According to the data, Black studies departments emerged on college campuses because of the advocacy efforts of students who were members of Black student unions.

The formation of Black student organizations subsequently led to the establishment of Black studies departments across the country. In their study groups, when sharing information about their courses, what and how they were being taught, the students found that a number of them were similarly disenchanted with the curricula. The decision to advocate for changes in curricula and the establishment of Black studies departments emanated from the discussions that took place in these groups (Rogers, 2009; Williamson, 1999).

After passage of the Higher Education Act and the Civil Rights Act, African American students arrived on college and university campuses feeling excited and optimistic about their futures. Many of them came from economically, socially, and educationally depressed communities. Their dreams were to achieve academically and realize upward mobility. Instead of feeling welcomed on these campuses, they suffered daily microaggressions by traditional students and faculty (Biondi, 2012; Solorzano, Ceja, & Yosso, 2000; Williamson, 1999). They felt isolated in a culture that had a philosophy of sink or swim and where they were being judged by a White standard. The students felt unprepared for the academically rigorous courses and were surprised at how African Americans were portrayed in the content of courses. Social and economic problems in African American communities were incorporated into courses; however, there was little or no information on their strengths as a people or the contributions of their people to society (Biondi, 2012; Solorzano, Ceja, & Yosso, 2000; and Williamson, 1999). The information that was covered was presented from a Eurocentric perspective, a perspective that was incongruent with their worldview and experience (Van Sertima, 1989). Because their reality and worldview differed from those of traditional higher education students and faculty, they were the other, something different, who was considered inferior to the White standard. They experienced rejection and cognitive dissonance. These microaggressions presented significant challenges for them (Solorzano, Ceja, & Yosso, 2000). In addition to advocating for the formation of Black studies programs, students desired role models that would articulate and/or validate their worldview. This need for representation led to advocacy for the hire of more African American faculty.

To create a greater understanding of African American student populations, the legitimacy of African Americans having their own philosophical base must be acknowledged and learning pursued based on their learning styles. Acknowledgement of African-centered culture is important because of the historical tie of African Americans to Africans in continental Africa – from ancient Africa prior to enslavement in America, to slavery when Africans were considered chattel, to the fights for freedom. African Americans have a rich history, beliefs, and practices going back to traditional Africa. To begin to understand African American perspectives, that content must be included in courses. One of the participants interviewed shared an example of the need for more information on Africa and African Americans in college courses.

> I met a man at the University of Georgia one time. I was down there talking about Africa and he said, "I'm getting ready to write my book for my Ph.D. in history and I have never studied one word about Africa." Most schools, White schools, and what have you, studied history and sociology, and left Africa completely out. So, we affected the whole system to make them add Africa and make them see us as human beings and see Africa as something that had made some kind of contribution.

4. Implications of the San Francisco State University Experience in the Development of a Black Student Union and a Black Studies Department Relative to the Black Power Movement and Higher Education

One of the first successful outcomes of student advocacy efforts occurred on the campus of San Francisco State College (Rogers, 2009; San Francisco State University, 2013). The first Black student union was established and the organization subsequently advocated for the establishment of the first Black studies department. After a five-month strike of a broad-based coalition that was led by the students in the college's Black student union, the Black studies department was established. The experience of students at San Francisco State University was used as a prototype for the establishment of Black studies departments at other pre-dominantly White and historically Black colleges and universities. Materials (e.g., student demands, policy paper) developed at SFSU were used as guides and the strategies they employed were emulated by students on other campuses.

5. Other Important Cases That Provide Information on the Effect of the Black Power Movement on Changes in Higher Education

A number of other colleges and universities had similar experiences that would be instructive. Some of these include Harvard University, which established the second Black studies program in the United States; and, activism at Columbia University, Northeastern Illinois University, Sarah Lawrence College, and Cornell University among others.

The Movement also changed historically Black colleges and universities (HBCUs) relative to curriculum and student organizations. Interesting cases include Howard University and Fisk University, where Black student unions and Black studies departments emerged in response to student unrest. Students on HBCU campuses also advocated for Black student unions and Africana studies departments. At Howard University, there was a struggle between the civil rights philosophy of integration and the Black power philosophy of cultural identity and self-defense. The students charged that, although HBCUs had a majority of faculty who were African American, the curriculum at HBCUs mirrored the curriculum at predominately-White universities, and they needed something different. There were debates in African American communities and at HBCU campuses about the terminology used to describe Black people - Negroes, Blacks, or African Americans; which resulted in agreement on the label, African American. Fisk University was the site of one of the first Black Power conference for African American student-activists and African American student protests. The protest was triggered by a beating of an African American man in the surrounding community. The issues Fisk University and Howard University confronted were similar to issues at predominately- White universities.

Limitations of the Study

Scope of the study.

The organizations and African American leaders in this study are a small sample of the organizations that were active during the era of the Black Power Movement.

Chapter II provided an extensive list of the Black power organizations that were active during the period. This study focused on 13 organizations that self-identified as cultural nationalist or revolutionary nationalist. The findings are representative of the organizations in the selected categories; however, the study did not address the full complexity of the representative organizations or the stages of their development. Most of the organizations were multi-layered and focused their energy on several areas simultaneously, such as housing, education, self-defense, religion, employment, nutrition, mental health, the arts, and building institutions. Further study is needed to understand the complexity and dynamics of the organizations and this period.

Lewin's theory of change and the elements of the critical race theory describe the dynamics and conditions the participants articulated and the turmoil of the era. Turmoil continued on campuses until changes were made to stabilize the tension between opposing forces. Counter spaces were created by students to help them cope with needed emotional support from microaggressions, the need for academic support, and validation of their reality.

Effects of age and challenges of participants in the study.

The findings of the study were driven by the memories of the personalities interviewed. The majority of the individuals interviewed were elderly and some could not remember some of the details of their organization's activities. Health was a particular challenge for them. One of the participants had Hodgkin's Disease and another prospective participant had to decline being interviewed because of brain injury that resulted from a stroke. Another participant had to schedule their interview around care for their spouse, who was ill. Age and ailments presented challenges for gathering data.

Effects of COINTELPRO on participant responses.

Another challenge was the participants 'suspicion of institutions and individuals because of their histories with the FBI's Counter Intelligence Program (COINTELPRO) (Ball, 2013; The Republic of New Africa, 2013). Of the 10 African American leaders interviewed, nine were targeted by COINTELPRO. All participants knew someone who was a target of COINTELPRO. The effects of the program have been long lasting and influenced the participants' full disclosure of events and activities. Former students at San Francisco State University who developed a Black student union and/or fought for a Black studies program refused to be interviewed because they did not know the researcher and were suspicious about how the data would be used. However, the university's archives and a published interview of a former student provided rich data on the SFSU experience.

Document analysis.

There is considerable information on the Black Power Movement and Black power organizations but it is widely dispersed and much of the information could only be found on organizational websites and in books as opposed to scholarly journals. This created a challenge for the researcher, as some organizations did not have a website. For the organizations that have closed, there is very little data on the specific dates they closed or the circumstances that led to their demise. A number of the participants interviewed could not recall the information.

Implications and Recommendations

Higher education institutions made significant changes to policies and practices in response to the era of the Black Power Movement. More changes are needed, however, particularly changes in student development practices and curriculum, and increased support for first-time African American college students. Recommendations emanating from the findings include continuing to enhance policies and practices for the support of African American students, particularly in student affairs. Campuses are now relatively calm and stable because of the responses of higher education institutions to the demands African American students made in the 1960s and 1970s. The resultant changes may erode if efforts are not devoted to maintaining past accomplishments, further enriching the curricula, and continuing to enhance the experiences of African American students and other students of color on higher education campuses. Information taught on the Black Power Movement should be separated from the Civil Rights Movement. Where needed, history of higher education courses should be revised to include the contributions of all people and to reflect the complexity of the Black freedom movement. Higher education institutions should continue to integrate information on the contributions and perspectives of Africans and African Americans throughout curricula, particularly to enhance the preparation of future educators who plan to teach in urban areas. Each area will be discussed below.

Black Studies Departments

The establishment of Black studies departments was a result of the advocacy efforts of students in the Black Power Movement on college campuses, and is considered a major achievement of African American students (Furniss, 1969; Rogers, 2009; Student Nonviolent Coordinating Committee, 2013). The absence of these programs helped to give rise to student rebellions and protests on campuses across the country. Continuation of the departments will serve to ensure that all students have the opportunity to learn about this segment of the population. As the San Francisco State University(SFSU) experience showed, achievement of the establishment of a Black studies department at the university led to additional diversification of curricula at SFSU and other departments, such as the establishment of Asian studies, Native American studies, Latino studies, world studies, women studies, and gay studies, among others. Some universities have included information on the Black experience in sociology and psychology courses. This diversity in curricula and personnel emanated from the advocacy efforts of the Black Power Movement for Black studies departments at higher education institutions.

Participants interviewed expressed concern that Africana and African American Studies departments are currently being eliminated on a number of campuses and funding support is being withdrawn. Black student groups are not receiving the support they received in the past. The rationale articulated for their elimination by higher education administrations is they are no longer needed. This sentiment is counter to the roadmaps of *Learning Reconsidered* and *Inclusive Excellence*. Because of the current trend, campuses may be at risk of becoming arenas of student unrest. The ramifications of ending Black Studies departments and withdrawing support for Black student unions necessitate a careful review.

African American Students and Black Student Unions

Developing mechanisms for institutional efforts to enhance the engagement and increase the retention of African American students is important because African American students have low retention and completion rates, particularly African American students who matriculate at predominately-White colleges and universities (Rodriguez & Nettles, 1993). The findings have implications for continued efforts to enhance the engagement of African American students.

The need for first-generation African American students to have counter spaces and emotional support after enrollment and during matriculation continues. Counter spaces, such as Black student unions, help to ameliorate the cultural shock many first-generation African American students experience when attending predominately-White higher education institutions side-by-side with privileged and legacy students. Black student unions serve as safe spaces where the different realities of African American students are valued, validated, and supported. Without the benefit of Black student unions, their feelings of being "the other" are exasperated. For these reasons, this type of support should continue.

Curriculum

The goal of higher education is to provide a transformational educational experience for students to prepare them to contribute to society. To accomplish this goal, higher education institutions should develop structures, andragogy, and support services to educate the whole student. Special attention should be given to improving educational conditions in local communities by enhancing the preparation of future educators.

During the Black Power Movement, many African American students came to universities from areas that had underperforming schools. This lack of educational preparation along with a hostile campus environment of daily microaggressions, a lack of support, and a lack of understanding of the reality of African Americans precipitated the activism of African American students. In addition to help with a rigorous academic program, cross-cultural and affinity opportunities are needed. The need for diversity education, didactic and experiential, cannot be overstated. One of the complaints of the participants in the study was the absence of information about African American institutions, contributions, and achievements in college courses. Participants in the study articulated feeling alienated because of how African Americans were portrayed in their courses or the total absence of information about African Americans in their classes. If andragogy, curriculum, and support activities were student-centered, and cultural differences and learning styles of a diverse student population celebrated, the activism of the Black Power Movement may not have spread from communities to college campuses.

Educators should be better prepared to teach diverse populations. To enhance the preparation of pre-school, primary, elementary, secondary, and post-secondary teachers, higher education institutions that prepare educators should revise curriculum in adragogy and content. Higher education institutions should ensure that future educators, teachers and faculty have knowledge of African American realities and skills to include and positively portray noteworthy African and African American people, events, and accomplishments in their classes. Knowing the information and using it to connect with their reality (ies) may serve to enhance the preparation of African American students for enrollment in higher education institutions.

Diversity education on higher education campuses.

Higher education administrators should ensure that all personnel receive training on race, ethnicity, and diversity, and use the tenets in the content of subject matter and andragogy in their classes. Faculty should study the nature of microaggressions and develop strategies to combat their devastating effects. Higher education administrators should ensure that all courses provide information that includes the contributions of all people in a culturally appropriate manner. Professors who teach about the Black freedom movement should seek additional information outside of traditional articles and textbooks and, as recommended by critical race theorists, invite authentic voices to share their experiences with students.

Since 1980, a number of models for teaching and supporting diverse student populations have been researched and implemented on some campuses. These models, which provide roadmaps for transforming the educational environment for diverse student populations in a manner that ensures their engagement, were created after the Black Power Movement era. To reduce microaggressions and help to eliminate the White standard that currently is the foundation of core values and norms in predominately-White colleges and universities, all college students should be required to take a course on culture. Many students have a variety of majors and do not enroll in courses offered by Black studies departments. Including the contributions of Africans and African Americans in relevant courses would ensure a broader exposure of all students to the information. Diversity should be taught; however, the concepts of culture and diversity should be treated as separate constructs. The study of African-centered principles and practices, such as MAAT and the Nguzo Saba, would help students understand the different philosophical bases and reality(ies) of African Americans.

Students should be encouraged to conduct field research in this area. These changes may foster a greater understanding of different cultures and enhance cross-cultural communications.

The inclusion of African and African American contributions to higher education institutions was recommended. The findings of the study clearly showed that the activities and accomplishments of the Black Power Movement were different from the Civil Rights Movement. The movements took place during the same period with similar aims but different foci and strategies. There is confusion about the activities and contributions of the activists in the Civil Rights Movement versus African American activists in other movements, particularly the Black Power Movement. In some institutions, the activism of African Americans during the 1960s and 1970s is solely attributed to the Civil Rights Movement. For example, civil rights activists are given credit for the establishment of Black studies departments. The findings in the study clearly showed that leaders of the Civil Rights Movement took a position against Black studies because they wanted to focus their message on integration. Two of the participants in the study stated that civil rights leaders viewed Black studies as another form of separatism. To correct this problem, higher education institutions should disaggregate information on the contributions and freedom struggles of African Americans to enrich the knowledge and understanding of the Black experience during this period. A study of curricula used to teach history of higher education courses at a representative sample of institutions across the country would inform academicians on needed changes to the course. Treatment of the contributions of Africans and African Americans in all history and humanities courses should be studied. Faculty in Black studies departments could be helpful with this effort.

Higher education administrators should solicit ongoing input from students of color to ensure their social and educational needs are being met. Commitment to diversity requires continual evaluation and adjustment. Higher education institutions should make this commitment. Ongoing discussions on diversity should be organized. Support for Black student groups should continue with a focus on first-generation students.

Recommendations for Future Research

This study represents a small sample of organizations and voices that were part of the Black Power Movement. The focus of the research was on higher education. The organizations that were part of the movement were diverse with a multitude of activities and strategies devoted to improving the lives of African Americans. To gain a deeper understanding of the varying aspects of the movement, additional research is needed. Higher education institutions that were sites for African American student activism should maintain an archive on the Black Power Movement to facilitate research on the Black Power Movement to provide increased access to the information for students and researchers. The dynamics and complexity of the Black Power Movement should be studied within the context of student led movements in the United States.

This study focused on the contributions of the Black Power Movement to higher education; however, the organizations in the movement were active in a number of other political and institutional areas. The findings of the study have implications for the need to acquire increased knowledge on other aspects of the movement. A number of other sub-movements emerged from the Black Power Movement. These include the Black Arts movement, the Black is Beautiful movement, the Black Anti-Apartheid movement, and the Independent Black School movement. The Black is Beautiful movement would inform academicians on African American perspectives because of its focus on using race and culture to enhance African American identity and self-esteem (Joseph, 2006; Karenga, 1977; Woodard, 1999). The Black Power Movement as a whole and its arenas of impact should be studied.

To ensure a nurturing enriching educational experience for students on college campuses, the conditions that led to the revolts on campuses should be studied with an eye toward ensuring the college environment is as supportive for diverse student populations as possible. Information on the Student Organization for Black Unity is sparse. Since this organization had chapters on a number of campuses, it would make a good case study. A study of the Black Power Movement relative to the theory of nigrescence and Lewins' theory of change would be informative.

According to the participants interviewed, the Counter Intelligence Program (COINTELPRO) of the Federal Bureau of Investigation had a significant impact on Black activists. The information and files on COINTELPRO have now been declassified. More research is needed on the details of the program and its effect on those targeted.

For many Black power activists, the Patriot Act represents a resurrection of the spying program. Further research on the contrasts and correlations between COINTELPRO and the

Patriot Act is recommended. Researching the areas delineated above would enhance knowledge on the African American experience and inform higher education policies and practices relative to this population.

Conclusions

The purpose of this historical research is to construct knowledge on the link between the Black Power Movement and changes that occurred in higher education between 1960 and 1980. An extensive literature review was conducted; and, African American leaders in the Black Power Movement, faculty, and students were interviewed. The framework for the analysis was Lewin's theory of change on opposing forces. The study was analyzed from the perspective of the social constructivist paradigm, specifically critical race theory, relative to the multiple realities of oppressed groups.

Based on the analysis, there are implications for the need to maintain the changes accomplished and continue to enhance the educational environment for students, particularly students of color.

There was consensus among those interviewed that the Black Power Movement was responsible for the formation of Black student unions and Black studies programs, an increase in African American faculty, and changes in curricula. Their responses were supported by the literature. The findings in the study showed a need to revise information taught on the African American freedom movement between 1960 and 1980, separating the accomplishments and successes of the Black Power Movement from those of the Civil Rights Movement.

The findings of the study have far-reaching implications for higher education, particularly in the practices of student affairs, adragogy, curricula, and the preparation of future educators to teach diverse populations. Black student unions provided much needed academic and social support for African American students. To ensure inclusion and representation of diverse student populations in curricula, higher education institutions should continue to support Black studies departments and hire more African American faculty. In addition to Black studies curricula, information on the contributions of Africans and African Americans should be integrated into all relevant education, history, and humanities courses. Because of the low retention and completion rates of African American students, it is important for higher education institutions to maintain and build on changes made in the past based on the lessons learned from the Black Power Movement.

References

Abramson, L. (2011). *Why is college so expensive?* Retrieved July 9, 2013 from http://www.npr.org

Ahmed, M. (2008). *Revolutionary action movement.* Retrieved May 13, 2013 from http://www.ram.org

American Civil Liberties Union. (2013). Reform *the patriot act.* Retrieved August 17, 2013 from http://www.aclu.org/reform-patriot-act

American College Personnel Association. (2004). Learning *reconsidered: A campus-wide focus on the student experience.* Washington, DC: The American College Personnel Association.

ARPS. (2013). The USA patriot act: COINTELPRO restored. Retrieved September 1, 2013 from http://www.arps.org/users/hs/fricket/fricke/CON LAW H/civil liberties/08-09/paul final.htm

Assante, M.K. & Abarry, A.S. (Eds.) (1996). *African intellectual heritage: A book of sources.* Philadelphia: Temple University Press.

Astin, A. W. (1993). *What matters in college: four critical years revisited.* San Francisco: Jossey-Bass Publishing.

Astin, A. W., Astin, H. S., Bayer, A. E., & Bisconti, A. S. (1997). Overview of the unrest era. In L. F. Goodchild &H. S. Wechsler, (Eds.), *ASHE reader on the history of higher education,* (pp. 724-738). Boston: Pearson Custom Publishing.

Austin, C. J. (2006).*Up against the wall: Violence in the making and unmaking of the Black panther party.* Fayetteville, AR: University of Arkansas Press.

Ball, J. (2013). COINTELPRO 101. *The Black agenda report.* Retrieved August 17, 2013 from http://www.blackagendareport.com

Baraka, A. (1997). *The autobiography of LeRoi Jones.* Chicago, IL: Lawrence Hill Books.

Beaumie, K. (2013). Social constructivism. *Emerging perspectives on learning, teaching, and technology,* (pp. 1-10). Retrieved November 5, 2013 from www.epltt.coe.uga.edu/index.php?title=Social Constructivism

Bennett, W. J. (1988). Why the west. In Sewell, G. T. (Ed.) *The eighties: A reader,* (pp. 274-280). Reading, MA: Perseus Books.

Biondi, M. (2012). *The black revolution on campus.* Berkeley & Los Angeles: University of California Press.

Bohman, J. (2005). Critical theory. *Stanford encyclopedia of philosophy,* (pp. 1-63). Retrieved October 9, 2013 from www.slu.edu

Brown, S. (2003). *Fighting for US: Maulana Karenga, the US organization, and Black cultural nationalism.* New York: New York University Press.

Brown, S. (1997). The US organization, Maulana Karenga, and conflict with the Black panther party: A critique of sectarian on historical discourse. *Journal of Black studies,* Vol. 28, No. 2, (pp. 157-170). SAGE Productions.

Busha, C. & Harter, S. P. (1980). *Research methods in librarianship: Techniques and interpretations.* New York: Academic Press.

Carmichael, S. (1971). *Stokely speaks: Black power back to pan-Africanism.* New York: Vintage Books.

Carruthers, J. (Ed.). (1984). *Essays in ancient Egyptian studies.* Los Angeles: University of Sankore Press.

Carson, C. (1981). *In struggle: SNCC and the Black awakenings of the 1960s.*

Cambridge, MASS: Harvard University Press.

Chang, M. J., Altbach, P. G., & Lomotey, K. (2005). Race in higher education: Making meaning of an elusive moving target. In P. G. Altbach, R. O. Berdahl, & P. J. Gumport (Eds.), *American higher education in the twenty-first century: Social, political, and economic challenges,* (pp. 517 - 554). Baltimore: Johns Hopkins University Press.

Children's Defense Fund. (2007). *America's cradle to prison pipeline report.* Retrieved April 4, 2008 from http://www.childrensdefensefund.org

Columbia University. (2007). The Black power rebellion. *Introduction to African studies.* Retrieved January 11, 2007 from http://www.columbia.edu/itc/history/marable/c1001/weeks/week10.htm

Creswell, J. (2007). *Qualitative inquiry and research design: Choosing five approaches.* 2nd ed. Thousand Oaks, CA: SAGE Publications.

Cross, W. Jr. & Fhagen-Smith, P. (2005). Nigrescence and ego identity development – Accounting for differential Black identity patterns. In M. E. Wilson & L. E. Wolf- Wendel (Eds.), *ASHE reader on college student development theory.* Boston: Pearce Custom Publishing.

Crotty, M. (2003). *The foundations of social research: Meaning and perspective in the research process.* Thousand Oaks, CA: SAGE Publications.

Delgado, R. & Stefanic, J. (2012). *Critical race theory: An introduction.* (2nd ed.). New York: New York University Press.

Denzin, N. K., & Lincoln, Y. S. (2000). Introduction: The discipline and practice of qualitative research. In N. K. Denzin & Y. S. Lincoln, (Eds.), *Handbook of qualitative research* (2nd ed., pp. 1-28). Thousand Oaks, CA: SAGE Publications.

DiscovertheNetworks. (2007). The Black power rebellion. *Introduction to African studies.* Retrieved August 3, 2013 from http://www.discoverthenetworks.com

Du Bois, W. E. B. (1903). *The souls of Black folk.* Chicago: A. C. McClurg and Company.

Du Bois, W. E. B. (1903). The talented tenth. In L. F. Goodchild & H. S. Wechsler, (Eds.), *ASHE reader on the history of higher education,* (pp. 551-561). Boston: Pearson Custom Publishing.

Eliot, T. H. (1969). Administrative response to campus turmoil. In *the campus and the racial crisis,* (pp. 51-64). Washington, DC: American Council on Education.

Encyclopedia Britannica (1908). Retrieved March 9, 2014 from www.britannica.com/EBchecked/topic/6747/African-Americans

Etzioni, A. (1969). Faculty response to racial tensions. In *the campus and the racial crisis,* (pp. 108-125). Washington, DC: American Council on Education.

Finkel, M. (2013). *Race riots in the 1960s – pictures, news, and articles.* Retrieved May 3, 2013 from http://www.highbeamresearch.org

Frederickson, G. (1971). *The Black image in the White man: The debate on Afro- American character and destiny: 1817-1914.* New York: Harper & Row Publishers.

Furniss, W. T. (1969). Racial minorities and curriculum change. In *the campus and the racial crisis,* (pp. 1-18). Washington, DC: American Council on Education.

Garraghan, G. J. (1946). *A guide to historical method.* New York: Fordham University Press.

Gillian, A. (2005). Garvey's legacy in context: Colourism, Black movements, and African nationalism. *Our African roots.* Retrieved January 11, 2007 from http://www.amonhotep.com/2005/1708.html

Glick, B. (1989). *The_war_at_home: Covert_action_against_U.S. activists_and_what_we_can_do_about_it.* Boston: South End Press.

Grant, J. (1968). *Black protest: History, documents, and analyses 1619 to the present.* New York: Fawcett Publications.

Grove, A. (2014). *What are legacy admissions?* Retrieved March 23, 2014 from http://collegeapps.about.com./od/glossaryofkeyterms/g/CommonApp.htm

Halisi, C. (1972). Maulana Ron Karenga: Black leader in captivity, *The Black scholar,* May 1972, pp. 27-31.

Heath, G. L. (1976). *Mutiny does happen lightly: The literature of the American resistance to the Vietnam war.* Metuchen, NJ: Scarecrow Press. Retrieved February 8, 2014 from http://www2. iath.virginia.edu/sixties/HTML. docs/Resources/Primary...

Herskovits, M.J. (1941). *The myth of the Negro past.* New York: Harper & Row. Hill, L. (2004). *The deacons for defense: Armed resistance and the civil rights movement.* Chapel Hill: The University of North Carolina Press.

Hilliard, A.G. (1989). Kemetic concepts in education, In I.V. Sertima (Ed., 3rd printing), *Nile valley civilizations.* Atlanta: Morehouse College.

Hirsch, E. D., Jr. (1983). Cultural literacy. In Sewell, G. T. (Ed.). *The eighties: A reader,* (pp. 243-253). Reading, MA: Perseus Books.

History Learning Site. (2013). The Black panthers. Retrieved May 3, 2013 from http://www. historylearningsite.org

Jackson, J.G. (1970). *Introduction to African civilizations.* New York: Carol Publishing Group.

Johnson, N. (1972). *Letter from Nelson Johnson of the youth organization for Black unity.* Retrieved May 4, 2013 from http://www.uncb.edu/ul/civilrights/Greensboro/nelsonjohnson

Joseph, P. E. (2006). *The Black power movement: Rethinking the civil rights-Black power era.* New York: Routledge, Taylor, & Francis Group.

Karenga, M. (2013). *Forty seven years of service, struggle, and institution-building; 1965-2012.* Retrieved May 3, 2013 from http://www.us.org

Karenga, M. (1977). Kawaida and its critics: A sociohistorical analysis. *The journal of Black studies,* Vol. 8, No. 2. *African cultural dimensions,* (pp 125-148). Sage Productions.

Karenga, M. (2008). *Kawaida and questions of life and struggle: African American, pan-African, and global issues.* Los Angeles: University of Sankore Press.

Karenga, M. (2013). *US: philosophy, principles, and program.* Retrieved May 3, 2013 from http://www.us.org

Ladson-Billings, G. (1998). Just what is critical race theory and what is it doing in a nice field like education? *Qualitative studies in education,* Vol II, No 1. (pp. 7- 24). New York: New York University Press.

Lang, C. (2001). 20th century Black Nationalism. *Against the Current,* Vol. XVI, No. II, No. 92. Retrieved January 11, 2007 from http://www.hartford- hwp.com/archives/45a/662.html

Lederman, D. (2008).House, focusing on cost, approves Higher Education Act. *Inside Higher Education.* Retrieved April 4, 2008 from *http://insidehighered.com/news/2008/02/08/hea.*

Lewin, K. (1948). *Resolving social conflicts: Selected papers on group dynamics.* New York: Harper and Row.

Lichtman, M. (2006). *Qualitative research in education: A user's guide*. Thousand Oaks, CA: SAGE Publications.

Marable, M. (1997). *Black liberation in conservative America*. Boston: South End Press.

Marable, M. (1992). By any means necessary: The life and legacy of Malcolm X. *The Black collegian online*. Retrieved January 11, 2007 from http://www.black-collegian.com/african//200.shtml

Mauk, A. J. & Jones, W. A. (2006). African American students. In L. A. Gohn & G. R. Albin, (Eds.), *Understanding college student subpopulations: A guide for student affairs professionals*, (pp. 69 – 86). National Association of Student Personnel Administrators.

McIntosh, P. (1989). White privilege: Unpacking the invisible knapsack. *Peace and Freedom*. Wellesley, MA: Wellesley College.

Moglen, H. (1988). Allan Bloom & E. D. Hirsch: Educational reform as tragedy and farce. In Sewell, G. T. (Ed.). *The eighties: A reader,* (pp. 284-293). Reading, MA: Perseus Books.

Monges, M.M.K. (1997), *Kush: The jewel of Nubia: Reconnecting the root system of African civilization*. New Jersey: African World Press.

National Archives and Records Administration. (2013), *The civil rights act in 1964*. Retrieved January 29, 2008, from http://www.archives.gov

National Association of Black Social Workers. (2007). Retrieved June 5, 2007 from http://www.nabsw.org

Nation of Islam. (2013). *A brief history on the origin of the nation of Islam in America*. Retrieved May 1, 2013 from http://www.noi.org/about.shtml

Norment, N. Jr. (2007). *The African American studies reader*. Durham, NC: Carolina Academic Press.

Okafor, V. O. (1999). The place of africology in the university curriculum. *Journal of Black studies*, 26(6), (p. 688-712).

Proctor, S. D. (1969). Racial pressures on urban institutions. In *the campus and the racial crisis*, (pp. 19-34).Washington, DC: American Council on Education.

The Republic of New Afrika. (2013). *The republic of new Afrika*. Retrieved April 30, 2013 from http://www.asetbooks.com/Us/Nationhood/RNARepublicOfNewAfrika

The Republic of New Afrika. (2013). *The republic of new Africa short official basic documents*. Retrieved April 30, 2013 from http://collections.msdiglib.org/cdm/printview/collection/tougaloo/id..

Robinson, C.R., Battle, R., & Robinson, Jr., E.W. (1987). *Journey of the Songhai people*. U.S.A.: Pan African Federation Organization.

Rodriquez, E. M. and Nettles, M. T. (1993). Achieving the national education goals: The status of minorities in today's global society. In L. F. Goodchild et al. (Eds.), *ASHE Reader on Public Policy and Higher Education.* Boston: Pearce Custom Publishing.

Rogers, I. (2009). Remembering the Black campus movement: An oral interview with James P. Garrett. *The Journal of Pan African Studies.* Vol. 2, No. 10.

ROOTS Activity Learning Center (2013). *ROOTS activity learning center.* Retrieved July 23, 2013 from http://www.ralc.org

Rudolph, F. (1990). *The American college & university: A history* (p. 253). Athens, GA: University of Georgia Press.

San Francisco State University. (2013). On strike: Shut it down. *The San Francisco State College strike collection.* Retrieved June 6, 2013 from http://www.sfsu.edu

Shulman, J. & Bowen, W. (2001). *The game of life: College sports and educational values.* Princeton, NJ: Princeton University Press.

Sokoya, K. (np). Personal testimony.

Solozano, D.; Ceja, M.; & Yosso, T. (2000). Critical race theory, racial macroaggressions, and campus racial climate: The experiences of African American students. *The journal of Negro education,* winter 2000, Vol. 69, No. 1/2, (pp.60-73). Retrieved December 20, 2013 from www. rochester.edu/.../solorzanoetal2001

Sparks Notes. (2007). The civil rights era (1865-1970: Black power: (1952-1968).

Spark notes. Retrieved January 11, 2007 from http://www.sparknotes.com/history/american/ civilrights/section6.rhtml

Stanford, M. (1986). *Revolutionary action movement (RAM): A case study of an urban revolutionary movement in a western capitalist society.* Retrieved April 30, 2013 from www.ulib.csuohio. edu/.../stanford.pdf

Student Nonviolent Coordinating Committee. (2013). *Martin Luther King, Jr. and the global freedom struggle.* Retrieved May 3, 2013 from http://www.sncc.org

Student Nonviolent Coordinating Committee. (2013). *What is SNCC?* Retrieved May 3, 2013 from http://www.sncc.org

Student Nonviolent Coordinating Committee. (2013). Retrieved June 6, 2013 from www.sncc.org

Taylor, Q. (2013). Republic of new Africa (1968-). *The Black past remembered and reclaimed.* Retrieved April 30, 2013 from http://www.BlackPast.org

Thelin, J. R. (2004). *A history of American higher education,* (pp. 269 & 338). Baltimore: The Johns Hopkins University Press.

Toure, S. (1975). *The African intelligentsia of Timbuktu.* New Orleans, LA.: Edwards Printing Press.

Ture, K. & Hamilton, C. V. (1992). *Black power: The politics of liberation.* New York: Vintage Books.

Tyson, T. B. (1999). *Radio free dixie: Robert F. Williams & the roots of black power.* Chapel Hill: University of North Carolina Press.

University of Michigan. (2007). *Cultural nationalism.* Retrieved January 11, 2007 from http://www.umich.edu/~eng499/concepts/nationalism.html

U.S. Department of Education. (2008). *Higher Education Act of 1965 as amended in 1998, Public Law 105-244,* Title IV, § 484® (1). Retrieved January 29, 2008, from http://www.ed.gov/policy/highered/leg/hea98/sec483.html

Van Sertima, I. (1989). *Nile valley civilizations.* Atlanta, GA: Morehouse College Warren, N. (1990). Pan-African cultural movements: From Baraka to Karenga. *The journal of Negro history.* Retrieved February 6, 2009 from http://www.jstor.org/pss/2717686

Washington, B. (1903). Industrial education for the Negro. In M. Lazerson, (Ed.), *American education in the twentieth century: A documented history,* (pp. 59-62). New York: Teachers College Press.

West, C. (2001). *Race matters.* Boston, MASS: Beacon Press.

Williams, C. (1987) *The destruction of black civilization: Great issues of race from 4500 B.C. to 2000 A.D.* Chicago: Third World Press

Williams, D. A.; Berger, J. B.; & McClendon, S. A. (2005). *Toward a model of inclusive excellence and change in postsecondary institutions.* Washington, DC: Association of American Colleges and Universities.

Williams, R. F. (1998). *Negroes with guns.* Detroit: Wayne State University Press.

Williamson, J. A. (1999). In defense of themselves: The black student struggle for success and recognition at predominantly white colleges and universities. *Journal of Negro education.* Retrieved February 6, 2009 from http://findarticles.com/p/articles/mi

Wisegeek. (2013). *What is critical race theory?* Retrieved December 10, 2013 from www.wisegeek.com/what-is-critical-race-theory.htm

Woodard, K. (1999). *A nation within a nation: Amiri Baraka (LeRoi Jones) & Black power politics.* Chapel Hill: University of North Carolina Press.

Woodard, K. (2013). The Black power movement. In J. Bracy, Jr. & S. Harley, (Eds). *A guide to the microfilm edition of Black studies research sources: Microfilms from archival and manuscript collections.* Retrieved June 5, 2013 from http://www.upa.org

Woodson, C. G. (1933). *The mis-education of the Negro.* Trenton, NJ: The Associated Publishers.

Worrill, C. W. (np). Introductions: Thoughts on the SOBWC II. *Summary of the proceedings of the 2008 state of the Black world conference.* New Orleans, LA.

X, M. (1990). *Malcolm X on Afro-American history.* New York: Pathfinder Press.

Yale University (1997). The Yale report of 1828. In L. F. Goodchild & H. S. Wechsler (Eds.). *ASHE reader series: The history of higher education* (2nd ed. pp.191-199). Needham Heights, MA: Simon & Schuster Custom Publishing.

Discussions with Participants:

Selected African American Leaders
Who Played Key Roles in the Black Power Movement

PART 1: CULTURAL NATIONALIST ORGANIZATIONS

THE CONGRESS OF AFRICAN PEOPLE (CAP)

Summary of the Organization

In 1970, following a series of Black Power conferences, a Congress of African People convention was held in Atlanta, Georgia. Over 3,000 activists attended. The focus of the convention was developing a Black agenda to build Black institutions. There were 11 workgroups. Each focused on an institutional area: economics, education, criminal justice, political liberation, social development, religion, media, self-defense, health, technology, and science. Each workgroup was charged with developing priorities in their area and following up on the decisions made during the convention by organizing similar groups across the country. Organizational representatives agreed to work together in operational unity even if they did not agree on all issues under the banner, "unity without uniformity." Heywood Henry was elected the first chair of the Congress of African People in 1970. In 1972, Baraka emerged as the organization's national spokesperson and key organizer. One of the outcomes of the convention was the decision to build a Black Political Party. In March 1972, a National Black Political Convention was held in Gary, Indiana. This initial meeting was followed by other conventions in Little Rock, Arkansas and in New Orleans, Louisiana. The conventions had mixed results because of ideological differences. Because of these differences, there was disagreement over certain elements of the platform.

Under the leadership of Baraka, the ideology of the Committee for Unified New Ark became a dominant force in the Congress of African People. In 1972, Baraka merged the Committee for Unified New Ark under the Congress of African People; however, in 1976, Amiri and Amina Baraka abandoned cultural nationalism and embraced communism as their political philosophy. These changes caused dissension in the cultural nationalist network and marked the beginning of the demise of the Congress of African People nationally and the Committee for Unified New Ark locally. In May 1976, the Committee for Unified New Ark (and the Congress of African People) was transformed from a Black Power organization to a Marxist-Leninist organization called the Revolutionary Communist League (Woodard, 2001).

Interview with Mtangulizi Sanyika, first Chair of the Congress of African People

1. What are your memories of the Black Power Movement during this period?

That's just a very long historical timeframe to try to remember and to recall. The first thing that I remember is the paradigm shift that it represented and I date the Black Power Movement itself in two phases. One is the formal articulation of the Black Power slogan by Willie Ricks and Stokely Carmichael in the summer of 1966 in the Jackson, Mississippi march. But prior to that, there was the Atlanta project that the Student Nonviolent Coordinating Committee (SNCC) initiated after the summer of 1964 in the Black belt, a college in Alabama, and in Mississippi, Georgia, and places like that, where Black people were in the majority. They raised the question of Black people being in control of the space that they occupied. So, there was the formal articulation of the slogan and its predecessor. I recall that because people think the Black Power Movement started in 1966 but there were predecessor activities including the rebellion that took place in Harlem in 1964 and the rebellion in Watts in 1965. But once the slogan was articulated, the precursors were dwarfed by the events that followed including the Newark and Detroit rebellions in 1967 and the successive Black Power conferences; 1967 in Newark and 1968 in Philadelphia.

A 1969 conference was planned but cancelled. I think it was supposed to be held in Barbados but the government there would not allow the Africanists to meet. So the 1969 conference was cancelled, which led to us trying to pull together the remnants of the 1969 Black Power conference that didn't happen and the continuation of the 1967 and 1968 conferences that did happen. What resulted was the 1970 Congress of African People (CAP), which I was blessed to have chaired for its first two years of existence prior to Amiri Baraka assuming the chair in 1972. The Black Power conferences led to CAP and CAP called for a Black Political convention, which was held in Gary, Indiana in 1972.

I was also part of, chair, of the Nationalist Caucus within the Black Political Convention. There was a convention in 1974 in Little Rock, Arkansas. That led to the convention in 1976 in Cincinnati, Ohio where we actually tried to run a Black presidential candidate, first Julian Bond and then Ron Dellums. That didn't really work out that way, but we were moving toward forming a Black Political Party as part of the thrust of the Black Power Movement. In 1976, there was a lull until 1980. In 1980, there was a declaration in New Orleans to form a Black Political Party, which I did not support because I didn't think the infrastructure was in place to do it. But the declaration went forth and the effort to form such a party went forward, but it did not last. It did not last very long because of ideological conflicts between the left and the middle of the ideological spectrum.

I also recall during that period, the change in our consciousness about Africa. That was reflected in the 1972 African Liberation Day and the African Liberation Support Committee. On May 25, 1972, we put at least 25,000 Black people on the street in support of Africa, which was the first time that had happened in the modern era - Black Americans reclaiming their relationship to Africa. We began the process of dismantling the Apartheid system of South Africa, which was a major outcome of the movement. We organized boycotts against products that were linked to South Africa's economy all over the country and all over the world. The Black churches played a role in developing resolutions at corporate meetings and the universities played a role. My students, for instance, took over the President's office. I was teaching at Harvard University in the Black Studies Department (1968 - 1972). The second Black Studies Department in the country was at Harvard and my students took over the President's Office (in 1969 or 1970) in protest of Harvard's investments in Gulf Oil, which was a major oil producer in South Africa. It was an important watershed moment.

I also recall the emergence of youth during that period. The Student Nonviolent Coordinating Committee (SNCC) formed an organization called the Student Organization of Black Unity (SOBU) that subsequently emerged into the Youth Organization of Black Unity or YOBU. Very little attention is paid to that movement in the record but it was a movement on college campuses that came out of the southern swing of the movement and the activists who stayed in SNCC in its transition from civil rights to Black Power and then to Pan-Africanism. That (YOBU) was a major movement because it was present on the campuses when I was teaching at Harvard, MIT, Brown, and the UMass-Boston during those days. And, it was present in our communities and certainly helped to raise our consciousness about the totality of the Black Power Movement.

I distinctly recall the shift that happened in the religious world, the National Committee of Black Churchmen whose board I was on in the mid-1960s. It developed a Black Power statement and had it published in the New York Times. That was a watershed moment that shifted the Black church from just an emphasis on personal salvation to social transformation, which included the emergence of James Cone's Black Power Theology and subsequently, Liberation Theology. The churches were involved in communities in ways that hadn't been seen before. Conversations about a Black messiah that had been initiated by Gerard Moge and Albert Cleage were taking place. There was the shrine of the Black Madonna. So the reawakening that took place with students, with youth who at the university level and at the level of the churches themselves, and the emergence of Islam as an important contribution to the way we practiced religion in the Black community was an important piece of everything that happened during that period as well.

There are so many memories that I have and experiences that I can recall, but certainly, those are among the highlights: the crystallization of our consciousness and a shift in the paradigm that we are African descended people in America. We're not just Black people trying to be Americans but we are of African descent. We stated in 1970, "We are an African people." "We are African Americans." We said that in 1970. It wasn't until 1984 that it became crystallized in the language of this country, in the senses, and all that; but the Nationalist and Pan Africanist movement had said that earlier in that day and in that time.

I also recall that there was a period where I made my first visit to the African continent as a guest of Mwalimu Nyerere for the 10th anniversary of Tanzania's independence in 1970-1971. Many of us did some nation-building work on the African continent particularly upon the request of the Tanzanian government and many people actually moved back to the African continent. We formed a new Pan Africanist relationship in the global context and even at the 6th Pan African Congress there, which was a challenge and a mess. This was also the period where the class struggle began to emerge in an ideological context. There was a left element and a Marxist element that began to insert itself into the Black Liberation struggle. People like Amiri Baraka became a Marxist. Owusu Sadauki, who was formerly a Pan Africanist, became a Marxist, and a whole range of scholar activists adopted the Marxist position and articulated the notion of class struggle. Of course, the Black Panther Party had already adopted that position, and that was also prominent in that era and in that period. There's so much to say but I think those are the highlights. Perhaps some other things will emerge during the conversation.

2. *Please share any information you have on the goals and plans emanating from Black Power Conference of 1967 that took place in Newark, New Jersey.*

I was there and did a presentation, a politics workshop. I also attended the 1968 Black Power Conference, which was in Philadelphia, and gave a presentation similarly in a workshop. I was an invited guest of Dr. Nathan Wright, who was the convener of the Newark Black Power Conference. I ended up doing some work in Newark that laid the groundwork for the ultimate election of Kenneth Gibson as the first Black Mayor of that city. One of the productive things that came out of the Black Power conference process itself was to use Newark as a laboratory to implement a Black Power agenda. We brought people from all over the country to learn Black politics in Newark and to run community development work in Newark. That came out of the Black Power conference along with "It's Nation Time" ideas and slogans. I was very much there and actively participated. I can see the images now and see the debates and discussions that were going on. Ahmed, who was a leader of RAM who came out of Philadelphia in a highly influential position, found himself moving underground and was not able to exert leadership. So, there was a gap in the Black Power Movement in terms of the Nationalists and Pan Africanists coming out of the Philadelphia conference. They found themselves unable to move forward.

Nathan Wright, I'm not sure what happened with Nathan, but Louis Gotthard was one of the other people coming out of the conference that Adam Clayton Powell had in his DC office (in New York). I'm sure you read about that first Black Power meeting that Powell had. Karenga, Gothard, and Nathan were among the people on the continuation committee to keep everything going. By 1970, Gothard was still around and he was with us. So was Chuck Stone who used to work with Adam. But, I can't tell you where Nathan Wright, who was the head of the Episcopal Diocese in Newark, was. Karenga was also off the scene. Nathan Wright convened the Newark conference. He was at that conference with Adam. The continuation committee was Nathan Wright, Louis Gothard, and somehow Karenga got to be a part of that, and there might have been somebody else. I think Chuck Stone represented Adam. So, we had Gothard and Chuck Stone at that meeting in Philadelphia where we put together the Congress of African People (CAP). I'm just showing you the continuation link. But, the Black Power movement, the conference, had basically gone into a lull because the 1969 conference did not happen and things were floating. There was no clarity about where to go next with the Black Power Movement. That's the result of what convening the CAP did. It gave validation.

The CAP was the result of the failure of the 1969 conference taking place. There was supposed to be an international Black Power conference in 1969 that a guy named Roosevelt Brown, who was once a military police, Stokely, and some other people had been trying to get together following up from 1968. 1969 was also the time when Karenga was having some internal problems on the West Coast so his leadership was waylaid around the time of the 1969 conference and the conference did not happen. We convened a meeting in Philadelphia to figure out what the next strategic move would be. It was at that Philadelphia gathering, which was a small gathering of about 15 people that the notion of a congress, which I put on the table, emerged. Baraka wasn't present at that meeting nor was Karenga. The notion was a congress rather than a conference. I saw the need to move beyond just having a conference, but to have a representative body of people who could make real decisions about their organizations and the community as we tried to move forward with a nation-building style and approach. There were divergent tendencies in the room and things were fractured. I was selected as chair at that meeting because everybody believed that I would be fair. There was a Pan Africanist tension and there was a Nationalist tension. Many of the Nationalists and, at that time, the Pan Africanists were arguing that we are an African people. The Black Nationalists were not yet willing to relinquish the slogan, "Black Power" or the emphasis on the United States. They were not willing to concede all of that. The orthodox Pan Africanists were arguing that we needed to focus on Africa while the Nationalists were still arguing that we needed to focus on the United States. I tried to bring those together through the notion of a congress of African people. That's how the name emerged. From there, we went to Atlanta to plan the actual event.

Baraka came into the process after those decisions and wound up chairing the politics task force. He put all of the Committee for Unified Newark (CFUN) into that movement. Karenga was locked up in jail and was very upset. He made some calls to us from jail that were not complimentary at all. At that time, Baraka was still very much the Nationalist and we got along except he wanted to make the whole organization a Kawaida organization. Other Nationalists in the group didn't want that. It looked like all of the workshop reports came back being preferenced with the Nguzo Saba and many of the workshop leaders said, "But, that's not what I said". So I confronted Baraka and asked how did this happen. His people were the recorders. I responded that we can't distribute these workshop reports because that's not what the workshop coordinators actually said in their workshops. I figured out what had happened. They just instinctively preferenced everything with the Nguzo Saba.

I knew that to keep the group together, we needed the perception of a diversity of Nationalists because that's how we got all of those diverse groups to participate in the first place. I'll never forget the time I had Farrakhan on one side and Whitney Young on the other. That's the famous picture that's in the Ebony picture book. They're very divergent people. That was the meeting where we blessed Farrakhan as Malcolm's successor. Betty (Shabazz) was there and Betty was still very much upset about the Farrakhan question. But I felt it was important that that part of the Black Liberation movement had to be present and to this day, the Minister thanks me so much for the way that we received him and accepted him at that early stage of his own career and development. Jesse was there. Julian Bond was there. Maynard Jackson was there. Ken Gibson was there. I'm not sure if Hatcher was there or not, but that list read like who's who in the African American world at that time. It was truly a congress of diverse Black political activists with political opinions and political ideas that all headed in a Nationalist and a Pan Africanist direction. We called for a convening of that convention. What led to the Gary convention was CAP. But by the time we got to San Diego two years later with me convening the CAP, I decided that the tide was heading toward Kawaida and I needed to let it go. I decided to leave the organization and left it to Baraka to do that. Subsequently, a number of us left the organization - Jitu, Haki, Mjenzi, myself, and all of our networks. We left the organization thinking they wanted to be Kawaida Nationalists. They didn't become Kawaida Nationalists; they became Marxists.

There was a conference at Howard University called "Toward Ideological Clarity." I think that conference was held in 1972 or somewhere like that. It was the year that Cabral was assassinated, maybe 1973. That's when a contingent came back from Africa arguing that the number one battle was the battle against Imperialism. They had talked to Sekou Toure after Cabral's assassination and that's part of what he told them. So they came back articulating the enemy as Imperialism, the need to fight against Imperialism, and beginning to echo some of the Marxist analysis at that time. Stokely had been playing with that because he was a student of Osajifu Kwame Nkrumah. It was only after the coup of 1966, that Nkrumah began using Scientific Socialism as his ideological framework. Prior to that, he was much closer to where Nyerere was on an African based Socialism. But, after the attempted coup or the coup itself, he moved towards Scientific Socialism. That had an impact on Stokely, who began himself pushing that line, and people like Owusu Sadauki also began pushing that line. Baraka also began pursuing that line. He was evolving that way after 1972 after the Gary convention. He didn't go to the Gary convention as a Marxist - that March 72 convention. He was still the Nationalist and Pan Africanist at that time. But it was post 1972, 1973, and 1974 that his worldview began to shift, change, grow, and evolve.

By the time we got to Gary, we had a battle inside the National Black Assembly in Dayton, Ohio and he and his cadre lost. In Little Rock, Arkansas, Ron Daniels emerged as the chair of that, the process. Well, actually, Daniels had been elected to something earlier but Hatcher and Diggs and all those people had left the assembly. Basically, in the post-convention period in 1975 after Little Rock, the Black elected officials who used to be a part of it disaffiliated themselves. And so Baraka had Daniels as the new leadership. Eventually Hatcher left and then Baraka left, leaving the remnants in Daniels' hands. But, there wasn't much left at that time. The Nationalists had split, the Black elected officials had split, and the Pan Africanists had split, so there was just a small cadre left which tried to keep it alive.

3. *Were you active with any other organizations and, if so, what organization(s), in what capacity, and for what period of time?*

I was the first chairperson of the Black Caucus in the Universalist Church. I was a founder of the Black Unitarian Universalist Caucus (BUUC), which functioned as an intermediary organization around empowerment and community development. We had talked the church into giving us unrestricted funds that we controlled to do work in the Black community. I was elected in October 1967. The Black Power conference was that summer. There was also the National Conference on New Politics. The Black Power conference was held in July and the National Conference on New Politics (NCNP) was held in August in Chicago. NCNP wanted to run King for president and Spock for vice president. It was a national organization that had recently been formed. I was the founding chair of BUUC from 1967 - 1972. I relinquished the chair of that organization so I could put more time into the Congress of African People actually.

4. *What global events influenced the formation and activities of CAP?*

I think that, broadly speaking, the struggle for liberation in Africa. I go back, I can only use my own consciousness here, to Ghana's independence in 1967, which was a distinct event and represented a huge massive paradigm shift in the liberation struggle on the African continent. The struggles in the Congo with the whole Lumumba, Casa Bubu, Mobutu battle that was taking place in the country; the independence of Tanzania in 1961 and the eventual merger of Tanganyika and Zanzibar; members of the liberation movement seeing the presence of African leaders at the United Nations. Almost every week, there was a new country achieving independence and we saw these African leaders in their royal garb embracing the UN in New York. All of those events had a profound impact and consequences on our consciousness. Our consciousness of Africa was being impacted very profoundly and deeply by those sets of global events more than any other.

I had studied in Russia in the summer in the early 1960s on a travel study fellowship. I had gone to the Soviet Union and then central Asia and met many African students who were at the University of Moscow. I gained first-hand knowledge of things happening on the African continent as it related to the struggle for liberation. That was the first time I had that kind of close encounter with Africans from the continent to get the story directly from them about the battle that was going on in their struggle, which had an enormous impact on my understanding. I was able to clarify things that the western media sources had conditioned and I think were leaving vague. I was able to develop a comprehensive understanding. That was a global event for me, leaving the US, seeing another part of the world, seeing how people think in the world, especially Africans, but seeing Europeans who were on the side of the African struggle and seeing the opposite European countries and governments who were on the side of the colonial powers.

So, all of that helped to shape my understanding of Africa and the world. That impacted my belief that we were an African people and we had a special place in history. I cannot articulate for others in this instance, what other global events may have affected their consciousness because I just really do not know that. Specifically, I can speak for myself. The Cuban missile crisis was a very important event in my political maturation process along with the independence of Ghana, the struggle for the Congo, the independence of Tanganyika, and encounters with Africans from other parts of the world.

All of those things helped to shape my consciousness - the CAP experience in 1970 and then, of course, the subsequent relationships we developed with African governments and African countries were critical. CAP used to have an annual reception at the UN, an ambassadors reception. We would get together as many African ambassadors as we could, link them with African Americans, and have this marvelous reception in New York. It was quite a colorful experience to see African Americans and Africans in a way we had not seen them. People in New York had not seen that before. Many of us had not either. It was a very important part of what CAP did. CAP did other things but it did some of that too. I just cite that because it was an important part of our statement about who we were.

5. What were the strengths and challenges of the organization?

<u>Strengths</u>: It was diverse. It had many strands in it. Some people would call themselves integrationists. Some people would call themselves Black Nationalists. Some people would call themselves Pan Africanists. It had all the strands of Black Nationalism in it. There were diverse strands. There was community control strand, there was the five-state hypothesis strand, there was the revolutionary replacement of government strand, there was we got to go to Africa to wage the battle strand, and we can wage the battle for Africa from wherever we are strand. We had 350

representatives from outside of the US. This is important. In 1970, we had 350 representatives and delegates from other parts of the world, including Australian Aborigines, three African Canadians, African Europeans, African Caribbeans, and continental Africans. We had Africans from every region of the Diasporas from the South Pacific to the Caribbean: the African continent, Europe, Canada, Asia, the United States, Central America, and Latin America. We had delegates representing all those regions where African people are. This was a U.S. based modern-day Pan-African Congress similar to the Pan-African Congress that had been held earlier in Europe. That was a strength and that was unique. Among African Americans, we had a spectrum of those who would call themselves integrationists, such as Whitney Young, to the Nation of Islam with the honorable Minister Louis Farrakhan. We had Black elected officials. We had activists. We had academicians and scholars. We had religious groups and clergy people. We had students. We had seniors like Queen Mother Moore and the reparations argument that she was constantly putting on the table. That's where Black Power theology kind of was born with James Cone and some other people out of the religion workshops CAP did that he coordinated. Preston Wilcox on education, the whole move towards independent Black schools was a very powerful, strong, and serious part of what we did. Cultural Gnostics like Larry Neal and Haki Mahibuti, who were both poets, were prominent and strong in that regard. We had a criminal justice movement. Earl Joyner, who subsequently represented the Wilmington 10, was a part of that, as well as the National Committee of Black Lawyers, which had just been formed as a variation of the National Black Attorneys. They were a new group, a progressive group. So, there was diversity of various kinds. I think that was the strength.

Secondly, we crystallized a global African consciousness. A global African consciousness was given form and shape in 1970. At the 1967 and 1968 Black Power conferences, the emphasis was overwhelmingly domestic. You didn't feel the power or drama on the African question and our relationship to it in Newark and in Philadelphia. And that's not just my perception. Back in 1970, there was an indelible imprint because we had among other things, Abdullaye Toure, who was the ambassador from Guinea, as a prominent speaker. In the process, we had representatives, again, from the totality of the African world. Some of this is in the Ebony History Book article in Sept 1970, I think. There are some pictures of some of those representatives from the rest of the African world. We had liberation movements and social movements in different parts of the African world. So, in many ways we were the first African American initiated Pan African congress in the modern era. It's not listed like that because I think, Manchester was the fifth Pan African Congress and the sixth was the one that was held in Tanzania in 1974. We were sort of in-between. But it was the first one on American soil like this. The others had been in Europe. This one was the first of this scope and this magnitude where we were African people claiming Africa. 350 representatives from other parts of the African world were attracted to this Congress of African People, and I enjoyed the privilege of chairing it. It affirmed Africa. It affirmed that we are an African people. It put us on the map.

The term, "African American" was codified in the 1980s but it was first articulated by CAP in 1970. And CAP is what made Gary happen. CAP called for Gary, a Black Political Convention. At CAP, we called for a Black Lobby, which became TransAfrica. We did much to dismantle Apartheid.

Weaknesses: A major weakness was the point where the Kawaida advocates wanted to make CAP a Kawaida organization. They wanted everybody to live, breathe, and die the Nguzo Saba the way they did. They wanted everybody to look alike, sound alike, talk alike, act alike, and be like themselves. I think that was part of what broke that organization up. I have no doubt in my mind that is what broke it up. That's what drove me out. I was not interested in being a Kawaidanist though I have a full healthy respect for the Nguzo Saba because we were Kwanzaa practitioners too. But we did not want to be part of a centralist organization under a mystical leader. That's just not who we were. The women in our organization would not allow that. Because of the position they (Kawaidians) took about women that just wasn't going to happen. We were not interested in trying to recreate 13th century African culture either. There was a deep perception that so much of Kawaida as practiced then was trying to recreate another time in history that had passed. And so, we didn't see ourselves trying to be Kawaida advocates. If others did, let them do so. We didn't have any problem with that. But many of us who were in the coalition, which made CAP in the first place, the majority of people were Nationalists, Pan Africanists, but were not Kawaidanists. So that was one of the weaknesses and that eventually broke the organization up. It probably was the major weakness that broke it up.

Now I can't speak for CAP once I left when Baraka became chair. I can't speak about that period and choose not to because he knows that history better than I do. I can only speak for the two years that I was the founding chair, the initial chair, and helped to put it together and make it what it was in its early days. I don't think it had the same impact again because it became an ideologically hegemonic organization with one distinct ideology. It changed the whole character of the place. That's the major weakness that I see, that people were driven out by the unspoken perception that there was a desire for CAP to be a Kawaida organization. And so folks said if that's the case, let them be that and we'll move on and do other things. That's kind of what happened.

There may have been some other local weakness. We were trying to organize chapters and people at differing places organizationally. I'm not sure we built local chapters that had all of the elements that we had put in place. But, we did build local chapters. That too was a strength. Where there were Kawaida organizations, we tried to create united fronts because that's what CAP was supposed to be - a united front, which was another one of its strengths - a united front with diverse tendencies. Operational unity is what we were preaching. But the presence of a centralizing personality with a cadre of advocates in the organization who were very well organized, well disciplined, and had a centralized approach to decision-making; that was not where the rest of us were. We thought that's what they wanted so we said let them have that.

6. What were the accomplishments of the organization?

I have to think about it. There probably are. There were some things we were doing in my own organization that sometimes we did in the name of CAP and sometimes we did in the name of the organization. It depended on what we were doing at the time. And then, there were some things done in the name of IFCO, the Inter-Religious Foundation for Community Organization, the group that Lucas Walker used to head that was the intermediary to do church funding. The different denominations used it to fund community based organizations and the work they were doing - voter registration, education, culture, land acquisition, farming - a whole bunch of things were done. So sometimes, we wore multiple hats. Sometimes we distinguished what hat and sometimes we didn't.

CAP, the Black Nationalists, gave birth to Gary because it was the Black Nationalists who engineered the Gary convention. Without the Black Nationalists, Gary was not going to happen that way. You would've had just a traditional milk toast meeting of people from the political parties but you wouldn't have Gary. We believed in the notion of a political party with diverse notions and Baraka was very strong on that too. The Black Power conferences of 1967 and 1968 made progress but they reached their maturation and couldn't go further. They got stuck.

Whether we acknowledge it or not, there's a link between what we did at CAP and Barack Obama's election. It goes like this: In 1970, we called for the formation of an independent Black political party, we raised the question of a Black candidate for President, we pushed the agenda to move Black Power in a progressive independent kind of way, we put pressure on the two-party system because we said we needed our own party, and we called for a Black political convention. That led to Gary in 1972. Gary moved the agenda even further and faster calling for a Black agenda and deepening Black political participation. In 1976, we tried to run a Black presidential candidate - Julian Bond or Ron Dellums. We had a convention in Cincinnati with 5,000 people. I'll never forget it because I gave a speech that I never gave again called "To the Hoop" about a Black presidential candidate. That's what led eventually to Jesse Jackson running in 1984 and 1988. At that 1976 convention, we tried to run someone who was well known and had some popularity like Julian and Ron Dellums. That led to Jesse running in 1980 and in 1984, which led to Sharpton and to Barack Obama. Now in the middle of all of that are Shirley Chisolm in 1972, Channing Phillips in 1968 from DC, and there was Kirkpatrick who ran in 1976. He didn't get anywhere. Ron Daniels ran, Fulani ran, and Dick Gregory ran. We had a committee of inquiry with John Conyers in 1968, who was also raising the question. These are the minor efforts. But, I'm saying that there is a link - an unbroken link between what we tried to do in 1970 with Black politics, then Gary in 1972, then Cincinnati in 1976, then Jesse in 1984, and Jesse in 1988, then Sharpton, then Barack Obama.

The CAP also gave us Kwanzaa. Karenga was the organizer and creator of the concept. He gave it to Baraka. It found its way into the CAP and many of us accepted the ceremony and the holiday at a time when there was little Karenga could do about it because he was locked up. It was CAP and the Nationalists and Pan Africanists who adopted and agreed to and supported the concept of Kwanzaa. That kept it alive and helped to spread it. Had that not happened in 1970, I'm not sure that Kwanzaa would have survived or not with Karenga having been locked up. With all the damage that the State did to his image and his leadership, I'm saying it could very well have ended right there. It could have been something that they did in the US organization in Los Angeles and that was the end of the story. But, it was the fact that CAP kept those seven principles alive in its ethos, and Baraka deserves credit for that and those of us who were not Kawaidians but who accepted the seven principles and the practice of Kwanzaa. Virtually everybody inside CAP with all of its diversity could relate to the Kwanzaa concept and the Kwanzaa principles. With Karenga locked up, it didn't have a future. It might have just died. I've heard Baraka say that he did more to keep Kwanza alive than Karenga ever did.

7.   What do you know about COINTELPRO?

When we left Philadelphia in 1968, there was a huge struggle about who was going to emerge as the leading Nationalist in the country and I think that Karenga had kind of established that that was going to be him. I was supposed to go to Los Angeles for the next conference except the shootouts happened on UCLA's campus. That compromised Karenga's leadership in the minds of many people across the country. That completely compromised his leadership. Then, after he got locked up for the alleged abuse of women, for a lot of people, that just compromised his leadership even further. Now of course we all know that COINTELPRO's hand was in a whole bunch of that stuff. I don't want to suggest to you that I believe the State's version of it at all because we know most things that happened negatively to Black folks during those days in the leadership of the movement, we know, COINTELPRO's hand was there. We know that. So I want it clear that that's a perspective that I have about it because I worked with Maulana and with, then, Imamu, and worked with them closely. As a matter of fact, the day that shooting took place, I was in Beacon Press' office with Baraka, Njenzi, and Karenga negotiating the publishing of his book by Beacon Press. The very day that the shootout took place. I asked him straight out, "Hey man, what's the deal?" He gave me his version and I just had to accept that he had not ordered the assassination of those brothers, but that was the dynamic of what happened. There had been struggles going on before that and I accepted that. But I'm saying that the image and impression for many people behind that and then the subsequent allegations of abuse of women was such that Maulana's leadership was very definitely compromised and marginalized. So he did not have the ability to spread the practice of Kwanzaa anywhere because he couldn't. He was in jail. CAP validated the concept and gave it broad national presence. Continuation is what I think saved Kwanzaa.

Regarding COINTELPRO, you can never put your finger on something and prove how it affected anything. It's not that easy to do. We had tense moments and people we thought were agent provocateurs. To be sure, that was happening at many different levels. But, I don't think that we were around long enough for that program to feel it had to launch a broadside attack on what we were doing. I don't know of specific instances where I would put my hand on something and say, "Aha. This proves that COINTELPRO did that." But we had many suspicions about how they may have been present and visible and caused confusion at the local level. A lot of incidences were at the local level where I suspect agent provocateurs were responsible for some of the confusion and mess. I know where I was located in Boston, I'm certain that that was the case, and I know of numerous incidents where there were disruptions. There were physical confrontations as well as political ones that I'm almost certain in retrospect that were induced by them.

8.   What is the current status of the organization?

It closed after 1974, but I don't know the exact date. After Baraka became chair, I let it go because it became more and more leftist with those crazy leftist battles and shootouts. We lost interest. We just thought CAP had lost its mind and Baraka had lost his mind. He was still in the Black Political Assembly into 1974. It was after 1974 that we had to wage a battle to take control of the Black Political Assembly. But, I'm not sure when you could date the formal demise of CAP.

9. *How did the activities of your organization affect colleges and universities on campuses and in the community?*

You have to ask the question based on correlation or based on causality. Certainly, there were the campus-wide movements of SOBU and YOBU, which the activists in SNCC initiated. But I think that the validation that CAP provided to the Pan African perspective blessed the work of that organization. And, of course, the Malcolm X Liberation University in Greensboro, North Carolina was also formed, and the Center for Black Education by Jimmy Garrett in Washington, DC. All of those were student-based organizations. No doubt that the work of CAP validated the work of YOBU and SOBU and blessed the notion that "We Are An African People", the Pan Africanist ideology which is where they were operating from. So I think CAP did a lot to validate a Pan African worldview for student groups and for Black Studies programs on different campuses because you had those struggles going on those campuses - about the Black Power question and Black Studies.

I think that we gave national and international voice as part of the formal Black Power movement because our colleagues in the middle and on the right who were still holding on to the vestiges of integration and assimilationist ideology had no counter to that. They had no response for young people that was believable or credible. Young people were decidedly to the left at that time and they were moving in a different direction. We blessed that impulse and gave our support to the need for academic institutions, the training of our young people, and who we were. We said what was appropriate and needed to be done. I think that blessing gave coverage and room for a lot of people in a lot of places because the CAP thrust kept the Black Power movement alive.

So we have to honor and respect the role that Black Nationalists in CAP played in the continuity of Black Nationalist and Pan Africanist thinking - for the country to see all of that and for young Black people to see all of that, and young people seeing that the elders were blessing this and think it's important. I think CAP did that though I could not document it causally but I can certainly do it through correlation, the impact that keeping the Black Power thrust had. It kept the energy going and it moved the agenda to the next level, which was Gary 1972. It led to the notion of really trying to seriously run Black candidates. But, it also continued to validate everything young people were doing in the schools and in their communities. So I think there's a correlation. I'm not sure about causality but the fact that CAP existed and we were all over the media blessing Black Power and blessing Pan Africanism, that's important. "We are an African people." That was the slogan.

10. *Did your organization's activities affect the development of Black student organizations and, if so, how?*

SNCC formed SOBU and YOBU. They were distinct organizations. You just don't find much about them in the literature. Nelson Johnson was a part of that. Cleve Sellers, who is now the president of a college in South Carolina, was a part of that. I think Owusu and Jimmy Garrett had something to do with that. The people out of the Malcolm X University, Mark Smith, some of the people in that shootout in North Carolina, Nelson and they had become members of the Communist Party there. They went that far. And there was a shootout and I think three people were killed. Mark Smith had been my student in my classroom and he was part of that. That whole piece of SOBU/YOBU, there's not much that has been written about that. They were not the Black Student Unions (BSU). However, BSU people were part of that. SOBU and YOBU had a distinct ideological worldview, a Pan Africanist worldview. BSUs were diverse organizations. They were united fronts with different tendencies and they focused their energy primarily on campus questions. SOBU had an ideological position and it focused its energy on global questions as well. Both entities were on campuses at the same time. I cannot accurately tell you which campuses. I can tell you at Harvard, SOBU existed because I was there and I know that but I can't tell you much else about their organizational presence at other places and how they may have switched hats sometimes too.

11. Did your organization's activities affect the development of Black studies departments at higher education institutions and, if so, how?

We (CAP) called for the formation of a Black University. We called for Black Studies programs in every university in this country whether they were Black or White. It didn't matter. Our students, our people, needed to take courses related to the history and contributions of African descended people. We called for those things. We gave blessings on African American history and studies as part of a curriculum not only at colleges and universities but at high schools as well.

12. Are you aware of any activities, programs, or benefits to higher education resulting from the efforts of your organization or other organizations in the Black Power Movement during the period from 1960 – 1980? Do they still exist today?

I have to do some thinking about that. People from the Black Power movement gave presentations on campuses, but there wasn't a pattern to it. Every student organization might invite a different speaker and there was no one place they drew their speakers from. They were across the spectrum about who they would have come and speak on campuses. But, certainly there was that effect. The movement provided a pool of people to draw from on the campuses for Black history celebrations and other activities on campuses. That's there, but I can't document with accuracy to make that link. I know it was there because I was one of those people who was invited to speak in my various capacities, but certainly, as chair of CAP. I was invited to speak but I also was invited to speak as a Black Studies professor, teaching the liberation movement. That was part of what I was teaching. So, I was invited to places wearing different hats too. Most people in the movement didn't wear one hat in those days.

It was clear that part of what was happening during that whole period was a shift in our consciousness and our understanding that we had been deceived. That was a wide spread sense back then, and that we had not properly taught our own history and culture. And we needed to be taught and part of what groups like CAP did was validate, say yes, that's true. We had people like John Henrik Clarke and Ben-Jochannan and Asa Hilliard. All of those people identified with CAP. We stuck to those kinds of people who were the bearers of our history. And Queen Mother Moore, bless her heart, and Preston Wilcox who had a group called AFRAM. Those were the outgrowth from the CAP process. Preston was member of CAP. So was Queen Mother Moore. All those New York Nationalist or Pan Africanists at one time were part of CAP.

13. Are there other persons you feel would provide helpful information on this topic?

I suggest you consult some other literature on that but I don't know of anybody who's written much about that. For the people who chose to write about that period, I've been unable to find much about SOBU and YOBU. I'm sure that Nelson Johnson would know some pieces and he's in North Carolina. Jimmy Garrett might know some piece of that. He's on the West Coast. Mukasa probably has some memory of that but there was a split with Stokely and he aligned with Stokely. There was split that Owusu Sadauki had with Stokely so I'm not sure how much detail Mukasa would have but it would be worth just asking him. I never associated Mukasa with the SOBU/YOBU side of it. I'm trying to remember now where Stokely was in this dynamic at that point. Wherever Stokely was, that's where Mukasa was going to be. I think Jimmy Garrett would be more authoritative, and Owusu and Cleve. Cleve was also close to Stokely. He was based here while Stokely was running around the world. Cleve Sellers would be an excellent source on this I think, along with Jimmy Garrett. But you probably would have to talk with more than one person to get that piece of the story because I think that's an interesting story.

14. I am collecting information on the sequence of events leading to the development of the first Black student union and the first Black studies department at San Francisco State University. Are there experiences at other college or universities that you feel would be informative?

Jimmy Garrett and Nathan Hare. The Harvard experience because it had the second (Black Studies) department after SFSU. The Rosovsky Report. You can go to Google and find that. The history of how that department came about is interesting. That was when Guinier was chair of that department. Guinier was from the New York area, a labor activist. He's Lani Guinier's father. Cornell and, both of them, were in my class, Lani and Cornell. I do not take credit for what my students do or do not do, however.

THE US ORGANIZATION

The US organization is one of the leading organizations in the cultural nationalist segment of the Black Power Movement. Because of the significant impact it had on the Movement, a summary of the organization is provided without an interview.

Summary of the Organization

The US organization is located in Los Angeles, California. It was co-founded by Maulana Karenga and Hakim Jamal on September 7, 1965 following the rebellion in Watts, California (Brown, 2003). Due to a disagreement on strategy, Jamal left the US organization in 1966 and formed another organization called the Malcolm X Foundation. Karenga then became the driving force of US. His vision was to promote African American cultural unity through service, struggle, and institution-building (US Organization, 2013). In the quotation below, Karenga explained Malcolm X's influence on the formation of the US Organization.

> "Malcolm was the major African American thinker that influenced me in terms of nationalism and Pan-Africanism. As you know, towards the end, when Malcolm is expanding his concept of Islam, and of nationalism, he stresses Pan-Africanism in a particular way. And, he agrees that, and this is where we have the whole idea of a cultural revolution and the need for revolution …we need a cultural revolution. He argues that we must return to Africa culturally and spiritually, even if we can't go physically. And so that's a tremendous impact on US" (Halisi, 1972, pp. 27-31).

During the 1960s and 1970s, the US Organization became recognized by Black Power organizations as the leading cultural nationalist organization in the United States. The list of accomplishments of the US Organization is lengthy. Kwanzaa, an African American holiday that occurs in late December, was one of the earliest successes of the US Organization. Through Kwanzaa, the US Organization and the Congress of African People promoted a Black value system (Nguzo Saba). The first Kwanzaa celebration was held in December 1966. US was also responsible for the establishment and/or development of the Black Congress in Los Angeles, PACO (a Black Federation in Dayton, Ohio), another Black Federation in San Diego, and the Committee for Unified New Ark in Newark, New Jersey. It co-founded initiatives such as the Brotherhood Crusade, the Mafundi Institute, the Community Alert Patrol, the Watts Health Foundation, the Young Lions (Simba Wachanga) youth group, and the Ujima Housing Project. US also claims credit for having a significant role in the development of the Black Studies discipline and the formation of Black student unions on college campuses (The US Organization, 2013).

The Organization continues its work today. With the exception of a short hiatus from 1971-1975, the US Organization has been active since 1965. Currently it operates an African American Cultural Center (a cultural school for children), the Kawaida Institute of Pan-African Studies, a men's group (Senu Society), a women's group (Senut Society), and a monthly study circle. It is also active in an extensive network nationwide. On its website (US Organization, 2013), the US

Organization lists the following seven future objectives. It will continue to sustain and promote African culture by:

1. providing models of excellence and paradigms of possibilities;
2. expanding political education;
3. training social change agents;
4. organizing and mobilizing people around their own interests;
5. participation in cooperative projects;
6. continuing to be a reference and resource center; and,
7. rebuilding and expanding the liberation movement (US Organization, 2013)

THE COMMITTEE FOR UNIFIED NEW ARK (CFUN).

Summary of the Organization

The Committee for Unified New Ark emerged from an organization called the United Brothers, which was established in 1967 in Newark, New Jersey. The initial purpose of the organization was to transform the political system in Newark. In 1968, the United Brothers changed its name to the Committee for Unified New Ark (CFUN) and later, in 1972, to the Congress of African People (CAP) (Woodard, 1999). In 1967, CFUN added an organizational unit for women called United Sisters. The Committee for Unified New Ark was led by the late Amiri Baraka (also known as LeRoi Jones), who became its spiritual leader with the title, "Imamu", and his wife, Amina Baraka, who was given the title, "Bibi". Other officers included a chief community organizer, a key political officer, a chief economic officer, and a political advisor. The men in the leadership of CFUN secured strategic leadership positions in public agencies across the city of Newark. The United Sisters formalized its division, with Amina Baraka as its recognized leader, and worked side-by-side with the men. In 1967, the United Sisters established the African Free School, an African-centered school for the children of its members (Baraka, 1997).

During the 1960s, Baraka became a protégé of Maulana Karenga from the US Organization, which was located in Los Angeles, California. Under Baraka's leadership, the Committee for Unified New Ark embraced the cultural nationalist theory and practice (known as Kawaida) promulgated by Karenga. Kawaida, a Kiswahili term that means "tradition and reason," was the driving force of the organization (DiscovertheNetworks, 2013, p. 1). The US Organization became known as the African-centered cultural giant of western United States and the Committee for Unified New Ark had a similar image in the East. Activists from all over the country commuted to their sites to attend weekly classes about manhood, womanhood, Kiswahili, Kawaida, the Nguzo Saba, politics, community organizing, and African-centered axioms and practices that flowed out of the US Organization. The men and women in the organizations wore traditional African clothing, had natural hairstyles, decorated their homes in African cultural themes, and conversed in Kiswahili in an effort to recapture traditional African values, reclaim traditional practices, and reconnect African Americans to their homeland in Africa. The Kawaida Doctrine provided the philosophical framework for this effort. In 1972, the Committee for Unified New Ark was subsumed under the Congress of African People.

Interview with Dr. Komozi Woodward

1. .What are your memories of the Black Power Movement during this period?

I was home schooled by my mother. She made me participate in a summer program at Princeton University. I did not know it at the time but it was an experiment. There were about 40 boys that were in the program. Their theory was that we were culturally poor. The intent of the experiment was to separate us from the Black community. They studied our eating and other habits.

Malcolm X was the one who inspired me because he talked about what I was experiencing. King's message was too weak.

2. *Please share any information you have on the goals and plans emanating from Black Power Conference of 1967 that took place in Newark, New Jersey.*

I attended the conference. Resolutions came out of the conference. See chapter 2 in my book (Nation Within a Nation). CAP (Congress of African People) replaced the Black Power conferences. H. Rap Brown also attended. I was most impressed by him because he spoke clearly and used regular language. He predicted what would happen to him. He doesn't get the recognition he deserves. Baraka told us we should be polite because we were representing the Black community.

3. *Were you active with any organizations and, if so, what organization(s), in what capacity, and for what period of time?*

I joined SNCC (Student Non-violent Coordinating Committee). After that, I joined the Black Youth organization (BYO), which came out of a Catholic youth organization in Queens Chapel Catholic Church. I left BYO because they kept talking negatively about Baraka and CFUN and they kept a book that they said had the true knowledge of African Americans in a restricted room on the top level of the brownstone house they had converted for the Chad School. I learned many skills there when I participated in renovating the building. I understood that no organization was perfect. Three other brothers and I did a list comparing the positives and negatives of the Panther Party, Nation of Islam, and CFUN. Based on our analysis, we decided to join CFUN and change it. We were young – 15 years old. At CFUN, I served from the lowest level and rose to be part of three men who ran the organization. I was mentored by Baraka, who made me in charge of economic development and housing development. I was given $6.4 million and later $24 million to develop a 100-acre plot of land. We traveled to the East and the Brownsville Center in New York, and to the US organization in California to look at their operations. Later, we attempted to build the Kawaida Towers with a complete community design. Because of racism, the Towers were not built. What we did build was a senior citizen's building, which was designed by the seniors. I also taught at the Political School of Kawaida, which was upstairs from the Hekalu (headquarters), and became managing editor of our newspaper. Activists came from all over the country to be educated. Later I worked in a factory, joined a union, and taught the history of the movement. My house was used as a school. After working at the factory, I ran the Children's Express, a program for rich children.

4. *What global events influenced the formation and activities of your organization?*

Malcolm X and Baraka visited Babu in Tanzania shortly before Malcolm's death. Babu led the revolution in Zanzibar. Babu also mentored Lumumba and Malcolm X. Baraka was apprentice to Babu, Nyerere, and Malcolm X. We were also influenced by the African Liberation activities taking place on the African continent.

5. *What were the strengths and challenges of the organization?*

We were doers. Our motto was "Kazi (work) is the Blackest of all". We were well organized with a lot of departments. There were roles for women in the organization that did not exist in other organizations like SNCC. We sent people to colleges/universities because we felt that we had to be experts. Two problems were we lacked technical skills and, as an organization, we were so successful that we caused other Black organizations to falter. We needed a united front. When we closed our doors, it created a gap in the Black community.

6. *What were the accomplishments of the organization?*

We opened and ran the African Free School, a 24-hour residential educational center for our children; helped to organize CIBI (Council of Independent Black Organizations); had a Spirit House and a Hekalu; organized a Black Arts group; had a newspaper; and, built a senior citizens building. We educated activists from all over the country and sent our people to school to be experts.

7. *What do you know about COINTELPRO?*

In 1974, they infiltrated CFUN and destroyed our investment program. They set up a health clinic opposite ours and began to recruit our people. They shot bullets into our childcare center and into my home. I remembered Bunchy Carter and left out of the window. I'm lucky to be alive today. My daughter still has nightmares about bullets coming into the center.

8. *What is the current status of the organization?*

The organization closed in the late 1970s.

9. *How did the activities of your organization affect colleges and universities on campuses and in the community?*

I was in college during my years at CFUN. When we learned that CFUN was forming a Congress of African People, we decided to form a Congress of African Students, a parallel organization. It was not known but the Ku Klux Klan was attacking students in Pennsylvania. We organized a student group at Dickerson College in Pennsylvania and developed a statewide newspaper.

10. *Did your organization's activities affect the development of Black student organizations and, if so, how?*

We sent CFUN members to school. CFUN members visited and lectured at the campuses. Students in the Congress of African Students demanded the formation of Black Student Unions. I formed the Black Student Union at my college. Initially, it was called Black Students for Community Defense. After Baraka spoke at our campus, we changed the name to the Black Student Union.

11. *Did your organization's activities affect the development of Black studies departments at higher education institutions and, if so, how?*

Baraka and Sonya Sanchez spoke at San Francisco State University and influenced the establishment of a Black student union there, and spoke about the need to change the curriculum. We provided structure and guidance for the Congress of African Students. These students took over buildings on campuses to demand changes in the curriculum.

12. *Are you aware of any activities, programs, or benefits to higher education resulting from the efforts of your organization or other organizations in the Black Power Movement during the period from 1960 – 1980? Do they still exist today?*

Everything is a continuation. We are now in the schools and mentoring students. Community folk are putting effort into getting students in colleges and universities, but the problem is the measure of success at this point. If we're successful, the graduates leave the community. We must do something about the brain drain from the community. Before we had the values but did not have needed technical skills. Now it is reverse. Our children have the skills but not the values or institutions in our community to apply their skills.

13. *Are there other persons you feel would provide helpful information on this topic?*

Haki Mahubuti. If he's too busy, contact his wife. I think her name is Carol Lee. If you search Google for Haki Mahubuti's wife, she will pop up. I suggest you read the *Black Spring, Something Torn and New* (by Nguzi), the *Business of Black Power, and the Chicago Black Renaissance* (analysis by Woodson and Dubois).

14. *I am collecting information on the sequence of events leading to the development of the first Black student union and the first Black studies department at San Francisco State University. Are there experiences at other college or universities that you feel would be informative?*

Look for information on Sterling Brown and Sarah Lawrence. Sarah Lawrence went from having no Black professors to many. I became the first Black professor at Sarah Lawrence as a result of the demands for diversity of the students. I have had the opportunity to teach the children of a number of Black leaders who attend(ed) the College. Check out the independent Black schools headed by Haki and his wife. They have ensured financial support for the schools by marrying them to Northwestern University.

THE NEW ARK SCHOOL (NAS)

Summary of the Organization

The New Ark School was a grassroots community organization that opened its doors in 1970 following the 1967 rebellion and Black Power Conference in Newark, New Jersey. The location of the school was the Central Ward in Newark, where the rebellion occurred. In that area, there was a concentration of high-rise 17-story apartments for low-income residents called "projects." The majority of the adult residents in the apartments were high school dropouts. Crime was a significant problem in the area. It was so severe that, because of safety concerns, law enforcement officers often refused to enter the dwellings when in pursuit of someone who had just committed a crime. The New Ark School emerged out of a movement to gain community control of the public schools and social services agencies that served their community, and to reduce the violence in the area. The mission of the school was to identify and mentor indigenous leaders so they would have a greater voice in their community.

The creation and expansion of program services at the school were driven by the needs of the population served. All programs services were provided free to residents. The first program the school offered was a high school equivalency (GED) program for high school dropouts. Many of the students that attended the classes were parents. They frequently missed classes because they did not have anyone to watch their children or funds to pay a childcare provider. To address the issue of childcare, the school established an early childhood learning center for their children. Because a significant number of students who enrolled in the high school equivalency program did not read at a high school equivalency (7th grade) level, they had difficulty completing the program. To address this problem, an adult basic education program for adults that functioned at a 5th grade reading level was established. Students, who needed it, could then begin in the ABE program, transition to the GED program, and graduate by successfully taking the GED test. The eligibility criteria for acceptance in the early childhood learning program was expanded to include all income-eligible children in the neighborhood because of the great need for childcare in the area. The childcare program subsequently expanded to include a primary school and a before and after school program for school age children. The after school program served a number of students who were referred to the program by the public schools because of behavior problems. This program became a day camp program that included both residential and non-residential components during the summer months. The school soon expanded and opened a residential treatment facility for teenage youth who had been diagnosed as socially maladjusted or emotionally disturbed. The majority of the youth were referred by a youth center, which was a prison for adjudicated youth. The two remaining initiatives of the school were continuing education classes for adults such as photography classes, martial arts, African dance, and nutrition classes; and, community education such as an annual Marcus Garvey festival to enhance awareness in Newark. Based on its development and expansion, it is apparent that the New Ark School responded to Black needs in Newark from the 1960s to the 1980s.

Many of the independent Black schools that emerged during the period were managed by umbrella organizations (such as the Chad School by the Black Youth Organization and the African Free School by the Committee for Unified NewArk). This was not true for the New Ark School.

The school, however, was led by Black Power activists who established an informal cadre. The co-leaders of the School were Robert Dixon and Kennedy Wilson. Other members of the cadre included Juanita Wilson, Jeannette Robinson, Kinaya Sokoya (me), and John Wilson. Kennedy Wilson and Robert Dixon were responsible for development; Jeannette Robinson oversaw the administrative and development functions of the School; Juanita Wilson and I were responsible for program development and implementation, and John Wilson was in charge of property maintenance and procurement. Four of the individuals above - Kennedy Wilson, Robert Dixon, Jeannette Robinson, and I served as executive directors during the life of the school. One by one, members of the cadre resigned to pursue other interests (e.g. higher education). It was difficult to find replacements that had the same passion and commitment to the School. The last person in the cadre left the school in 1982. Unfortunately, the individuals who followed us were unable to manage the grants that were the life-blood of the school and, in 1987, the school closed due to lack of funding (Sokoya, 2013).

Interview with Robert Dixon (Akendole): Co-founder of the New Ark School

1. What are your memories of the Black Power Movement during this period?

To me, the 60s meant the riots in Newark and the rest of the country and started me on a journey to try to make things better for the people in the community where the New Ark School was started. I think it's important to understand the starting of the New Ark Program. It was through the Department of Community Affairs that a lady named Katherine Evilepski and a priest named Robert Ulesky, started a program of para-professionals. They established three schools - one in Newark, one in Jersey City, and one in New Brunswick using paraprofessionals to run the programs. New Ark School started under the leadership of Lawrence Holder, a young lady named Jean Johnson, and me.

The New Ark School started out as a high school equivalency program to deal with dropouts from the Newark public school system. We started with 50 students. We registered them in the GED program and prepared them to take entrance exams for colleges. The program was successful that first year and when we saw the need to expand the program because of the many problems that were in the community, the School was transformed from a high school equivalency program to a multi-faceted resource center. This changed the direction of the School tremendously. It became a cultural entity providing all kinds of services for the people in the community – jobs; we provided information about sickle cell anemia, we got our people tested for that. We expected our board through a banker and Morris, a successful merchant, to help us and give us more credibility. That's some of the things that started the Program.

2. Please share any information you have on the goals and plans emanating from the Black Power Conference of 1967 that took place in Newark, New Jersey.

I didn't attend. I wasn't on board in 1967. We came into existence in September1970. I was working in the post office at the time and I left the post office to work full time as a mathematics and reading comprehension teacher.

3. Were you active with any organizations and, if so, what organization(s), in what capacity, and for what period of time?

Lawrence Holder was the first director (of New Ark School). Lawrence got the opportunity to go to Brown (University) and after a year (at New Ark), he said, "I'm out of here, man. You got it." I said, "Got what?" He said, "You got this program." I had no idea of where to go with this. And so, he gave me some information about getting an accountant to make sure all of the money was accounted for. Every time, I spent a dime, put a receipt in the bag and at the end of the month, take the bag to the accountant. And, when the people came, and they would come, they going to check on what I did with the money. And so, we hired an accountant. We sent them to him to answer their questions. I did that and he went about his business. After the first year that I ran the program, we got it funded again.

Kennedy Wilson was out of work and he passed by the school one day looking for a job and I said, "What can you do?" He said, "I've got some administrative skills," which I needed. So, he came in and after he looked at our files and all of the letters of commendations we had received, he said, "You have, a gold mine here, man, and I can help." So I hired him and gave him half the money - of what I made, and created a spot for him.

We got involved with CFUN (Committee for Unified Newark) and Amiri Baraka for help to develop a whole cultural stream for those that would come through our doors. We changed the concept of the New Ark School by adding a cultural aspect to the educational projects we had when we first started.

We then got involved with Don Saunders and the program that he conducted for AT&T, Bell Labs. Some of their staff used to come to the school for training. The purpose of the program was to raise the consciousness of White people in the corporate arena so they would provide upward mobility for Blacks in their company by opening doors for them to go from the mailroom to management positions. The program came out of a consent decree that came out of Washington. Don Saunders and Tim Harvey were instrumental in partnering with the New Ark School to provide a vehicle when these people, these directors and other managers from AT&T, would come to Newark as a part of their experience. We would take them and show them around the city of Newark, the destruction of the city, show them the problems that were created through neglect of the needs of the people. They had a different outlook because they had never experienced the Black experience. Many of them were coming from different parts of the country to AT&T and they had no knowledge of the Black experience. So, Tim and Don used the New Ark School as a vehicle to enlighten them on the problems faced in Black communities all over the country. We were just a prototype of the struggle that Black people were facing and the challenges that we had to overcome during the time and struggles after the riots.

We contacted Leon Moore, Founder of the Chad School, and Milt Campbell. They became a part of our cultural expansion. We got involved with them and they helped us tremendously in and providing information with regards to our child care program. They helped us put together a program to get the parents more involved in helping to shape the direction for the children. So, Chad was very helpful to us.

Prudential (Insurance Company) provided some money to help us go forward. Also the Victoria Foundation gave us money in the initial years of the program. There was a lot of involvement from the corporate section and we received a stipend from AT&T for their participation in our program. Hoffman La Roche gave us a lot of equipment for our science laboratory.

4. *What global events influenced the formation and activities of the New Ark School?*

The Black Nationalist movement that was prevalent in Africa was our source of inspiration. The Black Nationalist movement (in the US) came through Amiri Baraka. We were tied to him. During the weekends, New Ark prepared flyers that went out to the community to help get the people ready to go out and vote. That was the part of the school that got politically involved in waking up the community to the power of the community - the power of the people. The students of SNCC (Student Nonviolent Coordinating Committee), Stokely Carmichael, and all these organizations were coming to the forefront and were driving the direction of the Black community throughout the country. It changed the way people were thinking. Activists wore dashikis and had big afros. The lifestyle and thought patterns (of Black people) were changed in the big cities and throughout the country during that time.

5. *What were the strengths and challenges of the New Ark School?*

New Ark's High School Equivalency Program sent all of its students to college the first year. There were so many things going on. Kids were dropping out of school at such a tremendous rate and there was no place for them to go. That's what sparked the State not to limit itself to using professional teachers but also using paraprofessionals that had potential skills. Lawrence was the one with the degree. It was initially an organization run by paraprofessionals.

The one time we had a problem or the potential for a problem was when men from the State came to the School and saw these Black images, Black murals and photographs in the child care center where the big room was downstairs and the hallway going up the stairs from the first to the second floor. They questioned whether White children or people were allowed to come to the School. We had an answer for that. "Yeah, they could come but they didn't want to. Because, where we were located, they were afraid." One of them said there were all of these Black people on the walls and that's not allowed by the State. So I said, "Come on outside." We went outside and he looked around. I asked him, "How many people do you see that look like you?"

6. *What were the accomplishments of the New Ark School?*

When the public school teachers went out on strike, we took our students and sent them over to the _____ School. We were there with the kids that would come to school during the strike. We got a big write up in the paper about that.

The other programs (that were created in two other cities) folded after one year but we survived after the initial year and we got favor because we were successful in getting all of our students into college. The crown of our success was Bebee Wilson. She went to NYU, got a full scholarship, and changed her master's degree as a result of her starting and going to the New Ark School. She was the great success. She came back and worked in the child care center at the New Ark. She was New Ark's first student.

We raised the consciousness of Whites from Bell Laboratories. We took them on tours. We would walk down Springfield Avenue to Sidney's Restaurant for lunch. They would stop at the door (of the restaurant) and we said we are going to go in here. And we would say, "Come in. Come on in." They were afraid. We made sure they ordered food. Sidney's sold pastrami and roast beef sandwiches. The food was excellent. I would make them all pay and leave a big tip. They would sit there shaking in their boots and were very grateful to us for protecting them. It was an eye-opener for a lot of them.

New Ark Prep (a residential center) was an accomplishment that was established by the New Ark School. One thing that helped us was the New Ark School was the first organization in Newark that was allowed to go into the youth (detention center) to counsel the juveniles that were there. We were the first organization that was allowed to take the kids and... They (the detention center) provided the students for the New Ark Prep - the Youth House in Newark. They came out of the system. They were a step away from going to jail. They were considered incorrigible. We had 20 boys and 20 girls. The colleges were open to receive students coming out of informal institutional environments and giving them an opportunity to go further in their education. This was based on the fact that the youth went to a community school, an alternative school and showed an aptitude to do better. They were encouraged to do better and raised their self-esteem to the point where they would go out and achieve what the system said they couldn't.

We had a traveling summer program and after school program. We were able to take the kids out of Newark to the beach and we put them on a ferry. We went to a farm in upstate New York and down to Wall Street. We took them to the Yoruba Village in South Carolina. We took them to DC. I've been told that, "There is nothing out here now like the Newark School. "I heard that from Zakariah when I was interviewed by him on his radio program. Cheyenne still calls me. He came to an event. He is an artist. He opened an art gallery downtown in Newark. I am in touch with him. Every now and then I'll run into somebody. I ran into one of the students named George over in Newark. I was at a food place and he was there. I was talking to the fellow that was with me. George said, "Bob, this is me, George, from the New Ark School." I remembered him and his friends coming to the School together. They were the second and third students at the School. He had a business selling perfumes and men's articles. His business was doing well. He said, "It's good to see you. Thanks for the experience." I'm grateful to know that people out there remember, and it's been 50 years.

7.   What do you know about COINTELPRO?

I remember them vaguely. There's a brother from a church in Newark that's constantly bringing into the conversation COINTELPRO. It's to the point where they can pinpoint you anywhere in this country. It's down to showing your house and the inside of your house using satellites.

We had (a few) problems with the FBI. There was a brother that was part of the Black Panther Party who came to the school. He didn't have a place to stay so I let him stay down in the basement to watch the building at night. The FBI showed up one Friday asking to speak to me. I wasn't there at the time. That Saturday, I was on my way to Bloomfield College to take some literature and let them know about the School. Rosetta went with me. She told me when went back to the School, "See that car across the street?" It had two White guys sitting in it. "Those are the guys who stopped by the School yesterday looking for you." I said, "Let me go see what they want." I went over and knocked on the window. I said, "My name is Bob Dixon. I understand you guys were looking for me yesterday." He said, "We can't talk to you right now. We're undercover." Two White guys sitting in the community undercover. How can two White guys sit in the community and not be found out? They came back Monday. They showed me a bunch of photographs and asked if I knew any of the people in the photos. I said, "No, I don't know any of these guys." Then they gave me a card and went away. They watched us for a while. After about a month, they went away.

We used to meet every morning at 6 o'clock. There were about eight brothers: Kenny, myself, a brother from NY... I can't think of the names of the other brothers. But we would all meet and plan a strategy to launch the New Ark Prep program. We met every morning at 6 o'clock. And, you know how the police felt about a bunch of Black guys coming together. They would be watching us each morning. When we came in, I would always greet them, "How are you folks doing today?" That was to let them know that we were aware they were on their job.

8. What is the current status of the New Ark School?

It closed in 1986.

9. How did the activities of the New Ark School affect colleges and universities on campuses and in the community?

We were on Rutgers Advisory Board for their new students program. We served a few years on their Board. We had our own radio program on two stations - one in Newark (WNJR) and another on W... We would air a program on Saturday for an hour in the White community and air another program on Saturday for 15 minutes on the Black community station. So, the School got a lot of exposure through the media during those first four years. We would talk about programs that were part of the New Ark experience. Lloyd Henry (Ciuzi), developed the children's program that we aired. It was like a skit. After he came on board, we aired a program every week. He also worked with us over the summer in 1972. He added another dimension to the program. Brother Wabembe did the painting in the hallway.

10. Did the New Ark School's activities affect the development of Black student organizations and, if so, how?

One brother who was a graduate of New Ark School was very political. He's the only one I actually remember. College students came in and volunteered through Essex County College when J. Harry Smith was the president of the college. He provided resources and had an open-door policy for the students at New Ark School. As many students as we sent with their GED completed, he would find space in the school for them to continue their education. J. Harry Smith was very important. He told me "Whatever you need, the college is available for you to just come and take advantage to the max of all of the resources we have." "We got a lot of (first generation) students enrolled into that program. Dr. Jackson, the Dean of African Studies at Essex County College, became a member of our Board.

11. Did New Ark School's activities affect the development of Black studies departments at higher education institutions and, if so, how?

I think New Ark had a lot to do with that because we talked about the Black Movement going forward and the significance of the Black leaders that were emerging through SNCC. We talked about H. Rap Brown. We formed a group called the New Ark Ensemble. We used to go around. Lawrence had written a lot of poems. We put his poems to music and we went out to sing revolution. We appeared on stage with Dick Gregory. We sang ...and he was a good speaker at that program. So the brother was what was happening. We used to go over to Keane College and rehearse. We had students from Keane College in our program.

12. Are you aware of any activities, programs, or benefits to higher education That resulted from the efforts of the New Ark School or other organizations in the Black Power Movement during the period from 1960 – 1980? Do they still exist today?

What developed from our involvement in Newark was a sense of togetherness of trying to achieve a common ground, a platform on which we could build more unity in the community. There were a lot of things happening that was so negative during the time of our struggle in Newark. We had to project a different kind of image. There was a lot of involvement all over Newark where different organizations were trying different kinds of services. We were able to bring them all together for the common good so whenever somebody Black had a need, they would call the New Ark School and we would direct them to resources. Talk about networking - we were on the ground floor.

Now we talked about the change in clothing and change in attitude. That's been lost. That whole concept has been lost over the years. There's no more zeal and there's no more fire. It's like the fire has not gone out because there's still something to remember; but, for the most part, the Black community has gone backwards instead of going forward. We see that our children are without jobs, the education system is failing, and the curriculum that is being taught is not directed toward raising the consciousness of all people, including White and Black. By and large, the press, same thing we talked about. You don't find the struggle of Black people in the history books. Malcolm X, Farrakhan, and, Muhammad Ali; from a political perspective, they looked at as being very negative. The President of the US (Obama) is a whipping boy for the White establishment and they publicly denounce him and make him look like a fool. The walls on my basement have the slave narratives and so the question is how far have we come since 1863 as a people?

13. Are there other persons you feel would provide helpful information on this topic?

Most of the people that came through with me have gone on.

14. I am collecting information on the sequence of events leading to the development of the first Black student union and the first Black studies department at San Francisco State University. Are there experiences at other colleges or universities that you feel would be informative?

Seton Hall. Aaron Campbell ran the Black Studies Program at Seton Hall. We were able to go on campus and we would have permission to give some direction and help to get our students into their program. He's still around.

Epilogue: All of the members of the cadre at the New Ark School are now retired. Akendole Dixon continues to live in New Jersey. He is a pastor. Kennedy Wilson lives in the state of Washington, Jeannette Robinson lives in Georgia, Juanita Wilson lives in New Jersey, John Wilson lives in New York, and I live in Maryland. We all agree that our sojourn at the New Ark School was one of the best times in our lives. Black people still need organizations like this more than ever.

THE BLACK YOUTH ORGANIZATION

Summary of the Organization

The Black Youth Organization was established by college students in 1967 as an outcome of a summer tutoring and mentoring project in Newark, New Jersey. College students provided tutorial services for high school students in reading and mathematics. The students who provided the services found their mentees in great need academically. This experience was the impetus for establishing an organization called the Black Youth Organization with a primary mission of developing and operating an independent Black school. In the fall of 1968, the group opened the school with an initial enrollment of 70 children. They named the school after Chad, a country in Africa, because Chad is physically located in the heart of Africa.

Representatives from the Black Youth Organization attended a Black Power Conference held in Newark, New Jersey in 1967. After listening to the discussion at the meeting, they determined that the activities planned would lead to the death, injury, and/or imprisonment of a number of activists. Based on this assessment, they decided to work underground as an organization and focus their time and energy strictly on education. The Black Youth Organization had two divisions: The Chad School and a shadow group called the House of August. The Black Youth Organization was a coed group; however, the House of August was an all-male group. The purposes of the House of August were to protect the faculty and students of the Chad School, and develop and implement economic projects to provide funding for the school. Because the House of August division functioned primarily underground, there is little information on this group in the literature. Consequently, most of the information provided in this summary is based on the experience of the researcher, who was a teacher and parent at the school, and the testimony from a former leader of the Black Youth Organization.

The Black Youth Organization had a president, secretary, and board of directors. Leon Moore was president of the Black Youth Organization and the administrator of Chad School. Economic projects that were developed and operated by the House of August included a music store located in Liberia, Africa; an African art store in the United States; a printing press called Pyramid Press; and, a construction company called the August Construction Company. The printing press produced African-centered curriculum materials for the school and provided printing services for the public. The construction company renovated houses.

The Chad School was an African-centered tuition-based school that offered classes for African American children from three to 12 years of age. To teach at the Chad School, applicants had to successfully complete a high school equivalency examination and attend rigorous teacher training classes conducted by Mr. Moore, who was considered the sage of the organization. Throughout its existence, the school was recognized for its educational excellence. Students that graduated from Chad went on to be top performers at area high schools and most attended and received degrees from higher education institutions. Because of Chad's reputation, over the years, annual enrollment grew to 400 students.

The Chad School, as an institution, embraced and reflected the philosophy of Black Power. All of its students, teachers, and board members were African American. To ensure non-interference from the government, the Black Youth Organization refused to pursue or accept government grants for the school. In the early 2000s, the organization decided to allow White people to join its board of directors. The new board of directors attempted to change the cultural nationalist focus of the school and its policy on accepting grants. Staff and volunteers who had worked at the school since its formation objected to the changes. They organized another board of directors that was comprised of African Americans who had a history of being active and supportive of the school. A power struggle ensued between the two boards. This struggle exacerbated operation and funding problems. The school closed in 2005.

Interview with Babatu Y. Olubayo, Former Assistant Principal of the Chad School

1. What are your memories of the Black Power Movement during 1960 to 1980?

My memories, went roughly back from 1960 to 1980, I thought it was a period for advancement, for a segment of our population, of our group of people. There were opportunities created in housing, education, employment opportunities, and, to a certain extent, there was minor upward mobility for people in terms of the job marketing opening up, the housing situation expanding to allow people more access, and educational opportunities to further skills in order to remain competitive in this American environment.

KCS: What role did the Black Power Movement play in this era of advancement that you describe?

Well, if you take the Black Panthers as an example. They were able to bring together two different segments of the Black community. The Panthers themselves, who were viewed basically as roughians, tough people, or ex-felons if not felons, were able to initiate a breakfast program centered around our kids that was basically administered and handled through churches and other pillars of the Black community. I think Reagan recognized that, and subsequently the free breakfast program was established. I think that the militancy also allowed for employment opportunities. The union movements were beginning to pick up a little steam around the country, particularly in terms of Black participation. There was a bit of Black involvement in the union leadership, which had not happened since the thirties, and that allowed people to, again, to have greater access to certain economic opportunities that didn't exist prior to the Black Power Movement.

It (the Black Power Movement) certainly impacted schools. There was an increase in terms of people's consciousness. They were more willing to stick together over issues and things. I also think it fundamentally assisted the general Civil Rights Movement itself because it drew attention, stark attention, to the conditions of Black people in this country.

2. Do you know about the Black Power Conference in 1967 that took place in Newark?

Yes.

KCS: Do you know any or could you share any information you have on what came out of that conference in terms of the goals and plans?

Well, generally, the goals and plans of the meeting were to participate on a grander scale in

American life, politically, socially, certainly financially. Different factions or groups had their own ideas and methodologies for achieving those ends.

KCS: So, there wasn't one set of goals or plans that came out of the meeting itself?

There were certain goals. As a participant, the organization that I represented and was aligned with at that point in time, decided to take a different path because the forces to be and the factions that were involved in meeting those objectives. We decided not participate in the general political, specifically the political, effort. Instead, we chose to concentrate on an area that we thought that we could be successful in, which was education.

3. *Could you tell me a little bit about your membership in the Black Youth Organization? What capacity or role you played, and for what period of time? If there were any other groups that you belonged to, please share that information too.*

During that period, I was involved in several different types of organizations. I was very supportive, active, and became a minor member of the Newark Black Panther Party primarily because they had aligned themselves with creating employment and economic opportunities for Black folks through a project we had with the Ford Motor Company in Mahwah New Jersey. We also were affiliated with the Dodge Revolutionary Unit Movement out of Detroit, because, at that point in time, the Black auto workers were attempting to not only get jobs, but also to be eligible or able to participate and or be involved in managerial positions. At that time, I was an active member of a group at Western Electric. We formed what was known as the Western Electric Revolutionary Union Movement (WER), which we aligned with the Ford Motor Company and others.

KCS: The union movement. Can I ask, before you go into details, did this group have anything to do with the Revolutionary Action Movement Group? Or was it a different organization?

The Revolutionary Action Movement? No, it was a different organization. I guess you could say it was part of the Ford and Dodge Revolutionary Union Movement. There were union movements where Black people just began to have a say, and if not a say, they formed their own unions to advocate for clearer positions or demands than what the conventional unions offered at that time. For example, with the auto workers (United Auto workers Union) were under serving their Black membership. Western Electric was represented by two mainstream unions, which was the International Brotherhood of Electrical Workers and CWA, the Workers of America. I can't think of what the C stands for right now, but anyway they certainly didn't represent Black people's interest, so we formed our own union.

KCS: What about the Black Youth Organization?

The Black Youth Organization was a response to social conditions in this country, which was quite simply that Black youth were being misguided, misdirected in a general sense and specific senses, based upon the resources that they had available to them in their neighborhoods and communities. They were certainly underserved by the school systems. The Black Youth Organization was a spontaneous reaction to fill a void. We came together initially as a recreational athletic organization that primarily taught self-defense to young Black people at the YMCA. At that time, there were widespread discussions taking place on Black anything because of the Black Power Movement. There was a lot of Black rhetoric, a lot of Black information, being circulated. What we discovered was that our kids, the students or children who were involved in our program, just simply couldn't read and write. So, we did some testing, devised programs, created a curriculum, and began an experimental program.

KCS: You call it an experimental program?

That was how we initially started. Once the experiment was over, which was six to eight weeks, we decided the results warranted us forming an organization and providing a school. In order to do that, we needed to have an organizational structure. And because we didn't have the proper structure, we decided to pursue forming a 501c (3) under the name known as the Black Youth Organization. It was designed to promote educational, religious, social and civic efforts within the federal 501c (3) regulations.

4. What global events influenced the formation and activities of the Black Youth Organization?

At that point in time, there was a series of things going on, both nationally and internationally or globally. In the United States, we, Black people were engaged in what was known as the Civil Rights struggle, where people were looking to the government to ensure that they had basic rights as citizens in this country, whether they were voting rights, housing rights, employment rights, access to whatever the country is supposed to provide, education, health, etc. There were health movements going on at that same time. We were active on a lot of different fronts.

At the same time, our brothers in Africa and throughout the Caribbean were involved in a certain level of liberation. Between the 1960s and the early '70s, 30 - 40 countries in Africa became free from colonial rule. That certainly impacted the Civil Rights struggles of Black people in the United States. Those global influences, particularly the emergence of independent African states, influenced us to feel that we needed to acquire skills that would allow us to assist in building nations both here and abroad.

5. What were the strengths of the Black Youth Organization, and what were its challenges?

The strength of the Black Youth Organization was that it became a self-motivating entity. There was a period of time when there was a lot of enthusiasm and hope for Black people in general, and we were working with young people. Young people were the target of a lot of the social and civil rights activities that took place during the sixties. It was certainly the student movement that was in the forefront of the civil rights organizations, and it was also young people who were involved in the early expressions of many Black Power organizations. All of these grew out of student movements. It was students that had the intellectual capacity to analyze their situations and choose particular solutions for solving what they thought were pressing problems. The Black Youth Organization felt the same way, because of the various levels of control in this society. One of the most effective ways that we could impact our people would be to attempt to create structures that would impact the mind, impact how we thought, what we were taught, impact our thinking, and allow us to embrace an ideology. Simply put, our ideology was a very simple one. *We are an African people.* As an African people, we felt that it was our obligation to acquire the skills necessary to have an attitude and skills that would allow us to, again, develop African nations, no matter where they were, and our general Black communities.

KCS: When the Black Youth Organization was developing, where were the students? You all were students, right?

Yes.

KCS: Where did they come from?

They came from all over.

KCS: I mean, how did you come together?

The initial group was a small group at the YMCA in Newark, New Jersey. Once we put together that first group, and they were all local students, we began to interact with other Black youth groups around the country, because at that time there were a number of Black student organizations that were emerging on various college campuses. Specifically, there were actually two tracks. There was Black student organizations that existed on traditional American college campuses, basically White college campuses, and then there was the movement that expanded from Black organizations to Black student organizations, particularly in communities that were involved in historically Black colleges. For example, all of the local people (students) came from Howard University. They also came from Orangeburg State University and traditional Black colleges. Students joined these organizations to assist with civil rights and voting legislation.

6. *What were the accomplishments of the Black Youth Organization?*

Primarily our main effort was to establish and operate a school. We felt that we could effectively develop the minds of our young by having our own school, with minimal interaction with the larger society or the greater White educational institutions. We felt, using critical systems analysis, that they didn't serve our needs. We looked at models from the past. We went back in history as far as we could and examined all great schools of learning. We examined the attitudes of people who were enlisted and converted into supporting causes. At one point in time, for example, in the United States, there might have been almost a hundred medical schools that served Black people, particularly after reconstruction. But, there was an assault on Black education, just like what occurred with the Black codes during the reconstruction period. The greater population just chose to oppress people. Everyone knows the story of Virginia. I think it was Prince Edwards County that, rather than integrate its schools back in the fifties; chose just to shut down the public school system. We decided that one of the best and most effective ways for us to improve the condition of our people and children in general was to run our own schools. By that, we designed our own curriculum. We did not use White models. We just used information, and we chose four disciplines - mathematics, science, history, and language arts - to be the avenues for us to essentially excel.

7. What do you know about COINTELPRO relative to the Black Youth Organization?

Many organizations during the sixties were under the scrutiny of COINTELPRO. COINTEL was primarily the people who persecuted George Jackson, the Panthers, and the US Organization in California. There was not a single organization that COINTEL did not at least attempt to infiltrate or monitor. The Black Youth Organization was certainly one of them during those days and times, because we had relationships with other schools. There was a high period for what we liked to call African-centered educational institutions during the sixties, and they were scattered around the country. Quite naturally, we came under the investigative eye of COINTELPRO. COINTELPRO was an effort of the government that primarily attempted to destroy Black unity and Black movement towards whatever their purpose may have been, whether it was healthcare, education, etc. Their objective was to simply disintegrate, to destroy, any Black organization, and they certainly attempted to destroy the Black Youth Organization. We had instances of people who were what we used to call provocateurs back in the day. We had provocateurs just about on every level of community engagement.

As a member of the Black Youth Organization, for example, not only were my personal efforts centered on education, but at the same time, I was also concerned about urban renewal in the city of Newark. If I wasn't involved with the Black Youth Organization, I might have been involved in housing efforts. The same disruptive patterns would occur, no matter what effort the community was engaged in. It was the FBI, COINTELPRO.

KCS: Let's deal with this in separate streams.

Okay.

8. I know the school is closed now. What is the current status of the Black Youth Organization?

In 2013?

KCS: Yes.

In 2013, the original Black Youth Organization had dissolved. The Black Youth Organization dissolved years ago. I think there is an offshoot, because the Black Youth Organization started the school, which was known as the Chad School, which was really one of the most successful divisions (of the organization). With the demise of the Chad School, a foundation was formed. Its sole purpose is to, I guess, offer scholarship opportunities to Black youth or assistance in some sort of way. Maybe they do mentoring. I'm not sure of that. I know that the original organization died some time ago.

KCS: The organization died before the school?

Absolutely.

KCS: When did the organization die?

I couldn't tell you when the organization died. The organization itself had a series of rules and regulations. One of them was a posture that it would not allow the government or any foundations to have anything to do with Chad School's operation. So, they did not receive funding from them. It was the premise that no one could tell the organization what to do with its resources, with its funding. I think that once the organization decided to accept funding from government sources, they lost their identity. They lost their direction, and subsequently the demise began.

KCS: That was the Chad School?

That was the Chad School, the School being a division of the Black Youth Organization. I don't know the legality of that. I know that the Black Youth Organization probably exists on paper as an entity, but as a functioning organization, as far as being involved in the community, I don't think so.

KCS: Do you think that BYO's demise was tied to some event, like Leon Moore moving South because of illness?

No, I think primarily what occurred was the Black Youth Organization chose certain directions when we were involved in Africa. We saw Africa as being a critical point for the organization. We felt that we needed to develop businesses and have a presence in Africa. We needed to migrate back home.

Several events took place on the continent. Our base was in Liberia. I think that the assassination of Steve Talbot had a lot to do with us. The organization left Liberia and I left the organization at that point in time. I left prior to that, maybe not too long before that, but right about the time that Liberia began to disintegrate because of Sergeant …coming into power, I think that set the organization itself into disarray. A lot of the people who were members of the original Black Youth Organization decided to move on and it just disintegrated. It never replaced itself.

9. *How did the activities of the Black Youth Organization affect colleges and universities on campuses and in the community?*

Because of our successes locally, we got a lot of exposure, particularly in academic circles. We were on many, many radio programs and television programs. In fact, I remember one time we did a program in New York for one of the local Black programs and we received letters and phone calls from people all around the country that wanted to come and work with the Chad School. People from traditional Black universities, or people just out in the community felt that they wanted to contribute.

KCS: Did this include students and professors?

Absolutely.

KCS: From colleges and universities?

Yes, we had people who were highly skilled. We started our own teacher-training program of course. We took both people who had attitude and skills. The primary thing with us was attitude. If you had the proper attitude, you could be taught the skills. You could be given a body of information and taught to pass that on to your students. That's what we did. We also had people there who had degrees in the sciences, in math, or whatever. At one point, it was about fifty-fifty. We had people who had a tremendous number of skills that were easily transferable.

10. Did your organization's activities affect the development of the Black student organizations on campuses, and if so how?

We went on the lecture circuit. We interacted with Black student organizations and we spoke about our cause. We spoke about our methodology and our goals and objectives. That to a degree may have impacted students. Because we were part of a larger organization, which was the Federation of Pan African Educational Institutions, and they in turn had some impact on Black students in their local communities. To a degree, which I can't measure, but I can say that we were influential with people who really wanted to use the tools of education as a weapon. There were two organizations. There was also the Council of Independent Black Institutions, CIBI. CIBI was the second one and the Federation of Pan African Educational Institutions was the first group of alternative educational systems across the country. We went from California to Florida to Boston. There were various degrees of success and independence within the member institutions.

KCS: Was this only for people who were going to be teachers in the independent Black schools, or could anyone attend?

These organizations promoted developing strategies for the survival of the independent educational institutions and students were encouraged to participate, to volunteer, to do whatever, to make whatever contribution they felt would assist with their longevity, with their existence.

11. Did the organization's activities affect the development of any Black studies departments at higher education institutions? If they did, how?

I can't quantitatively or qualitatively answer that question. We chose to be an organization that tended to build a structure from within, and part of that was because of COINTELPRO. Because we knew that destructive forces were attempting to alter whatever successes we could manufacture ourselves, we tended to build internally. We recruited students from wherever they chose to come, whether it was Cornell or other schools. We had students come from Cornell. In fact, they were the guys that took over Cornell University. It was an armed takeover.

KCS: Was that Cornel West and his group?

Yes, a couple of them became members of the Black Youth Organization, at least the school and did quite well for a while.

12. Are you aware of any activities, programs, or benefits that higher education institutions experienced on campuses resulting from the efforts of either the Black Youth Organization or other organizations in the Black Power Movement during that period, 1960 to 1980?

I would say that the Black Youth Organization's role was miniscule compared to the role of organizations like SNCC and the Panthers. They had a tremendous impact on Black student organizations, particularly Black student organizations that were in White institutions. Blacks were beginning to have access to the Rutgers of the world, the Ohio States, and the UCLA's. So, these organizations were able to take advantage of the degree of intellectual curiosity and inquisitiveness at that time. A lot of young people became actively involved in other aspects of the struggle and they used their thirst for knowledge and information. They used the energy that grew out of the Civil Rights Movement to press for Black demands, not only on the campus, but in their respective communities.

KCS: Do any of these organizations exist today?

No, because I think that the organizations became co-opted.

KCS: All of them?

I wouldn't say all of them. I would say a great deal of them, because they tended to, at least in my opinion, to have lost their direction. For example, during that same sixties period, there was tremendous community unity expressed in various ways, particularly in urban centers and rural areas in this country. In addition to COINTELPRO, there were other ways that Black efforts were undermined. For example, for people who were in the forefront of community involvement or Black liberation, organizations were formed to co-op Black efforts, like the Black Affairs Council from Philadelphia, which became a funding conduit or organization that selected people in the Black community who would receive funding for whatever purposes. If you had a project centered on community health, then that particular group was the group that decided who would get the money. It took the leadership out of the community and put the leadership on those boards. Subsequently, those boards then decided who they would empower in the Black communities. The Episcopal Church did the same thing. It became a question of the steam actually being taken out of the sails of the Black community, and low and behold the next thing you know, you had some serious integration.

13. Are there any people that you feel would provide some really helpful information to me on this topic? Anybody you'd recommend?

Right here in this town (Washington, DC), I would suggest Tom Porter. I also suggest Tony Rather. Dr. Jared is at Morgan State University and he has a program called Dixon Bell. They mix music that I like. They can be contacted either at Morgan State or WPFW. They can give you insights into tremendous resources and identify people who are still active.

14. I'm collecting information on the sequence of events leading to the development of the first Black student union and the first Black studies department at San Francisco State University. Are there experiences that you know of at other colleges and universities that you feel would also be informative?

When you talk about San Francisco State, the first person that I think of is Danny Glover, who was instrumental in things like that. He has been consistent throughout his whole life. I think other people who came out of that experience are people like Sonya Sanchez and Nikki Giovanni because they were all part of Rutgers in New Jersey.

I wouldn't know where to begin to find these folks. For example, at Rutgers, there was a guy named Sam Sanderson if I'm not mistaken. He was more involved with the students, the Black student movement there. There are just so many people because that was a very rich period, but I can't remember because of my own posture at that point in time.

Epilogue: I had the honor of working at the Chad School for one year as a teacher of three-year-old children. My daughter attended the school for two years. It was an exhilarating experience. Staff there was truly a family. It was a safe zone and an enriching experience for the students. Knowledge was power. The only reason I left was recruitment to work at the New Ark School. The closing of the school is truly a significant loss for the children and families of northern New Jersey.

THE NATIONAL ASSOCIATION OF BLACK SOCIAL WORKERS (NABSW)

Summary of the Organization

The National Association for Black Social Workers (NABSW) is a membership association for professional and lay social workers who are devoted to the upliftment of African Americans. It is an African-centered cultural nationalist organization that was created in 1966 by the late Cenie Jomo Williams and a small group of social workers from New York after they severed ties with the Council on Social Work Education in protest of a perceived failure of the organization to address the unique concerns of African Americans. Currently, the National Association for Black Social Workers has 49 regular and 25 student chapters across the country. The 25 student chapters are located on the campuses of higher education institutions at schools of social work. The association provides education and training for social workers; participates in political discourses on issues that affect African Americans; and, provides education, training, mentoring, and scholarships for social work students.

The National Association for Black Social Workers' national office is located in Washington, DC. It is managed by an eight-member executive committee of elected officials who are supported by a staff of four people. It has a steering committee that includes the executive committee, committee chairs, and chapter representatives. Many of the members of the steering committee are professors at higher education institutions. The leader interviewed told this researcher, "The Steering Committee runs the Organization."

The National Association for Black Social Workers has 15 committees and four task forces. Major program activities include an African-centered Social Work Academy and a Sankofa Mentoring Project. Past presidents of the association belong to a council of sages that advises the sitting president. The organization uses African-centered ceremonies, rituals, and symbols extensively. Examples are conducting spiritual awakenings, pouring libations to honor the ancestors – the deceased founder, past presidents, family members, and s/heroes, reading a pledge at the beginning of each general session, reciting an oath, singing the Black National Anthem, holding processionals of dignitaries preceding major ceremonies such as the Opening Session and Harambee (closing) Ceremony.

The functions of the presidency include supervising staff at the national office, making decisions on national policy matters, appointing committee chairs, serving as the national spokesperson, chairing the executive committee, and serving as the organization's spiritual leader. The most important functions of the presidency are to strengthen the organization, maintain unity, and develop innovative programs. The organization's current stated priorities include documenting the history and programs of the association by overseeing the writing of two books - one on the history of the organization and past presidents; and, another which describes spiritual awakenings; fostering intergenerational pairing; and, raising the public profile of the association by strengthening media relations, increasing public policy activities, and increasing membership.

Conflict resolution, fund development, and engaging young professionals are the major challenges of the organization. Because of the voluntary nature of the organization's leadership and the strong passions connected to the organization's mission, often there are divergent views on methods for accomplishing objectives. To maintain its independence, early in its existence, the leadership of the National Association for Black Social Workers decided not to pursue or receive government grants. Because of this decision, fund development has continued to present major challenges. Currently, the major sources of the association's revenues are membership dues, workplace giving, and conference registration fees.

A number of members of the association's steering committee are pioneers who have served in various leadership positions of the organization for many years. The organization's surviving founding members are still active in the Association. Because the leaders of the association are aging out, the current president views the preparation of new leadership as critical for the organization's continuity and longevity (National Association for Black Social Workers Program, 2007).

Interview with William Merritt, former President of the NABSW

1. What are your memories of the Black Power Movement during this period?

Well, of course, my memories go back to the Civil Rights Movement – the sit-ins, especially the lunch counter sit-ins while I was in college, and of course, the bus rides and the different marches that were taking place prior to the Black Power Movement or as it evolved. And then the emergence of other organizations like SNCC. And, the debates and the differences of opinions in terms of the Black Power concepts v the civil rights non-violent movement and the various things that emerged out of the Black Power Movement, such as the different ways to look at things such as "I'm Black and I'm Proud," and the switch from nonviolence to, I wouldn't necessarily call it violence but the confrontation aspect of the Black Power Movement. Also, the various different groups that emerged like the Black Panthers and the US Organization, which added on to the civil rights groups.

2. Please share any information you have on the goals and plans emanating from Black Power conference of 1967 that took place in Newark, New Jersey. Did you attend that meeting?

No, I don't think I attended the meeting. Would you repeat the first part of the question? (Question repeated) I remember there was a meeting. I don't recall attending. I know I was very much involved at that time but in Plainfield, NJ - in a community action program. I had not yet been introduced to NABSW at that point. In fact, I was in graduate school at Rutgers during that period. So I sort of lost contact with a lot of what was going on except while I was in graduate school, I was part of civil disobedience - the community action organization in Plainfield. I was chair of the West End community action organization.

3. Were you active with any organizations and, if so, what organization(s), in what capacity, and for what period of time?

In 1967, when I was in graduate school. I had been working for the State Bureau of Youth Services. I went to graduate school and felt the need to stay involved in the community so I joined the community action program. In 1970 after graduate school, a friend and a colleague, someone who worked with me at the bureau of children's services, told me about Cenie Williams. Cenie wanted to meet with me and asked if I would organize a group of Black social workers to meet with him, which we did. That was when I was introduced to the NABSW and was asked to organize a chapter in New Jersey, which I did in 1971.

In 1969, I attended a Council on Social Work Education conference. I had just graduated from graduate school. At that time, I was introduced to the New York Black social workers. They were just organizing the national group. They took over the stage at that conference and they formed a coalition with the welfare rights people. They gathered a whole bunch of us to support taking over the stage. Actually, it was Black social workers from all over the country, but it was primarily led by the New York Black social workers and social workers that I knew. What can I tell you, you needed to be at this meeting. Jesse Jackson, I think, was one of the speakers. There were speakers and they went up on the stage and took the microphone to tell the people who were at that conference that they needed to get some priority as to what was happening in the Black community. They wanted everyone to donate to the welfare rights organization so they stationed people at every door with a welfare rights mother and blocked the doors until people contributed so they could leave. They made a statement of demands to the Council of Social Work Education saying that they needed to give some focus to the people that they were supposed to be serving. During that period, they were organizing. I didn't really get involved with them until 1971.

They were a fairly large group and that was the period when they really began to grow. It was Cenie's first term of office as president. A few of us from New Jersey went to a conference from NJ. It was held at Fisk University. I think it was on their campus. I was amazed to see all these Black people and the workshops that they gave. I went to a workshop on nation building that was conducted by xxxx, who is very much still involved, and another professor, Bill, who is now dead. The interesting thing about it was I had heard everyone using the term, "nation building", and I didn't know what that meant. I don't think anybody else did either. I found out later that it had been a concept discussed by Black social workers before. I went to this workshop and there were people there from all kinds of political ideologies. There were Muslims, the US people, the Panthers, and some civil rights organizations. Black social workers from all kinds of persuasions came. They were trying to explain their plan for nation building and defining it. Different people in the group became critical and everybody said well I got the plan and they went off and developed their plan. In the end, the leaders of the workshop said that nation building is an idea of people with different backgrounds and different interests being able to work together toward a common goal of creating a Black nation within a nation in nation building time. At the conference, a resolution was passed by the steering committee to create a committee called nation building and the next conference was entitled Nation Building.

KCS: The founders always talk about when they walked out. When they walked out, was it at the meeting of the NASW?

I think it was NASW. At that time, there were two organizations, the NASW and the Council of Social Work Education, which were not together. They later merged. In fact, I don't think there was a NASW at that time. There was another name and when the two organizations merged, they became the NASW.

My wife tells me that I get times and dates mixed up. I can't even tell you when I graduated from school. I can't tell if I graduated in 1965 or 1967 because I was so upset with Rutgers. I thought it was the most racist experience I ever had. When I got my degree, I put it in a drawer. At the school, there were five full time African American students among 104 students.

KCS: Were you one of the people who went to school because of the Higher Education Act?

Yes. The money came from my job because I was working for the State at the time. They gave out a stipend and tuition.

KCS: Are you a first generation student?

Yes.

4. *What global events influenced the formation and activities of your organization?*

I think part of it was there were people working for social welfare organizations and I think most people were very dissatisfied with the policies and the structure or, at least, the impact of those organizations on Black people. They really weren't serving the best interest of Black families. For me, learning about Black social work was significant. And, finally, I had a place to go to express how I felt, number one and number two, having a forum to join with other people. For most people, we had a place to be independent and, as a group, to work toward the betterment of the Black community. We could learn, there were workshops, and there were ways of learning. But, I think, even without the conference, we were organized as a group to serve Black people. We had meetings to discuss the issues around serving the Black community. I think of the impact of racism and the violence against Black people, that we had to come together. I think all those things impacted. I remember the Kawaida incident.

KCS: The Kawaida Towers in Newark?

Yes, the Kawaida Towers. In Newark, Plainfield, and Patterson there was civil disobedience, revolution, and riots. There was just so much going on at that time. Through community action organizations, the war on poverty empowered us in terms of how government works and we learned more about what we could do. Some of us became Black politicians and ran for office. Some of us did voter registration.

5. *What were the strengths and challenges of the organization?*

I think the strength of Black social workers is the fact that Black people could come together to share experiences, to share information, and to teach one another. I think that most people who participated became better or more skilled at their work. They were more informed. They became more global. They were culturally strengthened. I think that (culture) is one of the greatest strengths, although I get sick of all of the ceremonies. I think the organization is very much respected by other organizations that come into contact with it. Many speakers leave with more than they brought to the organization. I think it has had a tremendous impact on child welfare – on policy, on national policy on families, on kinship care, and that kind of stuff. It came from us, the Black social workers. The fight against trans-racial adoptions changed policies. I guess the next thing I'm going to say is contradictory in a way. On one hand, we have a committee or task force for everything and, on one hand, it's a weakness. It provides a forum for people with a variety of interests to express themselves.

One of the challenges (and I think it has always been a challenge in some way) is remaining constant in terms of our need to remain African-centered. Maybe that's not the way because everybody in the organization does not believe in Afrocentricity, but they do believe we need to be Black-focused and our membership should be Black. Some people think it's a challenge now, but some of us older members think it has always been a challenge. You will always have people who think that the world has changed and there is no need to be a Black only organization. From my point of view if you're not Black, you don't need a Black organization. You might as well join a multi-cultural organization. A challenge is recruiting students, although it has been impressive this year and we see a need to maintain this kind of interest. Hopefully, it's building a bridge between the young and old. I think the younger people now do see a need to keep the older people around. With this organization, it has been difficult because we were all young when we started. Most of the older generation was in leadership positions when we were young so we did not have that problem. We were young leaders who never went away. Often when considering a young person for a leadership role, older members would say, "Oh no, he's not ready yet," but we weren't ready either.

6. *You talked child welfare and trans-racial adoptions. What are some of your other accomplishments?*

I think the international conferences have a tremendous impact both for the people who participated in them and the host country. Members increased their knowledge; and, their experience going to other countries where people of African descent were in large numbers was invaluable. Some people would never have gone to Africa if we did not have those international conferences; and, would not have experienced not just going to Africa but would not have intermingled with people from other countries because of the kinds of tours and workshops they had that included African people. Over 1,000 people, and probably more than that, have had that experience of going to different African countries, Brazil, and the Caribbean. It's been enriching. I think the accomplishment of having a conference for 43 years is a tremendous accomplishment. We have an office, own a building, as small as it may be, but it is a great accomplishment. And, we accomplished it without having staff. I think an accomplishment is volunteerism. You don't have that kind of volunteerism in organizations such as this. We have been able to sustain ourselves because of people volunteering to be volunteer coordinators and to chair all these different meetings. I think it has not focused enough on some issues. The world is different and at that time racism was in your face.

KCS: What about not being government funding?

That is a tremendous accomplishment. We have accomplished being an independent self-determining organization by not accepting government grants or funding from traditional foundations. We will accept funding from Black groups but not predominantly White groups.

7. What do you know about COINTELPRO?

Oh, the FBI. We always suspected that we were infiltrated. There were even people that we thought might have been (agents). You know, for Black people, you always have to be, it's healthy to be paranoid, so we were paranoid about just about everything and everybody. And, of course, we had different kinds of people in the organization. Sometimes we had people who were ex-military. And, people often wondered about that. We never found conclusively that we were being observed. Today, for the first time, xxx informed me that at the conference in Los Angeles, two men, two Black men, approached him and showed him their FBI identification and told him that they had been sent by the FBI to observe us because of our exclusionary policy. They thought that we were doing something subversive. They said that they were going back and report that we were not doing anything subversive. But, we were talking mucho stuff (laughs). And, then they left.

8. What is the current status of the organization?

The organization has had some financial challenges, like every Black organization but, from my perspective, we're in better shape than most because we never did take any grants. Any organization that took grants, that depended on grants, is suffering. While we (NABSW) have problems, I don't think they're killer kinds of problems. I think that we are in a transitional stage. Today we were having a meeting on our exclusionary policies. Oh, I shouldn't say exclusionary - inclusiveness. My feeling, and I think most of us in there feel, there has always been Black people who have disagreed with it. Some come and some don't. Some people have a feeling that in this changing world of multiculturalism, we are going to lose people. The consensus of the founders and ex- presidents is that is how it's always been. Those that don't want to participate won't. Those that do, will. And we'll find people. My feelings are that as long as Black people are discriminated against and experience this kind of negative (treatment), we need Black organizations that will focus on Black people.

9. How did the activities of your organization affect colleges and universities on campuses and in the community?

We have (college) student chapters all over the place. Internationally, we have and have had chapters. We have one in South Africa. Nova Scotia, their students, is back here again this year. We have chapters in the Caribbean. Yes, we have chapters and I think they have influenced the increased number of Black faculty that are on college campuses. Now, I don't know about social work, but I know Black Studies is starting to lose Black faculty. Colleges no longer feel they need to have these Black programs. Part of our demand is more Black faculty. Now there are Black deans all over the place. That was the result of the Black social workers. There's mentoring going on, and, it always has been, through student affairs. That was created I think around YY's term of office. Our organization was actually started by a lot of MSWs.

The other thing...I don't know if it fits in this question, but there always has been a division on whether our focus should be on education or community activism v. being a professional organization. In the beginning, the original people wanted to focus on being a professional, an alternate professional organization. But Cenie, his focus and influence, was being an activist organization that works in the community. Cenie said we should be getting educated, but educated to do things in the community. Some people felt we should just focus on being an organization that develops the profession. We're still struggling with it but I think we are trying now. Like today, we heard they're giving awards to Black faculty and things like that. They're trying. I think there's a recognition now that we've (NABSW) lost a lot of Black faculty, although there's always been some Black faculty involved. There was a period when people would become faculty and we didn't see them anymore. There has always been a solid base of Black faculty that has been a part (of NABSW) but now most are not. There had been much more tension than there is now. Now there's much more encouragement for those faculty people to come back...for the educators to come back. We just started having a community service day a few years ago. Now we've always has had it internationally. We wanted to make sure when we visit, we took something there and left something behind. I think we've always done that. When xxx was president, I remember we went to the Caribbean. I wasn't there, but the service people at the hotel were on strike so NABSW members would leave the conference every day and go on the picket line with them. In St Louis, when the conference was there, we joined with the St. Louis chapter and took thousands of people out on the streets to protest the treatment of Black folks at the hospitals there. Everywhere we have gone, we have tried to do something in the community. Now we focus more on doing some kind of project in the community, like raising money and things like that. In the past, it was more things around activism in the community - boycotts, supporting community activism. Now it's more raising funds or providing some kind of social service. Before, we were more about activism.

10. Did your organization's activities affect the development of Black student organizations and, if so, how?

We talked about the student chapters: It was a debate at one time what the role of the student chapters would be politically. We decided that they would have the same privileges as other chapters, like voting and things like that. We decided it was important for them to be represented on our Executive Board and they should elect their person to participate on the Executive Committee. We felt very strongly that the organization needed to support them and we appointed a student advisor to work with them.

Other groups on campus are affected by the presence of student chapters. When you go on campus, you can see other groups. I know the Black Studies departments have been organizing students. I think the Black social workers have been a model for other groups – that you can have a Black organization and you don't have to compromise. Between 1967 and 1970, there were many new emerging Black organizations – Black psychologists, Black accountants, Black MBAs, Black everything...everybody. They determined that integration wasn't working.

11. Did your organization's activities affect the development of Black studies departments at higher education institutions and, if so, how?

I'm not sure about that. They all formed at the same time.

12. *Are you aware of any activities, programs, or benefits to higher education resulting from the efforts of your organization or other organizations in the Black Power Movement during the period from 1960 – 1980? Do they still exist today?*

We just spoke about Black studies. Black social workers hired faculty. They also encouraged people to get their MSW and doctorate, and encouraged people to write.

13. *Are there other persons you feel would provide helpful information on this topic?*

(Already answered)

14. *I am collecting information on the sequence of events leading to the development of the first Black student union and the first Black Studies department at San Francisco State University. Are there experiences at other college or universities that you feel would be informative?*

You may want to talk to my wife, XXX. She used to be the head of the National XXX.

ROOTS ACTIVITY LEARNING CENTER (RALC)

Summary of the Organization

ROOTS Activity Learning Center was founded by Dr. Bernida Thompson in October 1977 as an outcome of her experiences while she was a student at Central State University (then College), a historically Black higher education institution. The groundwork for the development of the school began there. The school opened as an infant care and early childhood learning center that served infants and children from six months to kindergarten. Since 1977, classes at the school expanded to serve children from birth through eighth grade. The structure of the school, which is tuition-based, is an infant center, a preschool, a primary school, and a middle school. Classes are multi-level so each student has the same teacher for three years and older students can mentor younger students. The teaching staff is African Americans who have either a degree or, minimally, certification. All staff receives year-round training, which becomes more intensive during the summer months.

The school curriculum is rigorous and African-centered. Students are taught Kiswahili and the center's philosophy embraces the principles of the Nguzo Saba, the African value system that promulgates the seven principles of umoja (unity), kugichagulia (self-determination), ujima (collective work and responsibility), ujamaa (cooperative economics), nia (purpose), kuumba (creativity), and imani (faith). The stated mission of the ROOTS Activity Learning Center is to promote and secure the connection of Mother Africa within its children; prepare students to break the chains of psychological conditioning that attempt to keep them powerless in all phases of society; provide students with a strong African-centered learning environment; guide students towards academic excellence, exemplary character, and social responsibility; and, encourage success leading to self-reliance and economic, social, and political contributions to society (ROOT Activity Learning Center.org., 2013).

Standardized tests, which are administered at the beginning and the end of each school year, are used as tools to gauge where students are academically, facilitate the development of individual educational plans, and evaluate the progress made during the school year. During the summer months, the school operates a summer day camp. New students who participate in the camp are given priority for enrollment in the school in the fall. The school operates a rites of passage program for students in its middle school called the Young Lions and Black Madonnas. Most of the school's graduates enroll in local parochial high schools. Since its establishment, the school has been recognized for its educational excellence. Several of its students have had perfect SAT scores. In 1999, the administrator opened a public charter school using the same curriculum (ROOTS Activity Learning Center, 2013). The school continues to serve students in the Washington DC metropolitan area.

Interview with Founder and Principal, Dr. Bernida Thompson

1. What are your memories of the Black Power Movement during this period?

I have a lot of fond memories about the Black Power Movement and that period. I graduated from high school in 1964 and graduated from college in 1968. In between that period of time, I went to a historical Black School to get my degree, Central State University (CSU) that my granddaughter now goes to. She'll be a sophomore this coming school year. At CSU I met a lot of people that were active in the Black Power Movement. We had study groups. We took over the campus to make sure they put Black studies in our curriculum. I just met a lot of people doing a lot of things, watching the demonstrations and marches on TV, talking and having brainstorming sessions, and so on. After I graduated, I started teaching and doing things with students in my school (public and Catholic schools between 1968 and 1976) for Black History Month. Then throughout the year I included a lot of Black history information in my lessons. In 1977, I opened the ALC. All of the things that I had learned were enveloped in the curriculum at the ALC. We started with an infant center (6 weeks old) and went to kindergarten. That was basically because I had an infant and a kindergartener. So, I really opened the school for me to teach my children and everybody else who wanted to be a part of what I was doing could come. As my daughter grew older, I added a grade a year up to 8th grade. It's still going on 36 years later, the ALC and the infant center.

2. *Please share any information you have on the goals and plans emanating from Black Power Conference of 1967 that took place in Newark, New Jersey.*

No, I didn't attend. I was in Ohio in school. I don't know anything by name but there were so many marches, conferences, study groups, meetings going on, so I didn't memorize every single one.

3. *Were you active with any organizations and, if so, what organization(s), in what capacity, and for what period of time?*

The college campus organizations, which included the Black history organizations and the Black studies organizations. The Black Student Union started in 1967. Before then, there were Black history study groups. There were groups where we would study on our own. We were called the Nkrumahs (for Kwame Nkrumah). That's the group I was in. We studied all of his works and we studied Karl Marx's works. So, that was what I was involved in. I was there at the beginning of their formation. The reason we were forming them was to educate ourselves so that we could educate our children. We were going to open up freedom schools. By the time we graduated, it ended up just being me but anyway, that was the point. We were studying to get all of the information we could; and, we were going to open a school that would give all of the information to children - the next generation. My major was elementary education. I went to school with the intent of teaching and eventually opening a school but the philosophical part, I didn't have that until I went to CSU.

During that time, the Small Business Administration (SBA) had an arm called Small Black Business Administration. And, the money was loaned. You could go to a lot of classes on how to open your business. You could get a wealth of information. They were trying. At that time, it was all about trying to open Black businesses. That was the era. So, I took advantage of all those classes that the SBA offered to see how to go about doing it. They would help you with your proposals to the banks; and, just help you all along on all of the things you have to do. I had already saved enough money to be my seed money but I had to borrow around $50,000 at that time. So, I was able to do it through Industrial Bank. Industrial Bank was about trying to help Black people with mortgages and how to open their own businesses. So, by 1976, the time was ripe. Between 1975 and 1976, I prepared and learned how to open the business. I already had the curriculum because I had attended study groups, taught in DC, and did all of the little things to put it together. Curriculum-wise I was ready but business-wise, I needed 1975 and 1976 to find out about licensing, get to know these people, get to know the places for licensing, get to know the loan people at the Industrial Bank, and get to know the SBA Black business group. I had to put all the paperwork together and have it go through or not go through, revise, and resubmit. The process and renovation of the building took a couple of years. In October 1977, I was able to open. Those couple of years, I had to take care of everything and I was able to open in October 1977. There was just me. There was supposed to be a group of us. Back in college, we were all gung-ho but by the time you got down to the nuts and bolts, I looked around and it was just me.

4. *What global events influenced the formation and activities of your organization?*

Apartheid was the big thing. We were active with the organizations here in DC (Trans-Africa) to end Apartheid. The children learned all about that and they went to different places to do a "Jump Rope against Apartheid" event and different activities that were going on to end Apartheid. Our goals were to have people take notice of South Africa and Apartheid.

5. *What were the strengths and challenges of the organization?*

Strengths are that ALC is African-centered with a strong curriculum. It has been around for 36 years and has a wealth of alumni that are doing exceptionally well in the community. They are leaders in the Black community. They know who they are. They show who they are. They know where they are and what they must do to liberate our people. They're leading their peers, organizations, and companies in that vein. I have no idea how many have graduated - a lot. I keep up with them, though, with my directory of graduates - where they are and what they are doing.

The challenges are, it's always challenging, for a group of people who are not wealthy people to have to pay tuition to go to school. But, back in the day, in the late 1970s, 1980s, and even the 1990s, parents would sacrifice. They seriously wanted their children to have the kind of education that was not the "mis-education of the Negro." They were serious. Nowadays in the 2012-13 era, there's a lot of smoke in the atmosphere that confuses new Black parents and makes them think that they have a choice that's free. I'm talking about the public charter school movement.

And, although we opened a public charter school, we opened the school with the understanding that if the government is going to fund schools, they just as well can fund an African-centered school too. But, that divided all of the people that were running freedom schools. We had a strong united Black school conglomerate of independent Black schools –the Council of Independent Black Institutions (CIBI). We supported each other financially and in every way. We had science fairs. We had conferences. We took our children to the Black science fairs and conferences and it was really a strong thing. But, once the public charter schools came into existence, it broke it up and even though they exist, you don't hear much about anything. What happened was about half of us agreed with my philosophy - that having a public charter school was part of our reparations. We were going to submit a proposal and they were going to fund our children too. We were going to do our African-centered stuff. That was half of us and the other half said, "You're sellouts. You're taking the White man's money. You can no longer be in CIBI." They refused to let us be a part of it, a lot of angry exchanges occurred, and people's feelings got hurt. It was just horrible. Anyway, you're talking about challenges. There you go. It still has not been resolved. It broke up CIBI.

All of my children are Black and they are taught by Black people, but I didn't have any problems because I made a point of saying that the philosophy will be an African worldview. There is only one race of people in the world and they are homo-sapien sapiens. They originated in African when the landmasses were together. Over time, the landmasses separated and people were peopling all of the continents and their features over 100s of years ended up changing. The word "race" is a man-made term and not a biological term. Therefore, when I talk about African people and the worldview, every race is invited as long as they know. Just as many Black people will go to the Catholic Church knowing they're Baptist. Many Black people go to the Jewish faith, Jewish schools, Catholic schools, and whatever. So, I never said, ever, that no race of people could come here other than Black people. I just say what our philosophy is, what we'll be teaching, and how we'll be teaching. Enrollment is open to everybody because everybody is a homosapien sapien. Everybody is actually African. Mixed children have come. There was a woman who adopted a Black child and she wanted her to come here. There were several parents where one was Black and one was White who sent their children here. I have never had two White people with a White child come. Black and Latino parents with mixed children have also sent their children here.

6. *What were the accomplishments of the organization?*

ALC has graduates who have done well. Almost definitely, I have been able to give Black people jobs and education. I've been able to employ lots and lots of people over the years and get them educated, sending them to conferences to raise their awareness - their African-centered intellectual knowledge. We've done this through the National Black Child Development Institute (NBCDI), the National Association for Black School Educators (NABSE), and all of the different arenas and groups that we belong to. NABSE has a conference coming up. The CIBI people don't attend any of the groups.

7. *What do you know about COINTELPRO?*

COINTELPRO back in the 1960s, 1970s, and 1980s was a federal spy organization that was initiated to break up Black groups so that they wouldn't be effective in the freedom movement. It did not affect my school that I'm aware of. You know the cartoon, Road Runner? The roadrunner goes along minding his business and the coyote keeps trying to kill or hurt him, and it always backfires. Well, I'm like the roadrunner. There may have been infiltrators/provocateurs but I was too busy running the school and they didn't get any energy from me.

8. *What is the current status of the organization?*

We now have two learning centers. We opened the public charter school in 1999. I opened the ALC as a corporation. With a corporation, you have to have a Board of Directors. You have to have an odd number of board members, so you can have three or more. I opened ROOTS with three people - me, my then husband, and our attorney. Now board members are Mama Nkechi, Ms. Jones, and me. Mama Nkechi was the first person I hired and I just promoted her to principal of the ALC. In 1999, I moved over to be the principal of the public charter school and I promoted

Baba Kamau to principal of the ALC, where he served until he died. The public charter school has to be a 501(c) 3 organization and it can't be owned by anyone. I developed the school and, in a practical sense, I'm in charge of the school. I looked and handpicked my Board members, who are likeminded people. We have seven on the Board of Directors The Board of Directors hires the principal, so they hire me, and then the principal recommends new hires the Board of Directors and the Board of Directors votes on it.

9. *How did the activities of your organization affect colleges and universities on campuses and in the community?*

There was really only one college who helped us, the University of Maryland. I looked for others and assertively asked Howard University, various staff and various professors, at Howard University and the University of DC if they would send student teachers over. They denied us. Throughout the years, they basically denied sending student teachers, but the University of Maryland would send student teachers. The people at Howard University and the University of DC said they only send students to public schools. Even after I opened the public charter school, which is a public school, they still denied us. The college students that came worked for a semester or a year at a time. There was a student that volunteered from another school that was far away in the west. The University of Maryland Black Student Union sent students to work with us.

10. *Did your organization's activities affect the development of Black student organizations and, if so, how?*

We just worked with them.

11. *Did your organization's activities affect the development of Black studies departments at higher education institutions and, if so, how?*

No, the Black student unions did.

12. *Are you aware of any activities, programs, or benefits to higher education resulting from the efforts of your organization or other organizations in the Black Power Movement during the period from 1960 – 1980? Do they still exist today?*

Because of the Black college student movement in the 1960s and 1970s, it's now commonplace to have Black studies in colleges and high schools. I don't think that the Black college movement had anything to do with practicing Kwanzaa on college campuses. Brother Karenga was the developer of Kwanzaa and the whole Pan Africanist group. It was very big and we're trying to make it stay that way but it's sought of fading now.

13. *Are there other persons you feel would provide helpful information on this topic?*

Baba Zulu, Baba Ageije Akoko, and Abina Walker

14. *I am collecting information on the sequence of events leading to the development of the first Black student union and the first Black studies department at San Francisco State University. Are there experiences at other college or universities that you feel would be informative?*

Central State University.

PART 2: REVOLUTIONARY NATIONALIST ORGANIZATIONS

THE (ORIGINAL) BLACK PANTHER PARTY

Summary of the Organization

The Black Panther Party for Self Defense (BPP) was not one organization but a coalition of organizations that grew out of local circumstances (Williams, 1998). The Lowndes County Freedom Organization, which was an Alabama-based group that used violence to retaliate against the barbarity perpetrated against Black people by the Ku Klux Klan, was the original Black Panther Party. It was organized by members of the Student Nonviolent Coordinating Committee and local residents following a freedom ride for a voter registration campaign. In 1966, Huey Newton and Bobby Seale founded the national office of the Panther Party in Oakland, California. Between 1966 and 1982, there were more than 32 chapters and 100 affiliates across the United States and abroad (Austin, 2006). The chapters differed based on cultural and regional influences. These differences were reflected in their ideology, methodology, and activities; however, the network of organizations (chapters, affiliates) ideologically embraced Marxism and advocated for the needs of the "lumpen proletariat" (the masses of people) (Williams, 1998, p. 65).

The Black Panthers recruited many of its members from colleges and universities. To expand their membership, leaders of the Black Panther Party gave presentations on college and university campuses. In Illinois, for example, the Chicago Police Department files listed the following higher education institutions as campuses where there was Panther Party activity: Chicago State University, Crane Junior College (now Malcolm X College), Illinois Institute of Technology, Northeastern Illinois University, Northwestern University, Roosevelt University, Southern Illinois University in Carbondale, University of Illinois at Chicago Circle, University of Illinois at Urbana-Champaign, Wilbert Wright Junior College, and Woodrow Wilson Junior College (now Kennedy-King College). In 1968, African American college students in Chicago organized students at college campuses across Illinois and formed the Congress of Black College Students (Williams, 1998).

In some states, activist groups were formed at higher education institutions and the activism of students flowed from the colleges to high schools. In Illinois, however, student activism began in the high schools and expanded to college and university campuses. The primary focus of college students was changing the curriculum while the advocacy efforts of high school students focused on community control of public schools. Support flowed both ways. University students helped high school students advocate for community control and high school students helped college students advocate for curriculum change.

The national office of the Black Panther Party network was located in Oakland, California. A majority of the chapters across the country replicated the operational structure of the national office. A collective called the Central Committee led the organization. The Committee was comprised of six people called ministers, three field lieutenants, and a chair. In some chapters, ministers were called deputy ministers; however, the responsibilities of their positions were the same. There was a Minister of Information, Minister of Communication, Minister of Defense, Minister of Culture, Minister of Labor, and Minister of Finance. Each minister was in charge of a cadre. Huey P. Newton was the National Chairman.

The overall mission of the Black Panther Party was to defend the Black community from police oppression and brutality. In 1971, after an initial focus on self-defense and arms, the organization decided to de-emphasize the military aspects of the Party and focus on the development and implementation of survival programs, community organizing, coalition-building, and electoral politics. The survival programs included a free breakfast program for public school children, medical research health clinics, a public awareness campaign on sickle cell anemia, free food for low-income families, free busing to prisons, free childcare centers, free clothing, a free ambulance service, and an emergency heating program.

The Party networked with diverse groups to combat racism. Some of the groups had White members and/or White leadership. The names of some of the organizations were Students for a Democratic Society, the Weathermen, the American Indian Movement, and the Puerto Rican Young Lords (Austin, 2006). The governments of North Viet Nam, China, Palestine, and Algeria also supported the Black Panther Party. Relative to electoral politics, a number of Panther Party members ran for elected office, several successfully (e.g. Bobby Rush, Bobby Seale). Some of the former members of the Party continue to serve as elected officials.

In 1968, then Director of the Federal Bureau of Investigation (FBI), J. Edgar Hoover, proclaimed that the Black Panther Party was the most dangerous group in America and began a public and covert campaign to destroy the organization. This initiative, which was established to destroy dissident groups, was called the "Counter Intelligence Program" (COINTELPRO) (Williams, 1998, p. 173). The activities of the Black Panther Party were monitored by law enforcement agencies across the country. In Chicago, the Red Squad (the intelligence arm of the Chicago Police Department), the FBI, and local media joined forces to discredit the Illinois Black Panther Party. During its existence, the Black Panther Party was the target of 223 out of 295 Black nationalist COINTELPRO activities (Stanford, 1986, p. 189). According to Williams (1998),

> "The FBI's secret war against the Panthers exhausted all of COINTELPRO's methods, including a media offensive, silencing the Panther newspaper, attacking the free breakfast for children program, preventing coalitions, neutralizing Panther supporters, exacerbating intergroup/intraparty tensions, infiltrating the organization, sponsoring raids and pretext arrests, encouraging malicious prosecutions, and even assassinating Panthers" (p. 173).

The word "assassinating" referred to the case of the late Fred Hampton, who was Chair of the Illinois Black Panther Party. In 1969, police killed Hampton during a raid of his apartment. The Hampton family subsequently filed a wrongful death suit against law officials and, in 1978, the court found the FBI, Cook County government, and the city of Chicago guilty of abuse of power and misconduct (Williams, 1998, pp. 215-216). In 1983, the Hampton family was awarded a $1.85 million settlement.

The Black Panther Party officially closed in 1982. The legacy of the Black Panther Party can be summarized into three areas – survival programs, formation of the original Rainbow Coalition, and the martyrdom of Fred Hampton. The most popular of the survival programs was the free breakfast program for schoolchildren. This program, which was adopted and institutionalized by public school systems across the country, continues today. Government also replicated the Panther Party's community health centers. The Panther Party established the original Rainbow Coalition predating Jesse Jackson's organization. The coalition is recognized as being responsible for the election of the first Black mayor (Harold Washington) in Chicago. The name, Fred Hampton, continues to be a catalyst for community organizing and development in Illinois.

Interview with Dr. Ahmad Rahman

1. What are your memories of the Black Power Movement during the 1960s and 1970s?

I have very strong memories of the Black Power Movement in that in 1963, three or four girls were bound and killed in Birmingham, Alabama. I remember very clearly that Martin Luther King said that, "No matter what they do, we're going to keep on loving them." I remember my friends and I, I was about 12 years old at the time, had just witnessed something disgusting. We said, "You know, keep on loving them?" They killed those four little girls that very Sunday I had been in my family's Baptist Church. I was the same age as those girls that'd been killed and I identified with them. I just thought Dr. King's response was so weak. So, when my mother's friend said that she saw a man named Malcolm X speak at the Nation of Islam Temple in Chicago and heard him said that Black people should get their own army and should go down South and protect our churches and people from being abused by the Klan and these racists... when I heard my mother's friend say that she had heard this man Malcolm X say that we should get our own army, I said right then that whenever that army started, I want to be in their army. I didn't care if they just let me stir grits or carry water, I want to be in that army. They're protecting Black people from the Klan and having our little kids blown up. So that was the first time I realized that there was a different way of thinking than Martin Luther King's way. Because the whole media focused on Martin Luther King's "I Have a Dream" speech and nobody else got any play. Every magazine rejected Malcolm X and the other way of thinking never got any respect from them. So we didn't think there was anything else. Really, there was but one Civil Rights Movement. We didn't know there was another way. So when Stokely Carmichael in 1966 shouted "Black Power," it resonated with those of us who were young in Chicago, and, I believe, in the North in general. When I was in the Panther Party, I got a chance to go to the West Coast, New York, Detroit, and Chicago. Young African-Americans, for the most part in the North, were knocked down with the Dr. King stuff. We respected him, but letting White people spit on you and kick you and you just keep singing and talking about you going to keep loving them and all that; most of the young people and teenagers in the North, we just were disgusted by that. We didn't support him. So, when Stokely Carmichael said, "Black Power," and we heard about Malcolm X as 15 and 16-year olds, that is what we identified with. That was my first encounter with the Black Power Movement.

2. *Please share any information you have on the goals and the plans emanating from the Black Power Conference in 1967 that took place in North New Jersey. Were you aware of that one?*

Yes, I'm aware of it. There was also one in New York.

KCS: Did you attend?

No, I didn't but I know people who did attend it. My understanding of the goals of Black Power, in general, were for us to have community control, first of all, of our economics, of our education, and of self-defense. Those three things to me were keys - economics, controlling education, and self-defense - because those were the three things that we actually lost when we were enslaved and never really regained. Others control our economics. Others control our education systems. Others control our defending ourselves. What is called "Second Amendment manhood" by Whites - that they had the right to own guns to protect themselves from being lynched and killed - we didn't have those rights. If we asserted those rights, then we were called Black hate mongers and ex-extremists. If I got a gun to protect myself from you, I'm an extremist, right? But if you have guns, you're a man. You're a Minute Man. You're carrying on the traditions of the Patriots. You see? The Black Power Movement overcame that paradigm, where we felt guilty to assert ourselves. They were the key things - to assert our own economics, to assert our own history, to assert our own defense of our own community, and to assert control of ourselves; not others. We overcame that guilt. I'll never forget when we pressed for Black education in schools and the NAACP (National Association for the Advancement of Colored People) denounced the effort as separatist. Almost all the pressure of the movement on college campuses that happened at that time, in '68 to '69 with Cornell, Columbia, and Northwestern, to get Black professors to teach Black history was denounced by the non-violent Civil Rights Movement as separatist. You know, that connected us with Black extremism. Never-mind they have a Judaic Studies Department. You know, what I'm saying? They have a Department of Russian History, a Department of Chinese Languages, and all that. We asked for African-American studies and we were separatists and hate-mongers. You see? The Black Power Movement overcame that. I really appreciated that whole spirit. They came out of 1967. In '67, there was a number of Black Power conferences. That was the big one. But there were Black Power conferences taking place all over the country. Brothers and sisters getting together saying, "Hold on. We're done with this." In Detroit, you had the Republic of New Africa and the Black Panther Party. We had the Revolutionary Action Movement and other groups coming together, and saying, "This is a new day."

3. *Were you active with any organizations, and if so, what organizations, in what capacity and for what period of time?*

I started out as a teenager in 1967 and '68 with an organization in Chicago called the Malcolm X Black Hands Society. I was just a teenager then. This was around '67. And then the Republic of New Africa came. That was around '68. But one of the things about the Republic of New Africa is their philosophy was five states in the south that Black people had built as slaves should be ours. We should have an independent state - an independent country; and, that Blacks, we, should go back down south. I used to go down south and visit my family every summer and I know my family, who migrated up north, wasn't moving back down there. I knew that the only way we were going to get that land from those rednecks in Mississippi was by revolution. Just because you got justice on your side doesn't mean they'd give you anything. So when the Black Panther Party started talking about a revolution - a socialist revolution - overcoming, overthrowing capitalism and imperialism, I also identified with that. That was in '69. I was in the Panther Party in '69, roughly to around '72.

KCS: Three years?

Yes, three years.

KCS: Was it the one in Michigan?

It was. It started in Chicago. In Detroit, the Detroit Panther Party. Everybody knows about Fred Hampton in Chicago. The leader who founded the Panther Party in Detroit, Michael Baynham, was found shot in the head before Fred Hampton was killed. What happened was he was in a building and there were Panthers in the building. They heard the gunshot and ran downstairs. He was dead, a bullet in his head, and the door was open. Somebody heard footsteps. Somebody was getting away. The office in Oakland didn't say who killed him. They felt there was an infiltrator in the party. There was and I found out later who it was. But, they didn't know who the infiltrator was. So they (the police) said, "We're going to place you all under the authority of Chicago." It was in that capacity that some people in Jackson, Michigan started a chapter, the Black Panther Party of Jackson, Michigan. I got commissioned in Chicago to go to Jackson, Michigan to help set up the chapter of the Black Panther Party. We didn't know about the FBI's infiltration and the program called COINTELPRO. We didn't know any of that stuff then.

KCS: We're going to discuss COINTELPRO in more detail.

Okay. All right. Well, I'll tell you how I got from Jackson to Detroit.

Jackson, Michigan already had an organization called the Black Messengers who wanted to become members of the Black Panther Party. We trained them, then they became members of the Black Panther Party. One of them, who was the leader of that organization, had given orders for guys to rob the Western Union; and as soon as they committed the robberies, they went to jail. The police were waiting for them at home. Now, when I got there, this stuff was already happening, and I didn't know what was going on. I didn't know who was who. All I knew was these guys went to jail and nobody's telling who gave them the order to rob the place because that's like snitching. You don't tell anybody that. I couldn't put this together, that this guy gave these people these orders, that they committed this crime, and they immediately got locked up with the police waiting at their homes. The same guy, a member of a big Black Baptist church, the biggest Black Baptist church in Jackson, Michigan, gave them (members) an order to go paint "Fuck Jesus" on the wall in big, bold letters - so big and bright that when they tried to paint over them, you could still see them. That totally alienated the community against us - totally alienated the community. We tried to organize the community with breakfast programs. There was a Catholic priest, who wanted to work with us. After that, we couldn't get anybody to work with us. I said, "We've got to go to Detroit, and we'll let this calm down here. We'll go to Detroit and we'll all work in

Detroit." I said, "This is ruined." I don't know if this guy is the same one who gave the orders - if he is the same one who was an FBI infiltrator. That was the kind of stuff that the FBI was doing to destroy the (Panther) Party. That was a successful distraction, a successful counter-operation. People don't know the kind of stuff that the FBI did. That's what they did.

4. What global events influenced the formation and activities of the Black Panther Party?

At that time, there were liberation movements going on. The main one was the anti-Vietnam War Movement. We all opposed America's involvement in the Vietnam War. Our leaders went to Vietnam. Eldridge Cleaver went to North Vietnam with Jane Fonda and broadcasted to the troops to let them know we have solidarity with the so-called Viet Cong. And, Eldridge, I remember, repeated to them what Mohammed Ali said. Mohammed Ali was the most outstanding example of Black manhood that we had. Mohammad Ali stepped up and refused to go into the military and said, "No Viet Cong has ever called me nigger." He was speaking for all of us.

KCS: Was that when Eldridge went to Viet Nam with Jane Fonda?

Yes, that was when the Jane Fonda thing blew up in the media. She was put on a Black list. While Vietnam was going on, there were liberation movements going on in Africa - Mozambique, Guinea-Bissau. There had been a liberation movement that was successful in Algeria. Che Guevara was in Bolivia trying to get them to liberate themselves. There were movements in Brazil and socialist national revolutionary movements all over the world. We were aligned with the Revolutionary Communist Movement at that time.

KCS: Was that different from what Nyerere promoted or are you talking just about communism?

Well, we wanted it (the Party) to be like the Communist Party of the United States that Angela Davis was a member of. Their basic philosophy was that the working class would have to overthrow the bourgeoisie, the upper class, and there would be a socialist revolution. But, we did not believe that the White workers were going to unite with Black workers or they would do anything because they gained so much from capitalism and racism that they identified with the bourgeoisie. They didn't identify with Black workers. So, we did not think that the Communist Party's philosophy would work for us. We believed that, with community control, for the purpose of us controlling our own community and fighting back against police brutality and racism, we had to organize what was called the Lumpen - the brothers on the street, the brothers in the hood. So that was a different philosophy, but we all believed that socialism was a better system than capitalism. That's what linked Mao Tse-tung, Ho Chi Minh, Che Guevara and Emil Cabral. What linked us all was the common belief in a socialist transformation.

5. What do you consider the strengths and the challenges of the Panther Party?

The strength of the Panther Party was we were young, energetic, dedicated, and somewhat fearless. The challenges and weaknesses were our leadership did not foresee the opposition that we had and, they did not know how to counter it. J. Edgar Hoover said in 1970 or '69, "The Black Panther Party is the number one internal threat to the security of United States." We're all 17 and 18 years old. I said, "You guys, I don't know about that. Us?" It was unbelievable. But he was serious. Now, White radicals had blown up the capital and had planted bombs in the US Capital. White radicals had blown up and started killing people. There were 500,000 soldiers in Vietnam. A 100,000 soldiers had come back to America crazy as loons, shooting dope and killing people, but we were the number one threat to the security of United States. When J. Edgar Hoover said that, he put a tag on all of us. At that point, Huey, who embodied the leaders of the movement, should have said, "Step back." We needed some kind of counter-espionage, counter-intelligence program. Because in any liberation movement, you are going to be infiltrated. We should have infiltrated other liberation movements too. We were all using a book called the *Mini-manual of the Urban Guerilla* written by Carlos Marighella. You can read the whole thing online. Look it up - The *Mini-Manual of the Urban Guerilla*. The police tried to infiltrate the Irish Republican Army (IRA). The IRA had their members join the police. Their members also infiltrated the FBI. We should have been on that level. We should have had our members become prison guards, police officers, and the FBI because the battle for the destruction of the Panther Party was on a physical level, was on a counter-intelligence versus intelligence level. It was a spy game. They had played this game for 50 years and had destroyed so many organizations.

I went to the FBI headquarters, the J. Edgar Hoover Building in Washington, D.C., and read the COINTELPRO files in the reading room of the FBI. All the techniques used against the Panther Party were used against Marcus Garvey's Movement (UNIA). The first Black person ever hired by the FBI was hired to infiltrate the UNIA. The letter is in the files. He wrote to Hoover and said, "We can't get anything on this guy." Hoover replied, "Keep on, we'll get something." That exchange in the FBI's file, that Garvey was the first Black person ever spied on by the FBI. The federal government pressed charges against him. They infiltrated Garvey's organization. All that stuff about White fraud, Garvey didn't even deal with paperwork. His underlings dealt with that, but because he was in-charge, the federal government was able to prosecute him (Garvey) for that. You can see it in the FBI files. J. Edgar Hoover plotted that stuff from the very beginning. So, Hoover did the same thing to the Panther Party. Huey and Bobby didn't have the smarts to recognize the battle so that we could win and counter that stuff. And that was one of the real shortcomings because people got killed. People I know got caught and a number were killed. I'm lucky to be alive myself. Oh, you don't know. I spent 21 years in prison. I'm a former inmate. I have a PhD. I'm a professor and was director of all of kinds of studies. I spent 21 years in prison because Huey and the Panthers could not counter the FBI's program to destroy it.

6. *What were the accomplishments of the organization?*

I think the accomplishments of the Black Power Movement in general, and the Panther Party being just part of it, was pride. To be Black was so shameful when we were kids. So, you blow off the Black thing. I remember, we would go to parties and everybody wanted to dance with the light-skinned girls. The Black-skinned girls couldn't get a dance. Just the fact that we now have pride in ourselves... Franz Fanon said, "Sometimes people must fight back even if they can't win. They must fight back just for their own self-respect." The fact was we fought back. And I think that time (the 60s) affected our development as human beings. The fact that we made the police reform themselves. At a certain time, I remember in Chicago, they talked to my dad, calling him "boy." They called my mother "girl." Some brother named Spurgeon Jake Winters, who I went to high school with, was in the Panther Party. Now 10 days before Fred Hampton was killed, nobody knows it, Spurgeon Jake Winter transported Black Panther Party guns from one building to another. The police came and attacked the Black Panthers with guns. They wanted to kill us anyway so we might as well fight because they were going to kill us. He knew he was dead so he shot it out. He killed three of them and wounded seven before they withered him with bullets. After that, the police started dealing differently in Chicago. It was "sir" and "ma'am". It wasn't "boy" and "girl" once they saw that we would fight them. The Panther Party led that movement. It wasn't just us. The brothers in the hood said, "Wait a minute. We ain't taking this ass kicking no more," and they started fighting back with their fists or whatever. Once they saw that we would fight back, they changed their behavior. Huey Newton said, "Nobody knew we could make them back down." They had the image of power and strength. In Chicago, they would ride around on big horses. They had tough looking leather jackets with big old guns and they were burley, big, old bullies really...Polish and Irish guys. They treated like us punks. I remember they'd just beat us and treat us like punks. Everybody was full of fear of them. Now we are full of fear of each other because we are in gangs. We're even shooting each other with no problem. But then, when we saw the police we would run like rabbits. We didn't know we could make them back down because of our history of slavery. Their image was one of total power and we were powerless. Somebody had to risk his life first to show us that we could make them back down and that was Huey P. Newton. He had some serious problems later. I and my other brothers who dealt with the guns in the Panther party always respected Huey because he was the first one to show us that we could make them back down. Now the thing about it is, we got a little reckless. Then I, I don't know if I told you about the incident. You saw the picture of me and Huey right?

KCS: Yes.

Huey was speaking at an urban mission. Every cop in the world was lined up in front of this theater and there were four of us who were Huey's bodyguards. We had to scout the situation to make sure there were no bombs and there were no snipers. Before Huey came, all of these cops were there because they thought we were going to riot because Huey was speaking. There were mainly White students from the University of Michigan at the mission. But, I had two guns. I had a 9-millimeter gun and a 38. One of the other brothers had a shotgun, a sawed off shotgun, which is illegal. He had it strapped to his arm under a big coat and a pistol. Others had different guns. There were four of us. This brother named Larry, he said, "Cover me." And I said, "What do you mean cover you?" He said, "Just cover me." I say, "Okay." I didn't know what he was going to do. All these cops were lined up. He walked up to them, opened up his coat, and put his hand on his shotgun as if he was going to draw. He didn't draw. I. thought, "Oh my God. Negro, what?" So I put my hands on my guns. I had two guns. I was ready to come out and the thing is none of them (the police) would budge. They wouldn't even flinch. They didn't want us to think they were moving because the first one who moved was going to die. Now they didn't kill us. They had more guns than us but not one of them wanted to be the first one to die. They didn't touch their guns. Having that shotgun was a federal crime. You couldn't have a sawed off shotgun. He had a double barrel shotgun and they were scared. They turned all kinds of colors of red and green. That was because of Huey Newton and the Black Panther Party. The slave master would back down. We didn't know that. And the fact is, it was after the Black Panther Party and the Black Power Movement they began to integrate police departments around the country. When brothers started shooting them in Detroit, the White cops did not want to drive in the Black community without a Black cop in their car. The same White cops who didn't want to integrate before, now they wanted to integrate the police department. So it was not marching and singing or whistle blowing that integrated these police departments in the Northern cities. It was the fact that Black people were shooting these cops. They just killed that boy in Brooklyn. You see that the other day?

KCS: Yes.

Yeah. That's stuff is big news now. That stuff happened everyday back then. And nobody did anything about it. Now it happens like once a year and it's a big blow up. Back then it was every day and nobody paid any attention to it. It was justifiable homicide. If you look at the Black Panther Party platform on the issue of education, it said that we must control our own people's education...that those who do not treat you right will not treat you right. The fact is the movement taught Blacks to educate ourselves and the community, and to control our education.

Our free breakfast program for children shamed the US government. There were no free breakfast and no free lunch programs in any public schools. It shamed the US government into doing what they do now so that my little boy can go to school and have a free lunch if he wants it. He doesn't want to eat that stuff. He wants us to fix his lunch. But for the kids whose families don't have the money to fix their lunch, they get free lunch and free breakfast in these schools now. And I think that was one of the great things that have benefited our children because you know a hungry child can't run, right?

7. *What do you know about COINTELPRO?*

I know a lot about COINTELPRO. As a matter of fact, I'm going to send you an essay that I wrote that was published about Detroit. It's called *The Rise and Fall of the Black Panther Party in Detroit*. It deals essentially with COINTELPRO and some of the stuff, for example, in Detroit. The main thing that the FBI wanted to stop was our newspaper, the Black Panther newspaper. I understood later that it was not our guns that were the number one threat. It was our ideas. And, one of the main problems, particularly why they killed Fred Hampton, is that he was trying to make the gangs stop killing each other and turn their aggression and attention against the government. The FBI saw that as one of the most dangerous things to the security in the United States. Think if the Cripps and Bloods with all those guns became revolutionary and start free breakfast for children programs, started acting like Panthers, started fighting back against the police, and started trying to change the government. This is the vision that the Panther Party had but J Edgar Hoover was seeing ahead of us. And he said, "That must never, ever happen." And that was the most dangerous thing, the real danger that the ideas would spread. The Black Panther newspaper was the vehicle for spreading these ideas. Hoover made sure that Sam Napier, who started the Black Panther newspaper, was shot, killed, and set on fire in New York. I worked with that brother in San Francisco. Beautiful brother. Always smiling. He was shot, killed, and set on fire in New York. I've got the FBI files where J Edgar Hoover gave an order to do two things: stop the free breakfast program and stop the newspaper. The agents in Detroit came up with an idea for our newspapers that arrived at the Detroit airport. They said, "We have this foul smelling spray that smells like the worst smelling species. We're going to spray it on them." I remember going to the airport to pick our newspapers, like 10,000 newspapers, and they all smell like that urine just like the whole plane had peed on the newspapers. I said, "How can they smell like pee?" Evidently, for the airport, the foul smelling stuff was too potent so they wanted them to spray them with stuff that smelled like urine. They (the papers) were ruined. This was the kind of stuff that the FBI did. In addition to painting those words on the church. Just undermining us in every way they could including misdirecting us saying, "Okay. We need to rob a bank for the revolution." You go rob the bank and as soon as you come to the bank the police are waiting on you. You'll be in prison for the next 10 to15 years. That was the kind of stuff that they did to through infiltration.

8.   What is the status of the organization today? Is it gone altogether?

Oh, it's gone. Now, there's like a loose association and we have a reunion every five years. But, it has no any affiliation with the organization called the New Black Panther Party because they frankly do not have an ideology similar to the Black Panther Party. There's a conflict between the New Black Panthers and the brothers in the original Black Panther Party. Some brothers in the Party tried to sue them or stop them using our name because of some of their bizarre behavior. It's bizarre. Let me give you an example. The leader was a guy name Khalid Muhammad, who passed away. He died. After Bush's first election when he stole the election in Florida, he had his inauguration in D.C. I lived in D.C. at the time. I was going to the Capitol to a demonstration where he was going to take the oath for office and drive down the street to the White House. I went down to demonstrate against him. There were hundreds of thousands of people from all over. People come from as far as Hawaii. They were so pissed off that he stole this election. And we were all there - White, Black, thin, thick, everybody. There were actually more people around opposing Bush than were applauding him. All of us formed this chain then here comes the so-called New Black Panthers. And the White boys said, "Oh, right on. Here comes the Black Panthers." So we were all facing the street and Bush's motorcade was coming our way. The New Black Panthers got in front of us with a bullhorn and one of them said, "Just because that White racist Jew was standing next to you doesn't mean he's your brother or your friend," and started attacking Jews. And, I experienced contradiction for a moment. Do you understand what I'm saying? Every race was there. What did the Jews have to do with this stuff? You see? That was just the most bizarre behavior and inappropriate really. What did Jews have to do with this? We were all together against Bush. But those are the kind of divisive tactics that the FBI used. I never trusted that method. One of the guys there from the New Black Panther Party recognized me, "Oh, we've got a real Black Panther here…blah, blah, blah, blah, blah." They asked me to come to a meeting. They were having a meeting the next day. Khalid Muhammad was going to speak at their meeting. I went to the meeting, me and this other brother. He said, "Let's go to the meeting." Okay, we're going to the meeting. It must about a hundred or so people in the meeting. Khalid Muhammad got up and said, "I want you to go in that White man's house and …I never trusted any of them after that - none of them. That's the new Black Panther Party

.KCS: Where are they based?

They're in a number of different places. In DC. There's a guy named Malik Shabazz. There's another man in Detroit named Malik Zulu Shabazz. I don't know where they're based. I just don't trust any of them.

9. *How did the activities of your organization, of the Panther Party affect colleges and universities on campuses and in the community?*

I think, at the time, it helped influence the movement for Blacks toward Black Studies. Not just the Black Panther Party, but look at the Black Panther Party as part of the Black Power Movement and this movement for Black Studies on campus. If you look at the movement that took place on Howard University's campus, where you got E. Franklin Frazier and all of them arguing against Black Studies. "You see, you got to assimilate. You don't need Black Studies." You got Amiri Baraka and all of them running around on campus. I remember, Amiri Baraka got so tired of Blacks were putting on airs at Howard University. One day, he and his partners got big watermelons and just sat right down and ate their watermelon with no forks. It sounds amazonic, but that was the movement. And there were students like Huey. Huey was a college student as well as Bobby Seale. Stokely Carmichael was a graduate of Howard University. There was this whole movement on these campuses for Black Studies, for Black identity, for Black pride, for hiring Black Professors on White college campuses, for establishing Black Studies Departments, and African Studies Departments. All of that was part of the Black Power Movement on campus. They had Black Power in the community and the Black Power Movement was in the military. One Black soldier said when Dr. King was in Vietnam, he asked the captain if they could have the Blacks attend so they can see Dr. King. The captain told him, "Hell, no." The captain and his other good old boys that night strung up confetti with a flag and had a party to celebrate the assassination of Dr. King. Somebody threw a hand grenade in there, killed the captain, and blew up some others. The guy who had asked for a memorial was arrested him for the killing. Since hand grenades don't leave any fingerprints, they couldn't prove it. But, they locked him up for nine months and he didn't get an honorary discharge from the military. That was the Black Power Movement in the military. There was a strong Black Power Movement in the military, particularly in Vietnam, among brothers who opposed that war.

10. *You mentioned Black students. How else did the Panther Party and the Black Power Movement affect campuses? What about the development of Black student unions?*

I think the development of Black Student Unions was influenced by the Black Power Movement. It was the students who organized other Black organizations, for example, the National Council of Black Lawyers. Now there is the Black Bar Association, the official one, but the National Council for Black Lawyers were the legal wing of the Black Power Movement. They became the main lawyers defending Angela Davis, H. Rap Brown, and members of the Black Panther Party. They still exist as a matter of fact. They are strong, still a strong organization. The Black student unions were the Black college and high school wings of the Black Power Movement. So, we don't, we see organizations in the Black Power Movement quite often as the Black Panther Party. We don't see that members of the Black Panther Party were college students and in high schools and were organizing and helping to organize Black student unions, or were influencing young people who are there to do it.

11. Did the Panther Party affect the development of the Black Studies Departments at higher education institutions? And if so, how?

I just think that the Black Panther Party was part of the Black Power Movement in general. Even if there wasn't a chapter of the Black Panther Party on campus, quite often the people would identify as being a Black Panther. I've met many people who said, "I identified myself as a Panther." By being a college student and identifying yourself as a Black Panther, what did you do? College campuses did not have a chapter of the Black Panther Party. But Black students identified with the Panthers anyway. So what did they do? Well, they started a Black student union. They demanded establishment of a Black Studies department. They demanded in your high school that students get books that are relevant to the Black experience. When I went to K-12, I never had a Black book except for one in the fourth grade and that was "Little Black Sambo." There was a White teacher from North Carolina who used to call us "Darkies," and she made us read "Little Black Sambo." So, there was a movement in high schools. We needed education that was relevant to us. Young people who felt like they were Panthers in spirit began to affect these changes on college campuses and in high schools.

12. Are you aware of any activities, programs, or benefits to higher education resulting from the activities of your organizations or other organizations in the Black Power Movement?

I think that the ongoing benefit is the fact that we successfully got Black Studies departments established. The fact is the non-violent Civil Rights Movement opposed the movement for advocating for Black/African Studies departments because they said it was Black separatism. Roy Wilkins gave a speech against it. I remember Roy wrote about it saying, "I have a red, black, and green thing. The flag that represents me is the red, white, and blue." This is what I witnessed at the NAACP. So, there was a clear dichotomy in the Civil Rights Movement where those who were fighting for racial integration felt that they could not at the same time fight for racial integration and fight for Black Studies Departments. They felt that we should integrate our history into American history. They did not see that if we did that, then it's going to always be at the back of the bus of American history. It was the Black Power Movement that pushed that. And, unfortunately, on most of these campuses where you have Black Studies Departments, they have selected leadership who don't appreciate that their jobs were created by the Black Power Movement. I was on a campus that dealt with the history of Black Studies. The chair of the department got up and gave a speech thanking the Civil Rights Movement and Dr. King for the fact that they had a Black Studies department. I remember when the battle was started for an African American and African Studies Department at that university, it was students with the big Afros and all that who were protesting and sitting there. They had never crossed paths with Dr. King. But, they have assigned people to those positions, who don't have the philosophy of those who fought to get those studies there.

KCS: Do they have the knowledge?

Like I said, this person who spoke didn't have the knowledge about things like the history of Black Studies and, in this particular situation, African Studies. Quite often the professors hired don't come to college campuses with a historical knowledge. They don't know our history.

13. *Are there other persons you feel would be helpful and will provide information on this topic that I need to talk with?*

Are you talking about the Black Panther Party or the Black Power Movement?

KCS: The Black Power Movement.

Black Power. Yes, well, I know one sister was at that meeting in '67. As a matter of fact, Stokely and Rap, elected her to represent SNCC. Her name is Gloria House. You know her? Gloria House. She's a professor at my university now. And there's this book about women and SNCC. I think it's *Hands on the Fleet of Flowers,* something like that. She has a chapter in that book. She would be a good person to interview. She was at the Black Panther conference and was elected by Stokely and Rap to represent SNCC at the Black Panther Party.

14. *I'm collecting information on the sequence of the events leading to the development of the first Black Student Union and the first Black Studies Department at San Francisco State University. Are there experiences at other colleges that you feel would be informative as well?*

Yes, Northwestern. What's that brother's name? Bracey? I think it's John Bracey. He's in Massachusetts now. He was part of that at Northwestern. There's a great book out now called, the *Revolution on Campus* by Martha Biondi, B-I-O-N-D-I. You can go to her website, see the bibliography and see the people she interviewed. Look up her name, Martha Biondi. She's a professor at Northwestern. That's a great book.

Dr. Kinaya C. Sokoya

Comparison of Black Student Union and Black Panther Party Platforms

Black student union (February1969)	**Black panther party (October1966)**
1. We want freedom. We want power to determine the destiny of our school.	1. We want freedom. We want power to determine the destiny of our Black community.
2. We want full enrollment in the schools for our people.	2. We want full employment for our people.
3. We want an end to the robbery of the White man of our Black community.	3. We want an end to the robbery of the White man of our Black Community.
4. We want decent educational facilities, fit for the use of students.	4. We want decent housing, fit for shelter of human beings.
5. We want an education for our people that teach us how to survive in the present day society.	5. We want education for our people that exposes the true nature of this decadent American society. We want education that teaches us our true history and our role in the present-day society.
6. We want racist teachers to be excluded and restricted from all public schools.	6. We want all black men to be exempt from military service.
7. We want an immediate end to police brutality and murder of black people. We want all police and special agents to be excluded and restricted from school premises.	7. We want an immediate end to **police brutality** and **murder** of black people.
8. We want all students that have been exempt, expelled, or suspended from school to be reinstated.	8. We want freedom for all Black men held in federal, state, county, and city prisons, and jails.
9. We want all students when brought to trial to be tried in student court by a jury of their peer group or students of their school.	9. We want all black people when brought to trial to be tried in court by a jury of their peer group or people from their black communities as defined by the Constitution of the United States.
10. We want power, enrollment, equipment, education, teachers, justice, and peace.	10. We want land, bread, housing, education, clothing, justice, and peace. And, as our major political objective, a United Nations supervised plebiscite to be held throughout the Black colony in which only Black colonial subjects will be allowed to participate for the purpose of determining the will of Black people as to their national destiny.

Note: From Up *against the wall: Violence in the making and unmaking of the Black panther party* (p. 353), by C. J. Austin, 2006, Fayetteville, AR: University of Arkansas Press and Mutiny *does happen lightly: The literature of the American resistance to the Vietnam war* (pp. 1-3), by G. L. Heath, 1976, Metuchen, NJ: Scarecrow Press.

THE REVOLUTIONARY ACTION MOVEMENT (RAM)

Summary of Organization

Undergraduate students at Central State University in Ohio established the Revolutionary Action Movement in 1962. Its stated purpose was "to educate African Americans on the economic, political, and cultural basis of the racial situation in the United States and the world; to develop unity with Africans in the United States and the world; and, to unite and organize African American students to become active in the African American liberation struggle" (Stanford, 1986, p. 204). In 1961, a group of Central State University students formed an organization called Challenge. In the fall of 1961, it decided to take over the student government at the university to politicize the students on campus. Their members ran successful campaigns and were elected to all of the offices. After the election, Challenge determined that its mission had been accomplished and decided to dissolve the organization. It formed a new organization called the Revolutionary Action Movement and its leaders became leaders of the new organization. The stated purpose of this national centralized organization was to coordinate the Black Power Movement.

The impetus for organizing the Revolutionary Action Movement (RAM) was discontent with organizations in the Civil Rights Movement (e.g., the National Association for the Advancement of Colored People {NAACP}, the Student Nonviolent Coordinating Committee {SNCC}, the Urban League, and the Congress of Racial Equality {CORE}). The students disagreed with the use of non-violence as a strategy for liberation and searched for a group that would involve itself in confrontational direct action. As individuals, the students had previously joined one or more of the civil rights groups and were dissatisfied. An example is one student who went from the National Association for the Advancement of Colored People to the Congress of Racial Equality to the Revolutionary Action Movement looking for a home. The students considered the aforementioned groups bourgeois and timid, seeking reform, rather than revolution.

From 1963-1964, the Revolutionary Action Movement organized local community groups for voter registration drives, conducted economic boycotts, advocated for jobs, and protested police brutality. In July 1964, student leaders formalized the Revolutionary Action Movement and developed a 12-point program that outlined its goals and objectives. These objectives included development of:

1. A national Black student organization movement,
2. Ideology (freedom) schools,
3. Rifle clubs,
4. A liberation army,
5. Training centers,
6. An underground vanguard,
7. "Liberation unions" for black workers,
8. Block organizations (called cells),
9. A separate country (nation within a nation; government in exile),
10. A war fund,
11. Black farmers co-operatives, and
12. An army of the Black unemployed" (Ahmed, 2008, pp. 1- 2).

The students planned to accomplish these objectives on three levels. The first level included organizing secret cells in cities. The cells would be the political bases for the organization and would provide financial support for activists to serve as full-time roving field organizers. The second level was establishing local chapters across the country and the third level was recruiting secret members who would fund the organization.

After Malcolm X left the Nation of Islam, he secretly joined the Revolutionary Action Movement and publicly established another organization, the Organization of African American Unity. Through the Organization of African American Unity, he planned to change the philosophy of civil rights organizations, moving them from civil rights to human rights; and, to internationalize the movement. The Organization of African American Unity and the Revolutionary Action Movement worked together. The Organization of African American Unity was the public organization and the Revolutionary Action Movement coordinating the Black Liberation Front underground.

The structure of the Revolutionary Action Movement was multi-faceted and intentionally confusing. A number of local student groups around the country adopted the name of the Revolutionary Action Movement. In 1964, the following officers were elected and installed:

- International Spokesman: Malcolm X

- International Chairman: Robert Williams

- National Field Chairman: Max Stanford

- Executive Chairman: Donald Freeman

- Ideological Chairman: James Boggs

- Executive Secretary: Grace Boggs

- Treasurers: Milton Henry and Paul Brooks (Naison, 1978, p. 37).

In 1965, James and Grace Boggs resigned their positions. New officers were elected and the organization decided to keep their names secret. These officers formed a secret central coordinating committee called the Soul Circle.

After 1965, Revolutionary Action Movement members led and participated in numerous demonstrations and protests but did not use the name of the Revolutionary Action Movement in the efforts. It closed all of its offices and published its materials anonymously to maintain secrecy. The organization created a code of ethics for cadres and rules for safekeeping secrets to maintain discipline and secrecy. These documents follow this summary. RAM established three membership categories: professionals, full-time field organizers, and general members. All persons who desired to join the organization had to complete training on ideology, politics, and activism.

During its existence, the Revolutionary Action Movement organized study groups that met weekly. Participants in these study groups were recruited for membership in the cells. It conducted free weekly Black history classes in northern Philadelphia for community members and organized three types of cells. Area cells were organized in cities, work units were established in factories, and political units were established to infiltrate civil rights organizations. The Revolutionary

Action Movement established local student chapters on college campuses on both historically Black college campuses across the country and at predominantly White college campuses in the North. It organized a youth self-defense section of ex-gang members that was initially called the Black Guards and later the Black Liberation Army. The Revolutionary Action Movement also helped to establish the Black Panther Party, the Republic of New Africa, the League of Revolutionary Black Workers, and the All African People's Revolutionary Party. It radicalized the Student Nonviolent Coordinating Committee and led and/or participated in numerous protests. In 1967, the FBI called Max Stanford, Revolutionary Action Movement leader, "the most dangerous man" in America. He was subsequently imprisoned (Stanford, 2013, p. 2). Because of problems with COINTELPRO, the national central committee dissolved the Revolutionary Action Movement in 1968.

Code of the Revolutionary Nationalist

(Revolutionary Action Movement Code; Stanford, 1986))

- A Revolutionary nationalist maintains the highest respect for all authority within the party.

- A Revolutionary nationalist does not promote or participate in gossip, rumor, and petty arguments either among fellow advocates or the masses.

- A Revolutionary nationalist is a brother or sister who has dedicated his total self and life to the liberation of the black nation.

- A Revolutionary nationalist is one who has submitted his will to the will of the nation

- A Revolutionary nationalist is one who respects and obeys all rules and directives issued by the party.

- A Revolutionary nationalist is one who will work to destroy the myth of individualism (me in spite of everyone) and will work to promote the reality of personality (me in relation to everyone).

- A Revolutionary nationalist is one who will promote the reality of Umoja (unity) through working in the closest forms with his black people, the black nation.

- A Revolutionary nationalist is one who will seize every opportunity to further his development in the vanguard political party through knowledge constantly repeating this cycle, thus rising to a higher level of unity of knowing and doing.

- A Revolutionary nationalist will never separate himself from the current revolutionary struggle but will instead maintain the closest identity with it.

- A Revolutionary nationalist will unhesitatingly subordinate his personal interest to those of the vanguard hesitation, will discuss freely and completely any conflicts, discontentment or disagreements with all parties concerned.

- —A Revolutionary nationalist will maintain the highest level of morality and will never take as much as a needle or single piece of thread, from the masses---Brothers and

Sisters will maintain the utmost respect for one another and will never misuse or take advantage of one another for personal gain---and will never misinterpret, the doctrine of revolutionary nationalism for any reason.

- A Revolutionary nationalist will always be honest with all of his people-the Black Nation.

- A Revolutionary nationalist will always preserve a cheerful spirit even in the midst of irksome tasks and weighty responsibility. He will maintain and display loyalty and love to all his brothers and sisters and all black people.

- A Revolutionary nationalist is the first to worry and the last to enjoy himself.

- A Revolutionary nationalist cannot be corrupted by money, honors or any other personal gains.

- A Revolutionary nationalist will hold in high regard the teachings of scientific socialism and will never violate the code and principles of revolutionary nationalism as taught and practiced in the party.

- A Revolutionary nationalist is totally dedicated to revolutionary nationalism using any means necessary to liberate the black nation.

(Stanford, M. (1986). Revolutionary action movement (RAM): A case study of an urban revolutionary movement in western capitalist society. Retrieved from www.ulib.csuohio.edu/.../ stanford.pdf)

Interview with Dr. Amad Muhammad (Max Sanford)

1. What are your memories of the Black Power Movement during this period?

RAM was formed in 1963 at Central State University. I did not form RAM. Its formation was spontaneous at the Central State College in Wilberforce, Ohio after the administration brought in the Ohio State Guard. It aligned its activities with SNCC, seeing itself as the student organization in the North like SNCC was the student organization in the South. RAM embraced the philosophy of Robert Williams who believed in armed self-defense. It participated in demonstrations and worked with other organizations and people such as Rev. Leon Sullivan and the NAACP. Robert Williams wanted RAM to challenge SNCC on the issue of non-violence. A conference for African American youth was held at Fisk University in Nashville, Tennessee in 1964. It was the first Black Power conference held in the country for African American students. SNCC was challenged about armed self-defense but because SNCC members did not want to talk about it, RAM formed on May 1, 1964. Most activists in the field, whether they were revolutionary nationalists or civil rights people, carried guns [before the discussion]. The public position was non-violence but they carried guns to defend themselves from attacks, especially from the Ku Klux Klan.

After RAM formed, RAM field activists were cut off the SNCC payroll. James Forman was SNCC's chair at the time. John Lewis put the RAM's activists on his payroll, although he did not agree with them. Muhammad Toure' began teaching Black history classes in Greenwood, MS.

2. *Please share any information you have on the goals and plans emanating from Black Power Conference of 1967 that took place in Newark, New Jersey. Did you attend that meeting?*

No, I did not attend the meeting. The Black Power Movement emerged much earlier than 1967. James and Grace Boggs had a conference and created an organization for Black Power before that. We felt that the community in Philadelphia was undergoing constant disintegration at that time, so we began to run Black history classes in the community and we worked with gangs. Because of our work with gangs, we became an early target of Mayor Frank Rizzo, who was racist. At that time, we were also fighting attacks from the Ku Klux Klan. In 1964, Uhuru in Detroit joined RAM making it a national organization. Our organization targeted young Black working class youth [for recruitment.]

3. *Were you active with any organizations and, if so, what organization(s), in what capacity, and for what period of time?*

I was in RAM from its inception until its end in 1968. I was the National Field Chairman. I was also in other organizations.

4. *What global events influenced the formation and activities of your organization?*

We were involved and followed many events: the Casa Blanca group, Viet Nam Movement, the death of Lumumba, the independence movements in Africa, Sekou Toure, Kwame Nkrumah, the African National Congress, Nelson Mandela's jailing, the Black Guard from the 1955 Bandung Conference in Indonesia, PAIGC, Ahmed Cabral, Free Elimu Movement, Mozambique, and events in Cuba.

5. *What were the strengths and challenges of the organization?*

Challenges: We did not learn much from our predecessors and we did not remain anonymous Strengths: We were discreet. We had no office. We avoided being targeted (by COINTELPRO) by joining other groups.

6. *What were the accomplishments of the organization?*

We started the Black Studies Movement, which became departments. When they became departments, however, they became cut off from the community. We helped elect Black mayors.

7. *What do you know about COINTELPRO?*

I was imprisoned because OF COINTELPRO. I think I might not be alive today if I did not jump bail. They arrested the key organizers, and court battles drained our resources. RAM members were told to stay away from me. If they found out they had contact with me, they would be gone. Today I am a felon because of COINTELPRO.

8. *What is the current status of the organization?*

It closed in 1968.

9. *How did the activities of your organization affect colleges and universities on campuses and in the community?*

The Black Student Unions opened space at Predominately White Institutions (PWI) and Historically Black Colleges and Universities (HBCU). RAM presented another alternative than what they were being taught. They took over buildings to get Black Studies in colleges.

10. *Did your organization's activities affect the development of Black student organizations and, if so, how?*

BSUs were started at Fisk and Howard universities. They wanted the colleges to teach Black students and not continue to teach from a White perspective. Under the leadership of Bill Strickland, Dave Richardson, and Amiri Baraka, the students started a Black Arts Movement, which led to Black Studies. James Garrett started the BSU at San Francisco State University. Classes were held in the Black community.

11. *Did your organization's activities affect the development of Black studies departments at higher education institutions and, if so, how?*

RAM presented another alternative than what students were being taught. They took over buildings to get Black Studies into colleges.

12. *Are you aware of any activities, programs, or benefits to higher education resulting from the efforts of your organization or other organizations in the Black Power Movement during the period from 1960 – 1980? Do they still exist today?*

BSUs and Black Studies departments. They are now under attack across the country. The BSU at Temple saved the Black Studies Department.

13. *Are there other persons you feel would provide helpful information on this topic?*

Ernie Allen organized the West Coast RAM. He formed the first Negro History class. Later James Garrett formed the BSU at SFSU. Through Jimmy Garrett, the BSU at SFSU pressured the school to establish a Black Studies Department and Nathan Hare was its first chair. Ibrim Rogers, professor at Temple University wrote a book about the Black student movement. Bill Strickland took over the Northern Student Movement [of RAM] to assist SNCC and was a leader in the Black Anti-War Movement. Nathan Hare was their mentor.
John Bracey, Jr. and William Sails were the organizers at Columbia University.

14. *I am collecting information on the sequence of events leading to the development of the first Black student union and the first Black studies department at San Francisco State University. Are there experiences at other college or universities that you feel would be informative?*

Many Black activists are now at The University of Massachusetts in Amherst, Massachusetts.

STUDENT NONVIOLENT COORDINATING COMMITTEE (SNCC)

Summary of the Organization

In April 1960, the Southern Christian Leadership Conference, then led by Rev. Dr. Martin Luther King, Jr., established the Student Nonviolent Coordinating Committee. Ella Baker, at the suggestion of Dr. King, was the primary organizer (Student Nonviolent Coordinating Committee (SNCC), 2013). This student movement was one of a few Black Power organizations that changed its philosophy from being a civil rights organization, embracing the strategy of non-violence, to a Black Power organization that embraced the strategy of self-defense. The change in philosophy resulted from the violence student activists experienced during voter registration drives in the South. From 1960-1966, the group was a civil rights organization. From 1966-1971, it was a Black power organization.

Also in April 1960, the Southern Christian Leadership Conference held a conference at Shaw University to organize students (SNCC, 2013). One hundred and twenty-six students who were activists at sit-in counters in 12 southern states and student activists from 19 northern colleges attended the conference. The establishment of the Student Nonviolent Coordinating Committee (SNCC) was an outcome of the conference. The late Marion Barry ("Mayor for Life" in the District of Columbia) was elected its first chair. From 1960 to 1966, members of the Student Nonviolent Coordinating Committee were active in the civil rights movement. It participated in sit-ins, freedom rides, voter registration drives, the 1963 March on Washington, and formed the Mississippi Freedom Democratic Party to challenge the then all White State Democratic Party.

In 1965, a crisis in philosophy (civil rights v. Black power) caused the organization to split into two factions and White members were expelled from the organization (SNCC, 2013). The transformation of SNCC from civil rights to Black power was reflected in its leadership:

Civil Rights era:
- Marion Barry, first Chairman, 1960-1961

- Charles McDrew, second Chairman, 1961-1963

- John Lewis, third Chairman, 1963-1966

Black Power era:
- Stokely Carmichael, fourth Chairman, 1966-1967

- H. Rap Brown, fifth Chairman, 1967-1969.

The cry for "Black Power" with a raised fist originated from the Student Nonviolent Coordinating Committee in 1966 in Greenwood, Mississippi. Although Carmichael popularized the term, it was actually Mukasa (aka Willie Ricks), another member of the Student Nonviolent Coordinating Committee, who cried "Black Power" while SNCC was completing a march from Memphis, Tennessee to Jackson, Mississippi. Previously, James Meredith had organized the march to encourage voter registration. During the march, Meredith was shot by a sniper and hospitalized. Black activists showed up the next day to complete the march. During the march,

Mukasa cried "Black Power." When queried about the meaning of Black Power, Carmichael responded,

> "We have to do what every group in the country did – we've got to take over the community where we outnumber people so we can have decent jobs"
> (History Learning Site, 2013, p. 2).

The Student Nonviolent Coordinating Committee was instrumental in establishing the Black Panther Party. In 1964, the organization helped form the Lowndes County (Alabama) Freedom Organization, which was the original Black Panther Party. In 1967, Stokely Carmichael left SNCC to join the Black Panther Party in California. H. Rap Brown, who, in 1969, changed the name of the organization to the Student National Coordinating Committee, succeeded him (SNCC, 2013). In 1969, Brown also resigned and joined the Black Panther Party as its Minister of Justice. When the Student Nonviolent Coordinating Committee changed its philosophy from civil rights to Black power, the government placed it under surveillance as part of its COINTELPRO initiative. In 1967, the Department of Defense stated:

> "SNCC can no longer be considered a civil rights group. It has become a racist organization with Black supremacy ideals and an expressed hatred for Whites. It employs violent and militant measures that may be definedas extreme when compared to those of more moderate groups"
> (SNCC, 2013, p. 6).

Because of a loss of funding and COINTELPRO, the Student Nonviolent Coordinating Committee closed its doors in 1971.

Interview with Mukasa Ricks, Student Nonviolent Coordinating Committee Pioneer

1. What are your memories of the Black Power Movement during this period?

In Detroit and Newark, where those cities were burned, the cry was "Black Power" and with Black Power, we integrated "Black is Beautiful" in the texture of our hair, our noses, our lips, and our skin. And, it pointed us towards our history in Africa and to a philosophy of nationalism. We began to be guided by theories of Malcolm X, Garvey, Nkrumah, and Sekou Toure. We then began to look to revolutionaries throughout the world including Fidel Castro, Ho Chi Minh, Mao Tse-tung, and others.

We had to defeat the civil rights leaders on the question of Black Power. We had to fight them. They condemned us - SNCC. They joined with the government against us. We stuck with Black Power and the masses of people endorsed Black Power through the rebellions that took place, the new movement, and the rise of the Nationalist Movement. SNCC was endorsed by other groups in the world - African groups - that were seeking independence, fighting against some form of colonialism and imperialism worldwide. Different groups inside Africa and in the Caribbean endorsed Black Power. So, Black Power became a theory that the masses could relate to and we were able to relate it to all aspects of our struggle and our liberation.

2. *Please share any information you have on the goals and plans emanating from Black Power Conference of 1967 that took place in Newark, New Jersey.*

I was in a car going to that conference – me, Ralph Silverstone, and some other SNCC people. When the car got halfway, we stopped and I got out of the car and told them I'd see them later. I took another path.

3. *Were you active with any organizations and, if so, what organization(s), in what capacity, and for what period of time?*

I joined SNCC in 1961 or 1962, from the founding of SNCC to the very end of SNCC. I was just one of the soldiers but I was a key organizer for SNCC and was a spokesman for SNCC in the field. I had the title of "Reverend Rick" and I was on the podium with Dr. King and all the rest of those so-called leaders. Anyway, I was the one that challenged them. I was a motivator and agitator for SNCC as well as an organizer. I was probably the strongest youth organizer that SNCC had.

4. *What global events influenced the formation and activities of your organization?*

We merged our activities with different international struggles that were happening. In the early 60s, we supported the Mau Mau movement in Kenya, the revolution that took place in Kenya. We met with Kenya's Oginga Odinga when he came to Atlanta and we realized that our movements were linked. Early on we sent people to Africa, to Guinea, and to other places. We always had a link with them and we also had different relationships and support from networks like Cuba.

5. *What were the strengths and challenges of the organization?*

The strength of SNCC was it was an organization rooted in the people and it was an organization that organized the people. It was organizing organizations that gave us strength. The other organizations - civil rights organizations - mobilized and we organized. We helped create all kinds of organizations and groups that were grassroots and we maintained good relationships with the people. SNCC was an organizing organization while Dr. King was a mobilizer. We created local leadership. We saw ourselves as organizers not leaders.

We had many challenges. As a matter of fact, challenging the system, being in the forefront of the movement, taking the leadership from all the other civil rights groups, and being a youthful organization; that was, I guess, a great challenge. They would say that the things that we did, we were the youth of the movement, were too dangerous. We took the struggle into Mississippi and into other areas. We went on the freedom rides and participated in the sit-ins. We took more of a militant position. SNCC became a vanguard of the civil rights movement where we found ourselves being the leaders and being the ones that forced or motivated the other civil rights organizations to come our way. SNCC was the organization that went into Mississippi. We went alone and then others came, but we were the ones that organized the state of Mississippi. SNCC led King and the so-called Civil Rights Movement.

I was not part of RAM (Revolutionary Action Movement), but I knew the people in the organization. I don't know what RAM had but SNCC had the organization, the territory, and the people. RAM tried to relate to SNCC in different ways but SNCC was the vanguard organization out there that most groups tried to identify with.

6.   *What were the accomplishments of the organization?*

We took our people to another level. We fought many, many battles. We struggled throughout the South and brought organizations to another level of consciousness. We were able to link our movement with movements throughout the world and we challenged America and its system of oppression, Apartheid, and segregation. We broke their back and we broke the back of the Democratic and Republican parties that were oppressing us and keeping us from voting and participating. We challenged the American government in Mississippi on the general oppression we found, the rebellions in the South, and the rebellions in the 60s. We shook the foundation of this country and made them change all of their policies toward African people. I think the rebellion shook this country to its foundation forcing them to pass laws that would open doors, like ending segregation and things that were closed to us, that we couldn't get in. We forced them to open those doors. By forcing them to open their doors, they couldn't discriminate against us on the job and in other areas. They were so frustrated that the government was forced to pass laws saying they could not discriminate. Anybody who got federal money had to have a certain percentage of people of African descent on those jobs and wherever the federal money was, there had been some Black representatives. We forced them to appoint Black officials and elect Black people. SNCC opened those doors. SNCC was the one that started registering people to vote and open the doors. SNCC ran the first Blacks for offices, helped form the Mississippi Freedom Democratic Party, and those kinds of things. SNCC was able to open the doors to a lot of things and we don't even know the effect of our activities because SNCC was influenced by and linked up with Africa. The African independence movement began to identify with SNCC and the different governments in Africa began to say to America as we exposed them, "How can you call yourselves our friend and treat Black people in America the way you do?" We embarrassed America on the international level and at different points we began to reach out to African governments. At some point, we joined our movement with the liberation movements in Africa and began to fight imperialism on the international level. It was SNCC that really took on South Africa. SNCC people demonstrated in 1963. In 1965, SNCC went to the UN, broke in, and beat up the South African staff. We beat up the ambassadors. I went to jail over that in New York and in DC for fighting against Apartheid. SNCC opened the gates to begin to educate people and link the African movement with our SNCC movement and let people know what was going on in South Africa.

7.   *What do you know about COINTELPRO?*

We all had problems in Mississippi with COINTELPRO because they were attacking us and doing all kinds of things to undermine our movement and our organizations. They attacked different members of our families. I know my family was attacked. They attempted to assassinate different members of my family. We lived through that so COINTELPRO was nothing but despised. It tried to undermine our movement. I've always been under the gaze of COINTELPRO and other elements of the FBI and CIA from my inception inside the movement.

8. What is the current status of the organization?

SNCC closed in 1969. We come together every now and then. We just had a big gathering in North Carolina for the 50th anniversary of the movement. We come together mostly, a few of us, White and Black SNCC people, who were involved in thousands of different movements and different phases that moved us forward toward humanity. SNCC people were involved in all kinds of things. Some people were involved in being revolutionary and linking with revolutionary movements around the world from North Korea to all the liberation movements in Africa, to Kwame Nkrumah, Sekou Toure, Maoism, and Marxism. So, the movement continued and different SNCC people took different paths.

9. How did the activities of your organization affect colleges and universities on campuses and in the community?

Well, during and after the Black Power Movement, after SNCC had organized the first Black Panther Party and after we began to talk about Black Power, it linked our people to countries all over the world. It also linked our people to students. We had a student brigade that organized students throughout the country. SNCC was made up of students so we always had a relationship with students. 1966 was when we made the cry for Black Power. In 1967, we had a conference on Black Power. This conference on Black Power was after the Detroit rebellions, where the cry for Black Power spread. Every household was divided on the question of Black Power. Where some people were against Black Power, you had somebody in that household that supported Black Power. So, Black Power became a very intense debate in the African community. In 1967, Fisk University had what was called the Black Power Conference. Fisk was the first school to go up in rebellion - Fisk and Tennessee State - they were the first schools to have rebellions. There were shootings and all that. They were blamed SNCC and Carmichael. One of the things we did was organize students on campuses and encourage them to organize organizations like Black student unions. SNCC went out to the White schools and began to encourage them (students) to organize Black student unions.

10. Did your organization's activities affect the development of Black student organizations (BSUs) and, if so, how?

We influenced BSUs (Black student unions). We encouraged students to get organized on White campuses. We encouraged them to demand Black books and include Blackness in the schools, which became Black Studies. So when they (students) were on White campuses, they could relate to the Movement. That was one of our purposes for doing that.

Regarding Fisk University: The students had endorsed Black Power. They were one of the first groups to endorse Black Power. They had a Black Power conference. While we were having the conference, the police shot a Black man in the neighborhood. When they shot the man in the back of the head right down the street from the school, the students got involved in it in some kind of way and we took the students to the streets. Then, we began to challenge the police by throwing bricks, bottles, firebombs and other things. And, before you know it, the city was in rebellion and it was coming from the campus at Fisk University. So now you had a rebellion on your hands at Fisk and Tennessee State. They blamed SNCC for that rebellion. They began to

191

terrorize and shoot students and stuff like that. On many campuses; including Black ones like Texas Southern, Orangeburg (the Orangeburg massacre), and other Black schools; we began to demand Blackness and set up Black Power chapters at all the Black schools; and, we asked the kids at the White schools to do the same thing. In doing so, they began to demand more from the schools and put together Black Studies programs and all those things.

11. Did your organization's activities affect the development of Black studies departments at higher education institutions and, if so, how?

The Black Studies program came out of the Black Power Movement. We began to encourage students to demand Black Studies programs. In some cases, like Cornell, students took up guns and took over administration buildings. All across the country, our children began to threaten to take over administration buildings and when they did that, most of the schools were so frightened. A couple of administration buildings were burned down. In fact, some members of the administration were kidnapped and held (hostage) and the students demanded different kinds of things like Black Studies and African Studies. We wanted the White schools to build a school where they taught something that related to us. So, all of that became the Black Studies program.

12. Are you aware of any activities, programs, or benefits to higher education resulting from the efforts of your organization or other organizations in the Black Power Movement during the period from 1960 – 1980? Do they still exist today?

Most of the students did not have any Black books, Black films, weren't able to attend Black lectures, or any of that. As a matter of fact, most schools taught history and left Africa completely out. I met a man at the University of Georgia one time. I was talking about Africa and he said, "I'm getting ready to write my book for my PhD in history and I have never studied one word about Africa." Most schools, White schools and what have you, studied history and sociology and left Africa completely out. So, we affected the whole system by making them add Africa, see us as human beings, and see Africa as something that had made some kind of contribution to the world. That's why we forced them to put millions and millions of dollars into Black Studies programs all over the country. So, all of these Black Studies degrees and Black Studies departments were established. Because they had Black faculty and Black Studies, they began to add us into other studies, like psychology and sociology. As a matter of fact, we brought civilization to this country where White people could sit in the same room with us and we could sit in the same room with them on an equal level.

On the response of HBCUs (Historically Black Colleges and Universities), they were scared to death of it - the administrators were. But, the students overtook the administrations and forced the issue. They tried to keep us out. As a matter of fact, Black administrators at colleges and Black high schools did everything in their power to keep us off their campuses. But, the students took over and forced them to let us on campuses. It went through the students. They were mostly college students. Anytime we went to a high school it was still mostly high school students. It wasn't the administration. It was the students. Every now and then, you had a professor that would invite us and be on our side. But, the administration as a whole, most of them were under the tutoring of the State and those kinds of people. Once we got African Studies departments in there, the FBI went to them and told them who to give jobs to. They gave people jobs who didn't relate to us.

One of the things they were supposed to do was keep Ralph, Stokely, SNCC, me and Black Power people off of the campuses. The Black Studies departments did everything they could to keep us off campuses. They began to work with the system to keep us off. Now they talk about Black Power and SNCC and all that and they don't invite me. I don't get invited anywhere.

Black Nationalism grew out of the rebellions and it linked us with Africa. We began to point toward Africa and began to have relationships with Africa, Kwame Nkrumah, Sekou Toure, and Lumumba - all kinds of worldviews. We created all kinds of world studies. When you look at it from the point of view of SNCC, all these groups attached their shit to us - women's organizations, women's rights - they began to attach their shit. And now, gay rights; they attached their shit to us. So a whole lot of people benefited from SNCC and what our movement was doing. As a matter of fact, they began to put international studies and all that kind of stuff on the campuses. That was a benefit from us because we created the opportunities by demanding Black studies on campuses. Women studies - there were no women studies on campuses until we picked up guns and demanded Black studies, African studies. Now you got women studies, gay studies and all those other studies.

13. Are there other persons you feel would provide helpful information on this topic?

I have to think about it.

14. I am collecting information on the sequence of events leading to the development of the first Black student union and the first Black studies department at San Francisco State University. Are there experiences at other college or universities that you feel would be informative?

Look up the Orangeburg massacre and Texas Southern University for the rebellion at Texas Southern in 1967. Look up Jackson State University on the rebellion in 1966 or 1967. There were a lot of schools. We had Black school rebellions, fights, and killings all over. We also had street rebellions like in Detroit and Newark and other places.

Epilogue: Baba Mukasa is still active and lives in the Atlanta metropolitan area. He describes himself as an African, a soldier, and a revolutionary. He is available for speaking engagements.

THE REPUBLIC OF NEW AFRIKA (RNA)

Summary of the Organization

In 1968, two brothers who were protégés of Malcolm X, Milton Henry (aka Gaidi Obadele) and Richard Henry (aka Imari Abubakari Obadele), established the Republic of New Afrika. They formed the Malcolm X Society and collaborated with another organization, the Group on Advanced Leadership, to organize a conference of 500 participants in Detroit, Michigan (RNA, 2013). At the conference, called the "Black Government Conference," they declared African Americans were free and formed a provisional government (PG-RNA). At the conference, 100 of the attendees signed a declaration of independence and a manifesto.

The Republic of New Afrika had three major goals:

1. Create an independent African American majority country on what they termed was subjugated land. This included the states of Mississippi, Louisiana, Alabama, Georgia, and South Carolina; and, in majority Black counties adjacent to the states in the states surrounding Arkansas, Texas, North Carolina, Tennessee, and Florida;
2. Advocate for payment of $400 billion in reparations from the US government for the injustices of slavery; and,
3. Advocate for a referendum to give all Black people the opportunity to determine their citizenship because they were not given the opportunity to state their choice after slavery ended.

A People's Revolutionary Leadership Council was established to build new communities and manage the new country. The following individuals were elected to office:

- First President: Robert F. Williams

- First Vice President: Gaidi Obadele (Milton Henry)

- Second Vice President: Betty Shabazz

- Minister of Information: Imari Obadele (Richard Henry)

- Minister of Health and Welfare: Queen Mother Moore

- Minister of Education: Herman Ferguson

- Minister of State and Foreign Affairs: William Grant

- Minister of Defense: Jalil Al Amin (H. Rap Brown)

- Co-Ministers of Culture: Amiri Baraka (LeRoi Jones); Maulana Karenga, and Baba Adefunmi (added later)

- Minister of Justice: Joan Franklin

- Minister of Finance: Raymond Willis

- Special Ambassador: Muhammad Ahmed (Maxwell Stanford) (RNA, 2013, p. 2).

The individuals listed above were already popular leaders among African Americans and several were leaders of their own organizations.

The leaders of the Republic of New Afrika realized that their organization would be controversial because of its goals. In preparation for anticipated encounters with law enforcement, they received training in weaponry and organized a militia for self-defense. Their activities were scrutinized by the FBI's COINTELPRO initiative and the Detroit Police Department. The Republic of New Afrika was involved in two well-known violent confrontations with law enforcement during which three police officers were killed. A number of the Republic of New Afrika activists were killed and the rest were jailed. The imprisonment of most of the organization's leaders left the organization without leadership and its popularity among African Americans significantly declined. By 1980, all of the jailed leaders were released from prison. The Republic of New Afrika continues to advocate for reparations for African Americans. Although the organization does not publicize the number of members in its group, it informally boasts a membership of between 5,000 and 10,000 people today.

Interview: Republic of New Afrika Activist

1. What are your memories of the Black Power Movement during this period?

I feel I was an integral part of it especially with the Black Panther Party. I learned at its feet. I guess you could say we looked at the difference between the Civil Rights Movement vs. the Black Power Movement. I was always drawn to the Black Panther Party as opposed to the Civil Rights Movement. I came up in the era of the 1960s, well really the 1970s, and we were reading the autobiography of Malcolm X. It had an impact on me even before reading Manchild in the Promised Land, and looking through a pictorial history of the Negro in America. A picture of 14-year-old Emmet Till, who was murdered, in my parents' reading room had an impact on me. His murder happened the same year or the next year after my birth so it really had an impact on me. So, for whatever reasons I was drawn more towards Black Power.

2. Please share any information you have on the goals and plans emanating from Black Power Conference of 1967 that took place in Newark, New Jersey.

I didn't attend the conference in 1967. I was in 7th grade at the time. If I had been of age, I would have been there.

3. Were you active with any organizations and, if so, what organization(s), in what capacity, and for what period of time?

I was involved very briefly with the Black Panther Party. I was in high school and at that time, the Black Panther Party was on 7th and T Street (in Washington, DC). I used to go down there to their political education classes and help them sell papers. I never was a Black Panther though. I used to hang around them all the time during high school. I know I did some things on sickle cell anemia. They were into those issues at that time.

When I went to college, I went to Howard University. One day, I happened to go to a lecture at Douglass Hall and there was a man. I don't know exactly who he was, but I recall how he looked.

I would say he might have been Khalid Muhammad. He was saying Black people in this country were not legally U.S. citizens. The 13th Amendment freed us but the 14th Amendment did not have a legal provision for citizenship. It was very very intriguing. I was a history major and I was just interested in things along those lines. I remember that being my first exposure to some of the issues that later I learned was part of the Republic of New Africa (RNA). I remember in 1975 or it might have been 1974, I went to a forum or some kind of program at the All Souls Church. It was a program sponsored by the RNA and they were planning for what they called the National Black Election. And I said, "This is very interesting." I went to this forum and they were talking about five states in the deep South. I wasn't into that but this whole thing about a separate nation intrigued me. Then I found out that the president of this group was in prison and I said, "Oh my goodness." For whatever reason, I wrote him. His name was Baba Imari. I wrote him and I said Brother Imari, I am a college student and I'm working on these national Black elections and if there is anything you need me to do, let me know. I was totally shocked out of my imagination when I received a letter back from him. And, it wasn't just a letter. It was a detailed a, b, c, 1, 2, 3; all of the things he wanted me to do.

And I said, "Oh my God." But, I did those things ranging from going to the post office in the wee hours of the morning, and filling out whatever those forms are to the different embassies, and to fight for brother Imari, helping to call for his release, to contacting people such as Congressman John Conyers, Congressman Ron Dellums, Congressman Diggs, Louis Farrakhan, Ronald Walters, James Turner, and Rev. David Eaton. I didn't really know any of these people, but Brother Imari had it all written down. I was to let them know what he wanted them to do. He wanted them to be part of this committee called the National Committee to Free the RNA 11, which was a Prisoner of War argument. I basically was Amara's, I don't know what you call it, but I did what he asked me to do to make things happen. And lo and behold, all these people came aboard and it was largely as a result of this that he ended up winning his freedom. Now at that time, I didn't realize until much later, I learned that the reason he turned to me was there was a big split going on in the RNA at that time. I didn't know anything about COINTELPRO at the time. I didn't know anything about it. I guess I did know a little bit but not much because none of that stuff was public at that time. None of it was. And so he really didn't have too many people to rely on.

4. What global events influenced the formation and activities of your organization?

The Black Power Conference on March 31, 1968 was a domestic conference. Imari was traveling nationally to address the war in America. Focus became international. There was a group called Advanced Leadership. Robert Williams was the Chair of Defense and Self Determination.

5. What were the strength and challenges of the organization?

Strengths: It heightened the consciousness of the movement, identified the importance of land, and internationalized the focus of the Black Power Movement. And you ask about the challenges, the setbacks. It was the COINTELPRO, bar none.

6. What were the accomplishments of the organization?

It heightened a new African political science. It was the basis for the New African independence movement. A lot of people got PhDs. You might hear about the Malcolm X Grassroots Movement, which was an outgrowth of RNA. NCOBRA (the National Coalition of Blacks for Reparations in America) was an outgrowth of the RNA. It was really started by Imari Obadele. A lot of people don't know that. So a lot of came out of that. While I was transitioning out of the RNA, I was transitioning into NCOBRA.

7. What do you know about COINTELPRO?

Its purpose was "to stop the long range growth of militant Black organizations, especially among the youth." That's a direct quote. To stop the growth of these groups among youth. It wanted to stop the rise of a Black messiah and get responsible "Negroes" to discredit Black militants. They and members of the White Left were jailed. It was interesting what was happening at that time. I remember clearly sitting at a bus stop and seeing a brother or sister at the bus stop with Don L Lee's book, "Don't Cry, Scream" or a copy of the "Autobiography of Malcolm X" under their arm. What happened a decade later? - drugs into the community. Anyway, between COINTELPRO and the RNA, I've seen the fire. Papa Wells, an elder in Detroit, went to his grave thinking that Imari Obadele was stealing money from the people because of scurrilous rumors that the FBI planted. They said that the tax money that people were paying to the RNA government was being used by Imari Obadele. I mean, this is dissention, fomenting distrust, and all that.

And that's just one person, one individual. All through the trial, Imari kept saying,

> "There's something more going on here. Something is just not quite right. They say they were there to serve a warrant on a person and the person wasn't even there. Something's just not hanging together with this trial in which I'm currently being charged with conspiracy."

Well, it wasn't until, in the law, you say discovery that things were revealed. Discovery is all of the evidence and documents, materials that could serve to exculpate your client. All this time, the government was saying, "There's nothing. We have nothing. There's nothing. There's nothing." Well, after the Supreme Court had denied the final appeals in the case, the FBI released 10 pages of FBI documents. I remember they said, "We are enclosing these at no cost." The documents showed that the RNA was a target generally and Imari Obadele specifically. Since that time, there has been 1,000s and 1,000s and 1,000s of pages, which we did have to pay for, redacted, heavily redacted, just whole pages blacked out, detailing the atrocities that the US government waged against this individual, Imari Obadele, and against the RNA group as a whole. I know one of the documents said, "Find anything that you can on this young charismatic person, Imari Obadele, because he is very influential. We must do something. Find something on him." Another document described when the FBI was interviewing Ku Klux Klan sympathizers in Jackson, Mississippi, they tried to foment something that they could do against Obadele.

He was a political genius, just an absolute genius and a prolific writer. If it were not for Rosa Parks, he might not have gotten out of jail in Hyde's County, Mississippi. They might have murdered him. The movement came out of Detroit. He and Rosa Parks were working at

Congressman John Conyers' office. He knew John Conyers. She made a call to John Conyers' office. Because of John Conyers' influence, they thought twice about lynching him. Conyers was from Detroit.

On March 31, 1969, the first anniversary of the RNA, there was an attack. There was a celebration at Franklin Stanley's Church. Something happened outside the church, like a Kwanzaa celebration. Nobody in the church knew what had happened. The church had all these men, women, and children all around. I remember, Imari telling them to "follow my voice, follow my voice." They were all herded into the indoor parking lot or garage because there were too many people. There were about 200 men, women, and children. If it wasn't for Judge George Crockett, who was newly seated on the bench just before he became Congressman, getting out of his bed to make sure these people were arraigned or got out, things may have been worse. They were all charged with murder or something like that. Of course, all of the charges were dropped and the two people who were outside were tried and acquitted. Like the Panthers, people never really had the leisure to develop - always having to be on the defense. It's amazing that people accomplished as much as they did.

8.   What is the current status of the organization?

They are still there. It definitely went down after Imari was incarcerated. The movement was totally destabilized. There are still some stalwart people hanging on. Regardless, the message is still there. They're doing things. They pursue reparations, observe Black Nation Day, and hold elections.

9.   How did the activities of your organization affect colleges and universities on campuses and in the community?

The RNA was not on college campuses. I think the politics of the organization caused a number of youth to shy away from it. They opted for the safer less radical organizations.

10. Did your organization's activities affect the development of Black student organizations and, if so, how?

Many of us were students but our focus was on creating a new government, not on higher education. We did help organize Student Organization for Black Unity (SOBU) and Youth Organization for Black Unity (YOBU), which were on college campuses. We helped to organize to advocate for the Wilmington 10 and the San Quentin 10.

11. Did your organization's activities affect the development of Black studies departments at higher education institutions and, if so, how?

Many of us were students but our focus was on creating a new government, not on higher education.

12. *Are you aware of any activities, programs, or benefits to higher education resulting from the efforts of your organization or other organizations in the Black Power Movement during the period from 1960 – 1980? Do they still exist today?*

Many of us were students but our focus was on creating a new government, not on higher education.

13. *Are there other persons you feel would provide helpful information on this topic?*

James Turner, Derrick Bell, and Ron Walters are good resources. Also Akindela Umoja from Atlanta and Ed Omaci

14. *I am collecting information on the sequence of events leading to the development of the first Black student union and the first Black studies department at San Francisco State University. Are there experiences at other college or universities that you feel would be informative?*

The Howard University experience. You can contact Donald Temple for that. Also, look up the All African People's Revolutionary Party (AAPRP) and the African Liberation Day Support Group.

THE NATION OF ISLAM (NOI)

Malcolm X was a significant figure in the Black Power Movement. Although he was the major spokesperson for the Nation of Islam, many activists in the Movement followed his teachings through his lectures and books. Following his death, his influence heightened resulting in the formation of cultural nationalist organizations, which embraced his concepts of healing and re-education; and, revolutionary nationalist organizations, which embraced the right to self-defense.

Summary of the Organization

Although the Nation of Islam (NOI) was established in 1930 by Wallace D. Muhammad, long before the activism of the 1960s and 1970s, because of Malcolm X (aka El Hajj Malik El Shabazz), it played a significant role in the Black Power Movement. Elijah Muhammad became the leader of the Nation of Islam in 1934. In 1952, Elijah Muhammad appointed Malcolm X as the national spokesperson for the Nation of Islam. During the 1960s, Malcolm X served as a counterpoint to Rev. Dr. Martin Luther King, Jr.'s philosophy of non-violence and promoted the right to self-defense. After the expulsion of Malcolm X from the Nation of Islam and his subsequent death, Louis Farrakhan became the national spokesperson and is the recognized leader of the Nation of Islam today.

The stated mission of the Nation of Islam is "to improve the spiritual, mental, social, and economic condition of African Americans in the United States and all of humanity" (Nation of Islam, 2013, p. 1). After 1946, Elijah Muhammad pursued the priorities of increasing membership, establishing a separate state for African Americans, adopting a religion based on the worship of Allah, and promoting African Americans as the chosen people (Nation of Islam, 2013). Malcolm X promoted these priorities when he was appointed the national spokesperson for the organization in the 1952. In February 1964, he was expelled from the Nation of Islam because of controversial statements he made after the assassination of President John Kennedy and allegations he made against Elijah Muhammad. After he left the Nation of Islam, he created the Organization of African American Unity. Through this organization, he planned to take the plight of African Americans to the United Nations. He was assassinated in February 1965.

Malcolm X's prominence increased after his death. During his life, he had given many speeches, which were transcribed, and had written several books and articles. His speeches and writings were studied and analyzed by young people who became activists in the Black Power Movement. Two different interpretations emerged from their analyses, one promoting self-defense another calling for a cultural revolution. The cultural nationalists of the Black Power Movement embraced the need for a cultural revolution and the revolutionary nationalists embraced the need for self-defense.

The Nation of Islam's platform explains what its members want and what they believe. There are 10 items that explain what they want and 12 items that explain what they believe. The items in the platform address the social and economic needs of African Americans as well as spiritual development, and align with the platforms and/or manifestos of other Black

Power organizations. For example, a summary of the first four items listed under "What the Muslims Want" are:

1. Freedom
2. Equal Justice under the Law
3. Equality of Opportunity
4. Establishment of a separate country for African Americans (Nation of Islam, 2013).

The two platforms are attached.

During the 1960s and 1970s, the Nation of Islam claimed a membership of 500,000 and had 75 Nation of Islam centers across the country. Currently, there are 10,000 to 50,000 members in the organization with 130 Nation of Islam temples in the United States, Ghana, London, Paris, and the Caribbean Islands. The organization has undergone numerous changes since its establishment in 1930 but continues to pursue its mission today.

Nation of Islam Platforms (www.NOI.org)

What the Muslims Want

THIS IS THE QUESTION ASKED MOST FREQUENTLY BY BOTH THE WHITES AND THE BLACKS. THE ANSWERS TO THIS QUESTION I SHALL STATE AS SIMPLY AS POSSIBLE.

1. We want freedom. We want a full and complete freedom.
2. We want justice. Equal justice under the law. We want justice applied equally to all, regardless of creed or class or color.
3. We want equality of opportunity. We want equal membership in society with the best in civilized society.
4. We want our people in America whose parents or grandparents were descendants from slaves, to be allowed to establish a separate state or territory of their own–either on this continent or elsewhere. We believe that our former slave masters are obligated to provide such land and that the area must be fertile and minerally rich. We believe that our former slave masters are obligated to maintain and supply our needs in this separate territory for the next 20 to 25 years–until we are able to produce and supply our own needs. Since we cannot get along with them in peace and equality, after giving them 400 years of our sweat and blood and receiving in return some of the worst treatment human beings have ever experienced, we believe our contributions to this land and the suffering forced upon us by white America, justifies our demand for complete separation in a state or territory of our own.
5. We want freedom for all Believers of Islam now held in federal prisons. We want freedom for all black men and women now under death sentence in innumerable prisons in the North as well as the South. We want every black man and woman to have the freedom to accept or reject being separated from the slave master's children and establish a land of

their own. We know that the above plan for the solution of the black and white conflict is the best and only answer to the problem between two people.

6. We want an immediate end to the police brutality and mob attacks against the so-called Negro throughout the United States. We believe that the Federal government should intercede to see that black men and women tried in white courts receive justice in accordance with the laws of the land–or allow us to build a new nation for ourselves, dedicated to justice, freedom and liberty.

7. As long as we are not allowed to establish a state or territory of our own, we demand not only equal justice under the laws of the United States, but equal employment opportunities– **NOW!** We do not believe that after 400 years of free or nearly free labor, sweat and blood, which has helped America become rich and powerful, so many thousands of black people should have to subsist on relief or charity or live in poor houses.

8. We want the government of the United States to exempt our people from ALL taxation as long as we are deprived of equal justice under the laws of the land.

9. We want equal education–but separate schools up to 16 for boys and 18 for girls on the condition that the girls be sent to women's colleges and universities. We want all black children educated, taught and trained by their own teachers. Under such schooling system we believe we will make a better nation of people. The United States government should provide, free, all necessary textbooks and equipment, schools and college buildings. The Muslim teachers shall be left free to teach and train their people in the way of righteousness, decency and self-respect.

10. We believe that intermarriage or race mixing should be prohibited. We want the religion of Islam taught without hindrance or suppression.

What the Muslims Believe (www.NOI.org)

1. WE BELIEVE in the One God whose proper Name is Allah.

2. WE BELIEVE in the Holy Qur'an and in the Scriptures of all the Prophets of God.

3. WE BELIEVE in the truth of the Bible, but we believe that it has been tampered with and must be reinterpreted so that mankind will not be snared by the falsehoods that have been added to it.

4. WE BELIEVE in Allah's Prophets and the Scriptures they brought to the people.

5. WE BELIEVE in the resurrection of the dead–not in physical resurrection–but in mental resurrection. We believe that the so-called Negroes are most in need of mental resurrection; therefore, they will be resurrected first. Furthermore, we believe we are the people of God's choice, as it has been written, that God would choose the rejected and the despised. We can find no other persons fitting this description in these last days more that the so-called Negroes in America. We believe in the resurrection of the righteous.

6. WE BELIEVE in the judgment; we believe this first judgment will take place as God revealed, in America...

7. WE BELIEVE this is the time in history for the separation of the so-called Negroes and the so-called white Americans. We believe the black man should be freed in name as well as in fact. By this we mean that he should be freed from the names imposed upon him by his former slave masters. Names which identified him as being the slave master's slave.

We believe that if we are free indeed, we should go in our own people's names–the black people of the Earth.

8. WE BELIEVE in justice for all, whether in God or not; we believe as others, that we are due equal justice as human beings. We believe in equality–as a nation–of equals. We do not believe that we are equal with our slave masters in the status of "freed slaves."

We recognize and respect American citizens as independent peoples and we respect their laws which govern this nation.

9. WE BELIEVE that the offer of integration is hypocritical and is made by those who are trying to deceive the black peoples into believing that their 400-year-old open enemies of freedom, justice and equality are, all of a sudden, their "friends." Furthermore, we believe that such deception is intended to prevent black people from realizing that the time in history has arrived for the separation from the whites of this nation. If the white people are truthful about their professed friendship toward the so-called Negro, they can prove it by dividing up America with their slaves. We do not believe that America will ever be able to furnish enough jobs for her own millions of unemployed, in addition to jobs for the 20,000,000 black people as well.

10. WE BELIEVE that we who declare ourselves to be righteous Muslims, should not participate in wars which take the lives of humans. We do not believe this nation should force us to take part in such wars, for we have nothing to gain from it unless America agrees to give us the necessary territory wherein we may have something to fight for.

11. WE BELIEVE our women should be respected and protected as the women of other nationalities are respected and protected.

12. WE BELIEVE that Allah (God) appeared in the Person of Master W. Fard Muhammad, July 1930; the long-awaited "Messiah" of the Christians and the "Mahdi" of the Muslims. We believe further and lastly that Allah is God and besides HIM there is no god and He will bring about a universal government of peace wherein we all can live in peace together.

THE STUDENT/YOUTH ORGANIZATION FOR BLACK UNITY (SOBU/YOBU)

The Student Organization for Black Unity was formed by the Student Nonviolent Coordinating Committee (SNCC) in May 1969 at North Carolina A&T College (Student Nonviolent Coordinating Committee, 2013). Founders included Nelson Johnson, Tim Thomas, Milton Coleman, John McClendon, Mark Smith, Alvin Evans, Victor Bond, and Jerry Walker. In August 1972, the name of the organization was changed to the Youth Organization for Black Unity (YOBU) to expand its membership to youth beyond college (Woodard, 2013). The organization's stated ideology, which is described in a 36-page paper, was Pan Africanism. The Youth Organization for Black Unity's priorities were to:

- advocate for the release of incarcerated African Americans, which they considered political prisoners;

- educate students and other activists through publication of a bi-weekly newsletter called "The African World;"

- support Black education by promoting and supporting independent Black schools and historically Black colleges and universities;

- redefine Black education on college campuses; and, inform Black students about the geography and politics (e.g. liberation struggles) of Africa (Johnson, 1972).

Events sponsored and/or organized by the Youth Organization for Black Unity included:

- organizing and sponsoring an African Liberation Day celebration in Washington, DC on May 19, 1972 in celebration of Malcolm X's birthday,

- sponsoring a Southern African Week, and

- operating a Pan-African Medical Program.

YOBU issued articles on the Pan-Africanism of Malcolm X and issued a report on the United Nations. From its founding in 1969 to 1972, the then Student Organization for Black Unity focused its organizational efforts on internal development. Chapters were established on higher education campuses across the country, however, the researcher could not find literature on how many chapters existed or where they were located. In 1972, the Youth Organization for Black Unity began to reach out to other student groups to form cadres across the country. The literature on this organization as a national entity is sketchy. Some of the colleges and universities where it had a presence, such as the University of Texas and Harvard, have information on the specific group on their campus in their archives. Although there is evidence that the organization was in existence during the 1980s, it is not known if it continues to exist today.

APPENDIX C: EDUCATOR AND STUDENT INTERVIEWS

THE SAN FRANCISCO STATE UNIVERSITY EXPERIENCE

As stated earlier, the first Black student union was established at San Francisco State University (then college) after a 5-month strike. An interview follows that details how the achievement was accomplished.

Interview with Dr. Nathan Hare, First Chair of the SFSU Black Studies Department

1. What memories do you have of the establishment of the Black student union and/or the Black studies department at San Francisco State University? Are there any popular stories you would like to share?

It was the first Black Studies Department in the country. It was called the School of Ethnic Studies and became the Department of Black Studies after a 5-month strike to make it into a department. The Merritt Community College also had a department of Black Studies but it was called African American Studies because it was more palatable - more friendly. At that time, they were toying with the question of Blackness. We had a Negro History course because of Carter G. Woodson's book. I finished the First Grade Reader, or whatever it was called. The Black Studies Department was established because of the advocacy efforts of the Black Student Union. The Black Student Union was the first by that name. A student taking the Negro History course took it and made it into an organization called it the Negro Student Association. Later it became the Black Student Union; and, after that, Black Studies. We were in the middle of a change in name. We were just starting to think seriously of "Black", "Negro", and "African American". It had been taught earlier in places like Harlem for a couple of years. I came across a book that told the truth about the word "Negro" and its uses. It was written by a committee to present the truth. On the committee were Langton Hughes, Queen Mother Moore, and John Henrik Clarke. I wrote this article about the issue of Negro and said that it seemed that Afro-American was coming in. I ended by saying that it didn't matter because any name would acquire the same old connotations of inferiority. It would not change our objective conditions. The article was in a magazine called Phylon that was founded by WEB Dubois when he was at Atlanta University. It is defunct now. For many years, it was quite significant. It was about race.

2. What was the impetus for their establishment?

In 1968 or 1969, I was promoted to the position of Coordinator for the Black Studies Program and we had to meet. A problem arose when the White administration did not fulfill its promises. It became a matter of whose side are you on and, I said, "If I had to choose, I would choose the Black side." When we got together, the committee developed a proposal asking for three faculty and submitted it to a liberal committee. The administration said that's not how you do it in America. You ask for more than you want and then you bargain down. So, we asked for 10 faculty. The Dean said you can't do it like that. You have to do it by a formula - FTEs. So, he showed us how to do it and the committee approved it. Then his boss came and said, "Oh, we can't do it. In fact, we can't give you any in September. We can loan you three but in September we have to wait and see if some of the departments don't use all of their slots." I told the students what the administration was telling me and so we got together and we met with the Black Student Union and the Black faculty union. We all agreed to strike for Black Studies. At that time, the students had recruited me to be their advisor on Black Student Union. The chairman had a wife who was suspicious of us so we met during the wee hours in the middle of the night. You had to be on time. If you were late, you had to pay a dollar for each minute you were late. I met with them and I was a member of the central committee of the Black Student Union. I participated in the strike and we were arrested. It was the longest strike in history - 5 months: from November 1968 – March 1969. There were 1,000 – 2,000 people who participated in the strike. They arrested 557 of us at one time. They surrounded us and wouldn't let us disperse and then arrested us for unlawful assembly and failing to disperse. Then, they, 1000 cops, backed up the wagon, formed a human chain, and arrested us one at a time. The majority of the people (arrested) were White. The student body was predominately White. There were the Students for a Democratic Society (SDS) and other left wing Whites. The World Liberation Front, which was a Spanish organization, was in the strike. The American Federation of Teachers (AFT) joined too. They added their own demands to ours. Everybody was striking and hardly anybody was going to class. So, a lot of Whites were out there striking. We had a rally every day and they tied to break us up. They said you can't assemble on campus but we assembled anyway. It was covered on the CBS evening news.

At that point, we had gone through integration and it didn't really work - the way things evolved in the general Civil Rights Movement - integration and non-violence. Black Power was the big cry nationally. It was a turning point. When Black Power hit in 1966, the students coming back to campus wanted to bring Black Power back to campus. All over the country, they tended to do that. SFSC was a State College and they had some groups there, the Equal Opportunity Commission and the war on poverty program and that sort of thing. Some of the students came from Howard University.

I developed my Black identity in 1961. I went to the University of Chicago as a PhD student and I passed the comprehensive exam. I became very conscious of race and didn't want to wait to read Black literature. I decided to read every Black book that I could find in the library downtown. I found a book about the name "Negro" and showed it to my professor. He said, "Where did you get that book?" He was fascinated by it himself because he was a specialist in race relations.

Anyway, the Black students had come back to campus in 1966, they wanted to bring Black Power to the campus, and they were concerned about what they were being taught. They were getting bad grades by comparison. They organized a group and out of the group came other notions and criticism of the classes. They disrupted classes and wanted to learn about their own heritage. Even some White students wanted to learn about the Black thing. They were curious about Black people then because Blackness was in the air. Black Power was the thing. It was exciting to the White students too. They were more receptive to Blackness than they are now. They wanted to be assimilated. They didn't want there to be two Black masses. They wanted to be White-friendly. They came into the rainbow era. In the 1960s, you could publish Black stuff anywhere. Black Power was the big cry - a signal. You could say anything you wanted to in the 1960s and Whites, down here on the ground, would love you especially if you allowed them to be accepted like the Black Panthers did. The Black Panthers were Black and feared but made room for Whites. They liked to hear them say how bad Whites were - "honky this and honky that" - as long as you let them get involved with something. They were the vocal minority of White liberals. The conservatives were part of the silent majority. They talked about other people and not about themselves. When you talked about how bad and sinful people were in the church, they knew you were talking about their buddies but not them. They were receptive for a few years, just a few years. The whole thing lasted about four or five years.

3. *Were there any particular events that were important?*

We decided to call a strike. George Murray, who was Minister of Education for the Black Panther Party and on the central committee, got up on a table in the dining hall and called for it. At first, it was going to be on February 28th for the birthday of Huey Newton, but it was moved to November 6th, which represented the day in 1967 when they raided the White Student Union building and beat up some of the staff members. They got put in jail for doing that. George still had a six-month suspended sentence over his head. So they honored November 6. They called it the "VADOR incident." They put the name in the newspaper that was run by Whites. We told everybody and on November 6th, everybody came. On November 5th, Carmichael happened to be in town. He had been recruited to the Black Panther Party as the Minister of Defense. He brought candles to speak to a group of students at the main auditorium. We had missing students. We handed them their rights and spoke out for them (missing students). There were 100 of them and they filled the auditorium. Stokely spoke to them that day. It was a great speech. Tomorrow came and we met in a small room in the auditorium. Finally, Mel Stuart, who was a Black actor who became a movie star, said, "We were just sitting around." _____, who was chair of the Black Student Union, said, "What are we doing sitting here when Black people are striking and students are going to class?" So, we went and told students we were striking. After 20 minutes, the campus squad came. The students went out on the campus and the strike was on.

The AFT said we don't want a police state so they joined the strike. The Third World Liberation Party joined us. There were students, predominantly White, out there. They arrested the ones that couldn't get away. We did that every day and nobody went to class. Then the AFT decided to pull out. Everyone was getting weary and tired and one woman in the creative arts area got mad at me for saying, "It was better to die on one's feet than to live on one's knees." One day while I was on campus meeting with the Black Student Union, I heard the AFT tell the Black students, "If you don't end this, we're going to end it anyway". So, they decided to end it.

We had done everything we could. They were arresting people. We had charges over our heads, pretty serious charges. They tried everything they could to break the strike. They (BSU) had a group meet and they worked out an agreement of what they wanted - a Black Studies Department, hiring and firing teachers, and faculty just like all the other departments had. We asked for 20 professors and they gave us 23 professors and 500 students. Any Black student that wanted to come could but they had liberal options. They got the School of Ethnic Studies, an Asian Studies Program, Native American Program, and a Latino Program. Everybody had a department. They put some students out of school. They had a blacklist of 500 students and some were put out. I became the first Coordinator of Black Studies.

4. *Who were the key people who participated in the effort? Who were the key students? Who were the key community leaders? Who were the key faculty?*

There were so many people. I don't want to miss anyone. Students included Jerry Varnado, Leroy Goodwin, Jimmy Stewart, Jimmy Garrett, George Colbert, and Claude Brown. Danny Glover, who became a famous actor, was also on the committee as a student. He was just a student you know. I knew Stokely Carmichael would become famous but I didn't know that he and Claude Brown would write <u>Manchild in the Promise Land</u>. George Murray, a Panther, taught Black English at an experimental college, which the university allowed. SFSC students sometimes taught courses and it was the same thing with Black Studies. But, they were not out there to get arrested. There were students breaking up the Black history class being taught by a White teacher. I was a Panther then because I liked their style. Baraka was a visiting poet in residence. He was on the campus staff for one year. He came by with members of RAM and asked them to speak.

Politicians were there too: Jerry West, Churchfield, and George Colbert. Jerry West and the City Council would come and speak as well as Congressman Rangel and Ron Dellums (He was a city councilman at Berkeley then). We had some faculty: A Calhoun. She was arrested. There was Fabio, a poet laureate; Sarah Papio, a professor at Merritt College; and, Laura Kiu, a dance teacher. They had a guy who was the troubleshooter. He didn't participate in the strike though. They wanted me to be a troubleshooter.

People from the community included Carlton Phillips (publisher of the local weekly newspaper), Queen Mother Moore, Cecil Williams from a Black church, a woman who became President of the Negro National Business and Professional Women, another woman who became the first president of NOW. There were many community people without names who would come out and march with us. Mohammad Ali came and spoke. They closed down the campus when they heard he was coming. We stood Ali on the steps of Frederick Hall so he could speak. The Black Power committee brought Ali there. When Baraka came, we put him on the steps of the School of Religion. I only saw Sonya Sanchez once during the strike.

God doesn't pick you out; it has to do with circumstance. What gets me is when people get up there and say, "I never gave up. I just have God-given talents." Everybody has God-given talents. The next time you have a party, have a talent show and let somebody sing or dance and see all of that talent there. I hate to see somebody say that they just worked hard and they never gave up. It's who you know but that's not sufficient either. That's not the only thing. Just like when you make a cake, everything has to come together, the heat, the timing. That's the same with life, being in the right time and place. You may not be good at first but you become better later.

When I was at Howard University before SFSC, students formed an organization called Nonviolent Action Group. Later it was renamed Student Nonviolent Coordinating Committee.

5. *Are there any records available that would be helpful in understanding how they emerged?*

The Black Student Union is getting ready to write a book. And, another group is writing a book. They're trying to get a book or two out. There are no university archives that I know of. They're getting their information by talking to - interviewing - each other. They are very knowledgeable about revolutionary stuff. They were a talented group of people in one place at the same time. The Black Student Union is still active and is supported. In the BSU, men assumed the leadership and women did most of the work. There wasn't a fight for leadership. The women wanted to restore the Black man to a position of strength. It was based on ideology. Queen Mother Moore was a mentor for me more than any man. Leaders of the Black Power committee would come and sit at her feet. She would say, "Grandma wants some demands. What demands will you make tomorrow?" She was responsible for most of the demands that were made. She didn't have any position but she told the men what to do. She was very respected in that sense but didn't have a position because they wanted the men to have them. I don't think you have anyone like Queen Mother Moore now.

AC Rogers wrote a book called <u>The Black Campus Community</u>. Martha Biondi wrote a book called <u>Revolution on Campus</u>. I'm writing my autobiography. I'm trying to get it done by my birthday next April. I'm going to call it <u>An Intruder in the Ivory Tower</u>. The revolution comes in stages. The problem is you a need a different actors - different people for each stage, like a relay race.

HOWARD UNIVERSITY

Historically Black Colleges and Universities were not immune from the activism of the Black Power Movement. Following is an interview of an alumnus of Howard University in Washington, DC.

1. *What memories do you have of the establishment of the Black student union and/or the Black studies department at your school? Are there any popular stories you would like to share?*

I went to Regina High School from 1970 -1973. I was influenced by the Black Panther Party. Used to hang out with them. I was always drawn to the Black Panther Party Movement as opposed to the Civil Rights Movement. I came up in the era of the 1960s, well really the 1970s, and we were reading the autobiography of Malcolm X. It had an impact on me even before reading "Manchild in the Promised Land" impacted me, and looking through a pictorial history of the Negro in America. My parents' reading room had an impact on me when I saw a picture of 14-year-old Emmet Till, who was murdered. His murder happened the same year or the next year after my birth so it really had an impact on me. So, for whatever reasons I was drawn more towards Black Power.

2. *What was the impetus for their establishment?*

The need to stick together and support each other.

3. *Were there any particular events that were important?*

Black History Month programs, Black Studies curriculum for high schools, in 1977 a Saturday school, called New Africa Shule, Council of Independent Black Institutions (CIBI) science fairs that were held once a year, martial Arts classes, and history classes I was a history major.

4. *Who were the key people who participated in the effort? Who were the key students? Who were the key community leaders? Who were the key faculty?*

Imamu Kuumba.

5. *Are there any records available that would be helpful in understanding how they emerged?*

COINTELPRO. Information on it can be found on the internet RNA's website;
A CIBI educator: jmshujaa@hotmail.com.

Printed in the United States
By Bookmasters